Enlightenment
and the
Shadows of Chance

Enlightenment and the Shadows of Chance

The Novel and the Culture of Gambling in Eighteenth-Century France

Thomas M. Kavanagh

The Johns Hopkins University Press
BALTIMORE AND LONDON

The Johns Hopkins University Press
2715 North Charles Street
Baltimore, Maryland 21218-4319
The Johns Hopkins Press Ltd., London

LIBRARY OF CONGRESS CATALOGING-IN-PUBLICATION DATA

Kavanagh, Thomas M.
Enlightenment and the shadows of
chance : the novel and the culture of gambling in eighteenth-century France / Thomas
M. Kavanagh.
        p.   cm.
Includes bibliographical references and
index.
ISBN 0-8018-4549-1
1. French fiction—18th century—History
and criticism.   2. Literature and society—
France—History—18th century.   3. Gambling in literature.   4. Enlightenment—
France.   5. Chance in literature.   I. Title.
PQ648.K38   1993
843'.509355—dc20   92-30732

A catalog record for this book is available from the
British Library.

To Monique

Contents

Preface

This study addresses the questions of chance, gambling, and the aleatory in the French Enlightenment. While my ultimate concern is with the literature of the period, and more specifically with the novel as that century's most important literary form, the real stakes of what is expressing itself through that genre become clear only when the novel is placed within its cultural and historical contexts. For that reason, part 1 examines the roles of chance and gambling in the epistemological, social, and economic histories of the period.

As I began researching the subject of chance in the eighteenth-century French novel it became clear that its significance is closely connected to what at first seemed a quite different subject: the formation and development of what we today call probability theory. First conceived by Pascal, and reaching its apogee in the works of Laplace, Poisson, and Borel, classical probability theory paralleled and in a very real sense sustained the emergence and hegemony of the modern novel. The more I learned about the cultural history of probability theory, the more it became clear that this history provides an important context for understanding the exactly contemporaneous age of the novel. The triumph of probability theory and the rise of the novel were part of a single shift in our understanding of the world and of how we represent our place within it.

In chapter 2 the focus of inquiry shifts to the tangible social practice most immediately reflecting the Enlightenment's changing attitudes toward chance. Gambling, all but omnipresent during the *ancien régime,* not only provided a thematics of choice for the novelists of the era but, as a form of social interaction central to the rituals of Versailles, both recapitulated and was defined by the crucial ideological conflicts of the period. The new moralizing of gambling by the rising bourgeoisie played a key role in that class's struggle against the traditional nobility of the sword as well as in its effort to consolidate control over the emerging urban proletariat. In these groups' different attitudes toward gambling there emerged the clearest expression of a profound mutation in the Enlightenment's fundamental understanding of individual merit.

Chapter 3, which deals with cultural backgrounds, examines the economic history of the period through the focal event of John Law's System, an event that, for a moment, equated wealth with chance. Law's volatile experiment with the dynamics of credit and speculation not only initiated the Enlightenment as we know it but revealed to society a dimension of the power of chance that France would spend the rest of the century trying to forget.

Part 2 uses the findings of these investigations to examine a number of individual novelists and the significance of their representations of chance. Four of the six authors I consider reveal important aspects of how the novel came to identify itself with an ability to evoke, yet limit, chance's power to disrupt narratives of mastery and reason. Jean de Préchac's late-seventeenth-century works *Les Desordres de la bassette* and *La Noble Venitienne* show how an explicit thematics of gambling linked the emerging form of the novel with the satiric representation of an aristocracy defined by its identification with the insubstantiality of chance. Moving to the eighteenth century, Prévost's *Manon Lescaut* offers the most extensive portrayal of the individual as submerged within an uncertain world of gambling and chance events. If, however, chance is a driving force within des Grieux's story, Prévost chooses to narrate it through a novelistic form consolidating a didactic identification of reader with character, promising an escape from the disruptive force of chance. Chapter 7 analyzes Voltaire's contribution to the development of the novel as the elaboration of a unique form of irony portraying the world as devastated by chance yet simultaneously defusing its threat through a textualized complicity of reader and authorial voice. My final examination of the novel's domestication of chance considers the case of Vivant Denon's *Point de lendemain* and the way that short work establishes the mutually sustaining acts of memory and writing as the basis of a reconciliation between pleasure as the product of chance and society as a construct of conventions excluding the chance event.

The last two chapters deal with novels working outside and against the genre's overwhelming collaboration in the taming of chance. Chapter 9 looks at how Crébillon *fils,* in his experiments with a narrative form lying between the novel and the theater, sought to preserve within the written text an indeterminacy of action and speech antithetical to the well-constructed story with which the novel had come to be identified. Finally, chapter 10 focuses on Diderot as the person who, more than anyone else, attempted to tell chance's untellable tale. *Jacques le fataliste*'s juxtaposing of its main character's fatalistic belief in the Great Scroll with the radically iconoclastic form of the work we actually read set in motion an ultimately unstoppable dialectic erasing the domination of chance by narrative with which the novel had come to be identified.

This study is, to my knowledge, the first attempt to relate the emergence of the novel to the problematics of chance, gambling, and probability theory. The notion of probability has provided the framework for two important studies of the novel: Douglas Patey's *Probability and Literary Form: Philosophical Theory and Literary Practice in the Augustan Age* (Cambridge: Cambridge University Press, 1984) and Robert Newsom's more diffuse *A Likely Story: Probability and Play in Fiction* (New Brunswick, N.J.: Rutgers University Press, 1988). Both of these works, however, take the word 'probability' in its quite different sense as a synonym for the verisimilar and the plausible. Patey's tightly reasoned study argues for an unbroken tradition of literary reflection and practice linking the term 'probability' as it was used in the Augustan age both to the classical doctrine of verisimilitude developed by Plato and Aristotle and to its continuation by the rhetoricians of the Middle Ages and the Renaissance. In choosing 'probability' as the key term for his title, Patey (and Newsom after him) explicitly rejects the position taken by Ian Hacking in *The Emergence of Probability* (Cambridge: Cambridge University Press, 1975) that the middle of the seventeenth century saw an epistemological break in the way that term was used. For Hacking, the word 'probability' was, before the 1650s, infrequent and of minor significance. After that decade, it began to appear everywhere and reflected a new understanding of the world having no precedent prior to the works of Pascal, Huygens, and Leibniz.

While I hardly claim to resolve this debate, it is clear that Patey and Newsom base their critiques of Hacking on a sometimes heavy-handed semantic tugging of the term 'probability' away from the larger cultural context of what the period called "expectations," *l'analyse des hasards,* and "the doctrine of chances." For them, the term must be limited instead to the more narrow rhetorical and philosophical tradition of literary verisimilitude. The problem with that semantic displacement lies in the dismissal Patey and Newsom make of the newer and clearly more forceful sense the word came to acquire from its use in the analysis of chance and gambling.

Hacking is certainly correct in his claim that the new force the word 'probability' acquired toward the middle of the seventeenth century was the token of a real change. The full significance of that change can, however, be understood only when we examine its implications beyond the limited contexts either of mathematical analysis alone or of theories of the verisimilar alone. The task before us is to extend our inquiry to the social, economic, and literary corollaries of that shift in which chance, gambling, and the development of the novel played so crucial a role.

A part of chapter 1 appeared in *French Forum* 15, no. 1 (January 1990), under the title "Chance and Probability Theory in the Enlightenment." I thank the editors for their permission to use parts of it here.

Material support allowing me the time to write this study was generously provided by the John Simon Guggenheim Memorial Foundation, the National Endowment for the Humanities, and the University of Michigan's Horace Rackham Graduate School. I am deeply grateful to all of them for their help and encouragement.

Enlightenment
and the
Shadows of Chance

Introduction

*Throughout the Age of Reason, chance has been called
the superstition of the vulgar. Chance, superstition,
vulgarity, unreason were of one piece. The rational
man, averting his eyes from such things, could
cover chaos with a veil of inexorable laws.*
—IAN HACKING, *The Taming of Chance*

Studies of the French Enlightenment have consistently neglected one of its most important paradoxes: while that
period was massively fascinated with chance, gambling,
and the aleatory in all their forms, its major figures suppressed that fascination in favor of ideals presupposing
coherent systems of reason, law, or nature. My intent in
this book is to examine how the refusal of chance played
a crucial but hidden role in the development of Enlightenment thought. The reality of chance functioned as a nexus
of disorder threatening, but at the same time producing,
the period's positive images of itself. I will thus be looking
at the French Enlightenment in terms of the denied yet
operative role played by the specter of chance in important
aspects of what the period proclaimed itself to be.

My use of the word 'chance' is not without problems.
Yet that term is, I believe, the best available in English to
evoke the particular challenge to the rule of reason I examine here. Were this study written in French, I would be
more comfortable with the associations and connotations
of *le hasard*. English, unfortunately, has no single word
that expresses everything brought into play by the French
term.

What is it about *le hasard* that works so much better than 'chance'? And why is it that the fetchingly yet deceptively similar English cognate, 'hazard', does not work? The English 'chance', as well as the German *Zufall*, the Spanish *casualidad*, and the Italian *caso*, all, in terms of their roots either in the Germanic *Fall* or the Latin *cadere*, evoke the idea of what falls out, what is coming down. They leave undecided the question whether the event is causally motivated or fortuitous. The word *hasard*, on the other hand, in what Clément Rosset refers to as its properly "tragic" sense, represents a mode of existence prior to and independent of any causal sequence established by reason and thus allowing us to situate and dominate the event.[1]

The term *hasard* was most probably derived from the name of a fortress in twelfth-century Syria. William of Tyre, in his chronicle of the Crusades entitled *Historia rerum in partibus transmarinis gestarum,* speaks of the Christian army's enforced halt in a castle called *Hasart*—a halt so long and so boring that the soldiers invented there a particularly fascinating game of dice which, when they returned to their homelands, became the rage throughout Europe.

Dicing had, of course, existed from the earliest antiquity. Archaeologists have long hypothesized that the disproportionately large number of astragali (the smooth, square-shaped heel bones of sheep and deer) found in ancient digs testifies to their use as randomizers in primitive games of chance. The tombs of the Egyptian pharaohs all contained exquisitely carved ivory dice. The word 'dice', the plural of 'die', derives from the Latin *data,* itself taken from the Latin *datum* as the substantive form of the infinitive *dare,* 'to give'. In late popular Latin, the term *datum* had the sense of "that which is given or decreed," most often by an agency considered to be beyond human control. As a part of the basic situation confronting any individual, such "data" were seen as a product of chance, of fortune, of an anthropomorphized Fortuna. To roll the dice, to ascertain the "data," was to learn whether good or ill fortune awaited. To roll the dice was to recognize a dialectic between individuals deciding their actions and a larger, engulfing world of forces over which humankind was powerless.

In the particular dice game introduced by William of Tyre's crusaders, the term *hasard* also signified one face of the die, the six—the point indicating that the player had lost his entire stake. As an echo of this we find, for instance, in Shakespeare's *Richard III:* "I have set my life upon a cast, And I will stand the hazard of the die" (act 5, scene 4). Hazard came to designate the very idea of risk, peril, or any menacing situation beyond human control. It is that meaning which, in the English 'hazard', as well as in the Italian *azzardo* and the Spanish *azar,* has prevailed in all European languages except French. The English, Italian, and Spanish words all imply, generally within a context of gambling, a stroke of bad luck, a surrendering of oneself to uncertainty in such a way that one's downfall seems always the most probable outcome.

It was during the seventeenth century that the sense of the French *hasard* took a different turn, one generating a meaning the word retains even today: that of an activity carried out against the backdrop, not so much of an almost physical danger, but of a radical silence, a fundamental inability of human thought to understand and dominate that which can be neither accounted for nor explained by the various narratives of reason. It was Pascal who, more than anyone else, gave this term its properly philosophical sense not only of something unpredictable, something outside the laws of causality and necessity, but also of an absence, a blank, a silence prior to the very possibility of human thought, reason, and understanding. *Le hasard* became for Pascal a synonym of hell itself.

The challenge of *le hasard,* of what I here call 'chance', cast a lengthening shadow across the eighteenth century. Our metaphors for that period—the Enlightenment, *l'age des lumières, die Aufklarung*—suggest that no matter how brilliant the illumination, certain shadows were inevitably intensified. These shadows were themselves evidence of a stubborn resistance to and refraction of the all-piercing powers of the illuminating source. My argument is that these shadows are not a meaningless defiance of the light but a nuanced variety of intensities telling us something that would otherwise remain unknown about both a reality unamenable to reason and the limits of the enlightening source. This subtle play of light and shadow lends to the terrain an otherwise absent relief adumbrating a new understanding, without which we would behold only the flatly illuminated plane of apparently obvious truth.

Chance, a resistance that casts a particularly sharp shadow, functions as a suppressed yet essential element within the defining polarities of eighteenth-century ideology. That period imagined itself as a series of oppositions, as a battle between conflicting forces of light and darkness. In terms of the period's mainstream, that opposition was between the secular and the religious, the natural and the theological, reason and faith. In the other major expression of this opposition, that most eloquently represented by Rousseau, the idea of "nature" retained its paramount importance but was contrasted not so much to the "religious" or the "theological" as to the "artificial"—that endless series of contrived and unnatural evils humankind had inflicted upon itself throughout history. This difference was important. Where the mainstream of the Enlightenment pointed to a shadowy past of Divine Right and abused privilege, Rousseau instead denounced what he saw as a resolutely secular and universal will to power, both flowing from and consolidating everything his contemporaries celebrated in the name of *les lumières*.

Rather than examine the polarities traditionally used to define the Enlightenment—the natural and the theological, the natural and the artificial—I suggest that we look at another opposition: that between everything the terms 'reason' and 'nature' came to signify and the recalcitrant challenge of chance. Standing against the century's proud beliefs in a world of reason or nature, and thus against a vision of the world as a potentially finite series of knowable and ultimately controllable determinisms, chance implied a resolutely tragic vision. To recognize chance was, more than anything else, to recognize our inability to reason toward and become part of any natural order. Chance speaks of the limits of reason as a faculty that, finally, reflects only its own presuppositions.

Within the newly secularized world of the eighteenth century, the emerging choice was that between an ever more triumphant faith in the ambitious yet fragile constructs of reason and a recognition of the world as chance. As the twilight of classicism compromised more and more completely any allegiance to a traditionally theocentric position, the newly palpable absence of the divine left two options: an ameliorative faith in the ability of human reason to understand and dominate a physical universe subject to knowable laws, and an antithetical vision of the world as ruled by the uncontrollable forces of chance and hazard. As alternatives to the rule of a divinity in which the intellectual elite professed more and more open disbelief, there remained the rigorous determinism of science and a disabused celebration of chance.

To choose science was to elect an understanding of the individual's role as one of participation in a struggle to fathom, describe, and explicate the laws governing a rigorously determined physical and social universe. To choose chance was to choose to understand the individual as a singular, isolated consciousness within a world of disorder and unpredictability shared with other, equally limited consciousnesses similarly stymied by the absence of any integrating principle.

Traditional histories of eighteenth-century France almost completely ignore the existence of such a choice. Narratives of the Enlightenment's triumph turn instead on the way that new experimental sciences, focused on and ferreting out the laws of the physical universe, departed from the abstractions of the previous century's Cartesian reason. Rather than projecting onto the world the categories and syllogisms of human thought, these newly enlightened sciences enthusiastically embarked on the discovery, understanding, and exploitation of the laws and constants of a physical universe independent of human interpretation. The validity claimed for the constructs of Enlightenment lay in their effort to enunciate a reality already there and already at work independent of human reason. In a recent study of chance and discovery, the chemist and historian of science Jean Jacques expresses with particular clarity both the shape and continuing relevance to the scientific enterprise of the Enlightenment's choice: "I draw the conclusion that my work depends entirely on one condition: that nature's laws, before being those of my reason, were her own. Our minds acknowledge them only because for thousands of years experience and discovery have confirmed them. It is not because I belong to a reasoning and rational species that I can hope to understand the real. . . . To the contrary, it is because the universe obeys laws which are also my own that I can penetrate its mysteries."[2]

Part One

Chance and the Culture
of Enlightenment

1

The Triumph of Probability Theory

La réflexion sur la chance dénude justement le monde de l'ensemble des prévisions où l'enferme la raison.
—GEORGES BATAILLE, *Le Coupable*

Fortuna was traditionally the very personification of surprise, . . . each unpredictable spin of her wheel turning the world upside down. The story of probability and statistics is one of the domestication of unpredictable Fortuna.
—LORRAINE DASTON, in *The Empire of Chance*

These two statements, the first from Georges Bataille's *Le Coupable,* of 1943, the second from the closing paragraph of a recent study of probability theory published in Cambridge's Ideas in Context series, evoke the two perspectives from which I will examine the development of probability theory from its origins in the work of Blaise Pascal through the Enlightenment and the early nineteenth century. Bataille's claim that an understanding of chance dissolves the cogency of any science born of reason is part of a series of philosophical reflections on liberty, fear, and *le hasard* collected in the chapter entitled "L'Attrait du jeu."[1] Daston's statement is from a collective work by a group of historians and social scientists subtitled "How probability changed science and everyday life."[2] Their focus, unlike Bataille's, is on the specific historical practices that resulted from the development and growing influence of what came to be called probability theory and would, in the nineteenth century, assume the more imperial demeanor of statistics.

9

Moving between the abstract and the concrete, I would approach the cultural history of probability theory through two figures from the classical period who played crucial roles in determining what would be the eighteenth century's most concerted strategies in responding to the challenge of chance. Pascal's Jansenistic theology, his conviction as to our utter dependence on divine grace and our inability to merit salvation through works, was part of a radical skepticism concerning humankind's ability to dominate, understand, or control the world of which it was a part. At the same time, and very much in relation to that skepticism, Pascal, in his correspondence with Fermat and his *Traité du triangle arithmétique*, laid the foundations for a mathematical assault on chance, promising in the most optimistic tones that our mastery of blind fortune could achieve all the exactitude and certainty of the geometric method through which he would analyze it. Speaking of what before him had been the incomprehensible puzzle of chance, Pascal wrote: "eam quippè tanta securitate in artem per Geometriam reduximus, ut certitudinis ejus particeps facta, jam audacter prodeat."[3] In *The Emergence of Probability*, Ian Hacking analyzes *Les Pensées*'s famous meditation on the wager. He shows that the sequence of stages in Pascal's debate between the believer and the libertine in fact results from a precise application to that subject of the mathematical analysis of expectations Pascal had developed in his earlier works on probability.[4] This coherence between Pascal's scientific and philosophical work, between his all but obsessive mathematization of every human situation and his acute awareness of the ultimate limits of human reason, suggests that we must look for the real motivation of his work on chance beyond the reductive legend attributing his role as the founder of probability theory to an encounter with an aristocratic gambler as incongruous as it was fortuitous. It was the nineteenth-century mathematician Siméon-Denis Poisson who first consecrated this legend in the opening page of his 1837 treatise on probability theory: "A problem related to games of chance, put to an austere Jansenist by a man of the world, was at the origin of the calculus of probabilities."[5] If Pascal was to impose upon chance a methodology and a rhetoric holding out a promise of certainty where before there had been only an insuperable challenge to human reason, it was not simply because he counted among his acquaintances the devoted gambler, the chevalier de Méré. The real motivation for Pascal's fascination with what would come to be known as probability theory lay in his far more fundamental compulsion to work through and against an acutely somber vision of the limits of human understanding.

René Descartes, in a well-known passage in *Le Discours de la méthode*, reveals a similar obsession with salvaging from a situation of complete uncertainty some nonetheless certain method for "advancing," for "moving forward." He adopts as the second maxim within his strategy for escaping his starting point in radical doubt the obligation to act as firmly and resolutely as possible in all actions. Descartes justifies this paradoxical response to the challenge of doubt with his metaphor of a man lost in a forest. With no idea where he might be, no sense of which direction he should take, it becomes all the more important that he feign an at least provisional certainty within his objective uncertainty: "Acting in this way like travelers who, lost in a forest, must not wander about, turning now one way and then another, and even less remain set in one spot, but must march ahead in one direction in as straight a line as possible, never changing their course for slight reasons, even though at the outset it was only chance that led them to choose that direction."[6] Thanks to the bootstraps effect of this strategy, a situation first defined as depending on *le hasard seul* yields both escape and salvation when approached through the protocols of certainty.

The examples of Pascal and Descartes are important because each shows in a different way how, against a background of radical skepticism, there emerged both the desire and an actual mathematical method for arriving at a new form of certainty based on a permutational analysis

11

of human contingency and thus possessing none of the abstract universality associated with the scholastic concept of an indubitable and apodictic *scientia*.[7] This new certainty was, finally, a particular valence of doubt. And without that origin in doubt, its rhetoric of promised understanding could never have achieved the imperious militancy it was so consistently to display.

In the second forward to his *De Ratiociniis in aleae ludo* (1657), Christiaan Huygens speaks frankly about the dizzying aspirations of this new science. The task before mankind, an endeavor in which Huygens sees himself as a principal contributor, is to make others aware of the large and previously unsuspected domains over which "our marvelous Algebraic Art" extends. In conquering these provinces of real life experience, the new algebra of hazards will use what first seemed an impossible challenge to produce the most convincing proof of its efficacy: "The more it seems difficult to use reason to analyze what is uncertain and subject to chance, the more the science accomplishing that feat will appear admirable."[8]

Pierre Rémond de Montmort offers in his *Essai d'analyse sur les jeux de hasard* (1708) the first application to card games of the mathematical techniques developed by Pascal, Fermat, Bernoulli, and Huygens. In fact, the careful descriptions Montmort gives of the card games before his analyses of their probabilities constitute the best summaries we have of what were some of the most popular card games of the late seventeenth and early eighteenth centuries: pharaon, lansquenet, le jeu du treize, basset, piquet, and hombre. In his introduction Montmort explains that his careful scrutiny of so apparently frivolous a subject as the intricacies of popular card games carries with it the serious advantage of allowing him to vanquish, on its home ground, that most decried of all Enlightenment evils: superstition. "It is especially in games of chance that the weakness of the human mind and its tendency toward superstition manifest themselves. . . . And it is much the same for people's behavior in all those areas of life where chance plays a role. The same prejudices govern them, and imagination dictates their conduct, blindly giving birth to fears and hopes."[9]

If superstition exercises so great a sway over our actions in the domain of card playing, it is because we are ignorant, because we remain unaware that there are in fact hidden laws regulating every turn of the cards. The task before Montmort is obvious: "I thus thought it would be useful, not only for gamblers, but for mankind in general, to show that chance does obey knowable rules and that, for not having learned those rules, we make mistakes every day whose unhappy consequences should far more reasonably be attributed to us than to the destiny we lament" (vii).

Montmort's analysis of card games, his contribution to the development of probability theory, is philosophically conceived as a demonstration that there exists no capricious superior power, no Fortuna or *hasard,* determining the fall of the cards. The only divinities at work in what the superstitious mistakenly persist in seeing as a brush with fortune are the mathematically calculable ratios between the chances for the card we want and the chances for all other possible outcomes.

This, however, is not the only lesson of the cards. Within the perfectly systematic calculations sustaining Montmort's analyses, the truly wise reader is invited to discover the careful hand of the Creator, the presence of a Newtonian first cause responsible for a perfect order. Anticipating Laplace by more than half a century, Montmort redefines *le hasard* as nothing more than an index of our ignorance: "Strictly speaking, nothing depends on chance. In studying nature, one soon learns that its Author acts everywhere and always with wisdom and infinite foresight. If we are to give the word *chance* a meaning congruent with true philosophy, we must conclude that as all things are determined by fixed laws, only those whose natural causes remain hidden from us are seen as depending on chance" (xiv).

The purpose behind Montmort's analysis of card games

is consonant with the fundamental endeavor of the Enlightenment. Our natural world, even that of apparent chance, is regulated by hidden rules structured in so orderly a fashion that mankind will one day surely complete his understanding of it. As we move toward that goal, we will, territory by territory, conquer the purely illusory realm of chance—a pseudo-power incarnating nothing more than our waning ignorance of natural causalities.

In his *Doctrine of Chances* (1718) Abraham De Moivre, the Huguenot mathematician who chose lifelong exile in England after the revocation of the Edict of Nantes, makes clearer than any of the major writers on probability theory what the real goal of this new science was. Examining those spheres of human activity where chance was assumed to play a part, the doctrine of chances will reduce that concept to one of utter insignificance, to a "mere word" fit only for those "blinded by metaphysical dust." "But *Chance,* in atheistical writings or discourse, is a sound utterly insignificant. It imports no determination to any *mode of Existence;* nor indeed to *Existence* itself, more than to *non-Existence*. It can neither be defined nor understood; nor can any Proposition concerning it be either affirmed or denied, excepting this one, 'That it is a mere word.'"[10]

Each of these passages from prefaces and addenda to early works of probability theory bases the value of their collective enterprise on its contribution to the emerging understanding of a system of laws banishing all belief in chance. But what, we must ask, is actually happening within these treatises on probability? The real order and systemicity offered the readers of these works lie within the mathematical analyses themselves. The truly new order being revealed in these works is that of the theory itself, of the theoretic construct through which the finite permutations of a given aleatory situation are inventoried and compared.

The theory of probability does offer a response to

chance, does generate a distinct scientific enterprise. It is able to do so, however, only by first relinquishing any claim it might make to speak of what, from the viewpoint of the player, the gambler, the person awaiting the outcome of the chance event, is most crucial: the present moment, what will actually happen next, the specific event. As a science of chance, probability theory may speak of the real; but it does so only by first stepping outside the real, by adopting as its vantage point a distant, removed position excluding all real involvement with any one outcome as opposed to another.[11] The reality about which probability theory speaks is always an abstracted real without compelling pertinence to any specific moment or situation.

Probability theory can say a great deal about the expectations I might legitimately entertain that a given number will appear when I roll two dice. What the theory tells me about those expectations forms a relevant context to my decision whether and what I will wager. Probability theory has, however, nothing to say about what number will actually come with the next roll. Thanks to the lessons of probability theory, I feel I know more, and I do know more. But there where I most want it to speak, it remains forever mute.

Like any *theory* of reality, probability "works" only to the extent it is able to substitute its representation of the real, its model, for the reality it sets out to explain. To the question, What *will* happen? it offers an exquisitely refined understanding of what *may* happen. As a science, the eighteenth century's doctrine of chances offered no new knowledge of any specific event. Instead, it spoke eloquently of all possible alternatives within the anticipated event. Coaxing us away from what it dismissed as a compulsive and primitive fixation on *the* result, probability theory asked its readers to focus instead on complex combinatorial permutations of all possible results. Silent with regard to the one, it spoke endlessly of the many.

Addressing this question of the limits of probability theory, the twentieth-century philosopher of science A. J.

Ayer expressed its fundamental paradox in the following terms: "No conclusions about any matter of fact can be derived solely from the calculus of chances. There are no such things as the laws of chance in the sense in which a law dictates some pattern of events. In themselves the propositions of the calculus are mathematical truisms. What we can learn from them is that if we assume that certain ratios hold with respect to the distribution of some property, then we are committed to the conclusion that certain other ratios hold as well."[12] Probability theory has in fact carried off an enormously seductive slight of hand, making the embarrassingly visible rabbit of our ignorance vanish into the decidedly thick air of complex equations. There where we feel most acutely the limits of our knowledge—as we try to know what specifically will happen next in a situation governed by chance—the calculus of probabilities offers a demanding and rigorously mathematized discourse bristling with apparent proofs of our mastery over a situation that in fact escapes us completely.

The new understanding suggested by probability theory carried with it cultural implications that were to change profoundly the way we think about the world, about society, and about the individual's place within it. What was happening in the development of this new science, in the contour of the very different way it asked us to look at the world, was perhaps most apparent in the elaboration, first by Jakob Bernoulli in 1713 and most completely by Poisson in 1835, of a "law" endowed with the convenient power to guarantee that, properly understood, the pronouncements of probability theory would always be correct: the law of large numbers.[13] Claiming that the frequency of events will, over the long run, always conform to the mean of their probabilities, this law dictates that the theorems of probability hold true on the one condition that the number of occurrences within the sample be sufficiently large. If we toss a coin only twice, it can easily happen that, rather than one heads and one tails, we encounter a 100 percent frequency of one alternative or the other. As we increase the number of tosses toward infinity, however, the fifty-fifty distribution predicted by this simplest level of probability analysis will prove more and more valid.

The law of large numbers, confirming probability theory's inability to speak of *this* event within *this* situation at *this* moment, implies that this new science may speak of the specific event only to the extent that it has become part of, cosubstantial with, a larger group, a larger number, outside of which the calculus of probability holds little validity. What we now call the law of large numbers is important because, more than any other single aspect of probability theory, it shows the role played by this new science in the consolidation of specific sociopolitical practices crucial to the development of Enlightenment ideology. What we see happening in this newfound branch of mathematical investigation, first modestly known as "the doctrine of chances" but, with Laplace, ambitiously rechristened "the calculus of probabilities," is an elimination of chance that carries with it both a redefinition of the individual and a foundation for the period's most important ideological constructs. The premise that the understanding of the individual can be complete and effective only when that individual has become one within a large number, one member of a group, is a guiding principle of the most important aspects of Enlightenment thought.

Rousseau's theory of the *volonté générale* depends on a structurally similar transformation through which the individual ascends to the higher moral level of the citizen. Rousseau's model of the modern state demands that each individual merge into and identify with all other members of the community in such a way that as each becomes a citizen, all come to participate equally in the collective privilege of sovereignty. Rousseau's analysis of the relation between the individual and general wills directly parallels the way probability theory addresses the question of the specific chance event through an abstraction from the single turn of the card or roll of the dice toward a higher level of reflection situating that event within the repertory of all possible outcomes. In both cases a superior value is attributed to that which concerns the collectivity as opposed to the individual.

At a different but again structurally similar level of reflection, Kant adopts as the foundation of his ethics an imperative implying that the individual's access to a norm of correct conduct hinges on his being able to extend *to all others* the dictates of any position the self would adopt individually. Everything that might once have been framed in the context of the single individual finds itself redefined by the presupposition that any true understanding of that singularity necessitates the individual's being absorbed within the group, the large number, the ambient community.

Inspired by the same lesson of probability theory, Condorcet set out to apply the work of his younger friend Laplace to the specifically political question how one might guarantee that such deliberative bodies as judicial tribunals and legislative assemblies will make correct decisions as they judge the guilt or innocence of an accused and as they frame laws for society. In his *Essai sur l'application de l'analyse à la probabilité des decisions rendues à la pluralité des voix* (1785), Condorcet carried out a careful if somewhat laborious analysis of how society might be sure of achieving such results. For Condorcet, this involved exercising control over a series of numerical variables. On the one hand, there was the number of members sitting in such bodies and the majority required for a binding decision. On the other hand, there was a different kind of variable: the probability that each member of such a body, as a more or less rational individual, would arrive at the correct decision in a specific situation. And here, Condorcet argued, the real value of his proposed system lay precisely in the fact that an adjustment within one of those variables could easily compensate for a deficiency in the other. When dealing with educated and objective individuals, from whom the likelihood of a correct decision was high, their total num-

ber, as well as the majority required for closure, could be
quite low. When, however, the deliberating body was composed of individuals in whom one had less confidence,
both the total number of members and the majority required for closure could be increased. Even though, in
other words, some members (and even many members)
might be wrong, this deficiency at the level of the individual could be recuperated as an avenue toward truth once
all such individual judgments had been integrated within
a larger collectivity and a more rigorous definition of the
required majority.

In attempting to understand the social and political implications of classical probability theory, it is instructive to
look beyond the eighteenth century to that science's continuation and culmination in the work of a figure such
as Emile Borel, the early twentieth-century mathematician
who stands as the most eloquent heir to the French Enlightenment tradition. Borel enunciated, more clearly than
any other single voice, the implications of probability theory and its development into statistical analysis in what he
called *les mathématiques sociales*. Only a firm grounding in
such "social mathematics," Borel insists, can guarantee a
correct appreciation of the relation between the individual
and the group, an appreciation recognizing that the only
true individualism is what he calls a "collectivized individualism":

> Is there then no basis to the opposition between probability
> theory and individualism? To the contrary, there is a very
> real one in that individualism is antisocial, whereas proba-
> bility theory lays the foundation for what might be called
> *social mathematics*. Its study reminds us that we are part of
> society and that social phenomena have their own existence
> and their own interest. Probability theory tells us that even
> though individuals differ in many ways, they are similar in
> their liability to accident, to illness, and to death. . . . For

that reason the study of probability theory has great educational value. As a discipline, it should be taught to all who aspire to a role in the administration of men and of things.[14]

What is most intriguing about this statement is the way Borel, in making his case for a "collectivized individualism," attempts to clinch his argument by referring to precisely that instance of chance over which probability theory can most obviously exercise no real power at the level of the individual: "they are similar in their liability to accident, to illness, and to death."

What emerges even from this rapid overview of the triumph of probability theory and its expanding political corollaries is the way this new understanding of the individual through the group relies on a process of circular reasoning. Throughout the eighteenth century, the individual was called upon to act in accord with various dictates of nature and reason. Yet those dictates become most audible and compelling only when, according to the same mechanics we have seen at work in the theory of probability, the individual was approached, not as a specific case defined by its singularity, but as a random sample from, and potential illustration of, probable laws valid only at the level of the large number, the encompassing group.

Given this reliance on the law of large numbers, on the necessity of the sufficiently large sample, it is not surprising that probability theory, at the service of (and itself well served by) a progressively more centralized state, should have found its most ambitious applications in the development of statistics.[15] More than any other single figure, it was Adolphe Quételet, Laplace's Belgian disciple, who, exploiting the ever more massive statistical data gathered by state offices, articulated the crucial ideological implication of this new discipline: that of *l'homme moyen*. According to a dynamics that the various coercions of the twentieth century have made eminently clear, this mythic "average man" quickly became not only a mathematical mean but the always eloquent spokesperson of a comminatory social imperative denouncing all difference as deviation.

The development of probability theory from the writings of Pascal through its nineteenth-century mutation into the discipline of statistics brought with it profound changes in the form of the historical consciousness imposed upon the individual. The early doctrine of chances, with its promise of at least partial knowledge in those vast areas where before there had been only the uncertainty of chance, contributed in an important way to the Enlightenment's emerging ideal of rational man. More than anything else, probability theory was a mathematized protocol providing individuals with the tools necessary to quantify and carefully measure the array of alternatives before them and thus ensure what seemed to be the ultimate rationality of their actions. Ideally, any situation falling within the realm of what Locke called "the twilight of probability" could now be broken down into a series of options each of which could be assigned a quantitative probability in relation to the desired outcome. As a series of major scientific works effecting what has been described as the most important mutation in human thought since Aristotle, the works of Pascal, Huygens, Leibniz, Montmort, Bernoulli, De Moivre, Condorcet, and Laplace assumed as their audience a new elite of fully rational individuals capable of understanding and applying the lessons of this new science both to themselves and to their political participation in the life of the community. Developed by and addressed to such an elite, the calculus of probability was based on and militated in favor of a vision of the individual as a consciousness freed from prejudice, superstition, and the unexamined ballast of tradition. Those who would calculate probability theory's complex permutations of the possible present were unencumbered by any allegiance to a past or a history extending back beyond their canny analyses of the specific situation in which a decision had to be made.

This concentration of the self within a faculty of reason situated entirely in the present represented a major shift away from a quite different ethos dictating that individuals locate their most profound sense of themselves within a concrete history linking them to, and defining them through, the temporal continuities of family and class. For the noble, this was the obvious continuity of an illustrious ancestry to be honored and perpetuated. For the merchant or tradesman, it was a commercial position defined and safeguarded by the continuity of a guildlike economic system. For the peasant, it was a piece of land passed down from generation to generation.

Very much in opposition to this diachronic sense of the self as the continuation of an identity anchored in a history of families, institutions, and inheritances, probability theory proposed and consolidated a new form of subjectivity structured as the pure synchrony of rational individuals living within and carefully evaluating the complete paradigm of lateral options available at each successive moment of their lives. For Laplace, classical probability theory's most eloquent and most influential spokesman, the ultimate value of this new science lay in its imperative that rational individuals, acting within a rigorously deterministic world, model themselves after the ideal of a superior, all-knowing intelligence for whom all subjection to human temporality, to the plodding sequentiality of past, present, and future, would cease: "Given for one instant an intelligence able to comprehend all nature's forces and the respective situations of all it comprises—an intelligence vast enough to analyze all those data—it would include in a single formula the movements of the greatest bodies of the universe and those of its lightest atom. For it, nothing would be uncertain, and the future, like the past, would be present to its eyes."[16]

The subsequent development of probability theory into

the ever more pervasive discipline of statistics consolidated yet at the same time shifted the orientation of this new consciousness of self. Rather than to the traditional Enlightenment ideal of the single, rational consciousness confronting and mastering the uncertainties of the present, the new science of statistics coaxed the individual toward an always comparative understanding and valuation of the self. The statistical consciousness came only by measuring the self against a potentially infinite series of averages and means. Statistical understanding juxtaposed the self, as one in no way privileged unit, with data relating it to all other such units throughout society. The growing force of such concepts as the "average man" and the "normal man" proclaimed the necessity that one's actions be understood through their integration within all the similar and different actions undertaken by that vast mass of others from whom the data and conclusions of statistics were drawn.

The most important premium accruing from this recuperation of the one through the many came with the probabilist's ability to elaborate a new and compelling science of what at the level of the individual could only appear to be pure chance. Once the whim of the individual had been integrated within the norms of the conglomerate, there emerged a knowledge that could present itself as the orderly and predictable working out of societal laws: "Statistical writers persuaded their contemporaries that systems consisting of numerous autonomous individuals can be studied at a higher level than that of the diverse atomic constituents. They taught them that such systems could be presumed to generate large-scale order and regularity which would be virtually unaffected by the caprice that seemed to prevail in the actions of the individual."[17]

The statisticians' "average man" also had a very definite doctrine to proclaim. The epitome of society as conglomerate, his perfect incarnation of the mean was such that all individuals, should they hope to understand anything of themselves, were obliged to ask how they compared with that universal standard. Consolidating one of the fundamental paradoxes of modern democracy, all could now be equal because all risked an equal insignificance should they cease to refer themselves to an exalted average that could, at the same time, claim to be nothing other than the mathematical summation of each as an individual. With all now equally subject to the rule of the average and the normal, the idea of a "census," of a one-by-one and one-for-one counting of the population, left the realm of the absurd. As Porter points out, "It makes no sense to count people if their common personhood is not seen as somehow more significant than their differences. The Old Regime saw not autonomous persons, but members of estates. They possessed not individual rights, but a maze of privileges, given by history, identified with nature, and inherited through birth. The social world was too intricately differentiated for a mere census to tell much about what really mattered" (25).

The individual consciousness posited by the science of statistics is no longer the practical, applied rationality of the early doctrine of chances, but the new thinking of a "mass man" hemmed in by and always receptive to the lessons to be drawn from a quantitative averaging of the one with the many. Probability theory offered the paradise of a purely present rationality freeing us from the burdens of history, family, and class. Its mutation into the imperial discipline of statistics redefined the individual as one unit cosubstantial with and quantifiable in terms of all others. Individual actions took on meaning only as a function of how they related to the actions of all others with whom the individual was compared.

Early probabilists such as Jakob Bernoulli, Leibniz, and De Moivre looked on their science as the beginning of a new apologetics, as a way of offering a rational defense of their Christian and providential world-views. For them, while the individual event may appear to be a product of chance, the working out of a divine plan for humankind could still be glimpsed in the broader contours of a whole into which the individual fit and for which providence provided the abiding law. In the course of the eighteenth and nineteenth centuries a profound mutation occurred. For Laplace, Quételet, and their progeny of sociologists, economists, and criminologists, the world was still deterministic, but it was a determinism cut off from any cause or principle of coherence beyond its material substance. For these scientists of the statistical, the world had become determined but meaningless.

The triumph of probability theory within the Enlightenment is important to our modernity for the boldness with which it was able to generate any number of rational and civic "moralities" whose control of the individual relied on an evacuation of all real reference to the individual and whose treatment of the specific demanded that it be subsumed within the general. For us, living in a time when the only conceivable ethics is one of what is probable within a context of large numbers, the eighteenth century holds a particular fascination as that moment when, perhaps forever, what began as an ethics of the individual freed from the weight of the past subordinated itself to the far more oppressive ideologies of the probable and the normal.

In examining the development of probability theory and its relation to the guiding ideals of the Enlightenment, we are inevitably led to ask what, finally, was at stake in this struggle to tame, domesticate, and render innocuous the brute reality of chance. The beginnings of an answer might be glimpsed in a 1777 text by Buffon entitled *Essai d'arithmétique morale*.[18] Buffon begins the explanation of his "moral arithmetic" by drawing a distinction between physical certitude and moral certitude. Physical certitude, he states, is the certainty we have of an event, such as the rising of the sun. Our certitude that the sun will rise is "physical" because it is "composée d'une immensité de probabilités" (458). Moral certitude, on the other hand, occurs when our certainty is only analogical and based on a comparison. Moral certitude is an only relative assurance based

on similar situations and most often is derived from what
has *not* happened in similar circumstances.

Conveying a clear sense of what he means by moral
certitude is important to Buffon because, he insists, it is on
its terms that we are forced to act in the greatest part of
our lives. Struggling to clarify this concept, to the question
where certitude begins, he offers a quantitative answer. A
moral certitude, he decides, is one at least equivalent to
our certainty that we will live another day. Relying on the
primitive actuarial tables available during the period, Buffon then calculates that the probability that a man of fifty-
six will die within the next twenty-four hours is approximately 1 in 10,189. This, for Buffon, provides exactly the
benchmark he needs. Any event whose probability is less
than 1 in 10,000 is one we can be morally certain will
not occur and one to which we should accord no more real
importance than we do to the possibility that we may die
within the next twenty-four hours. Therefore, to cite Buffon's practical example, only a fool would invest in a lottery
ticket when more than 10,000 other tickets are being sold.
Like our death within twenty-four hours, the possibility of
any event for which the odds are less than 10,000 to 1, he
concludes, "should neither affect nor occupy our feelings
or our minds for a single moment" (459).

It is the way man lives with but can and must forget his
mortality that allows Buffon to clarify his crucial concept of
the probable, of the morally certain. The fact that Buffon
defines this category in terms of a customary dismissal of
our death, which must one day be wrong, underlines a
profound complicity between probability theory's concerted emasculation of chance and our own continual rejection from consciousness of any real sense of our impending death. In her study of classical probability theory,
Lorraine Daston points out that while gambling problems
continued to provide the most numerous applications for
probability theory, an important part of the truly new discoveries within that science after 1700 occurred as a result

of attempts to establish what might be called an algebra of human mortality:

> This history of classical probability theory's treatment of risk is largely the history of mortality statistics and their applications. . . . Beginning with the work of Edmund Halley, Jakob Bernoulli, and Abraham De Moivre, the role of statistics in mathematical probability grew steadily, and for most of the eighteenth century the statistics of choice dealt with human mortality. Therefore, any account of the mathematical theory of risk in this period must begin with why, when, and how contemporaries kept track of death.[19]

Death was, it would seem, very much a silent player in the games of probability theory and the fascination they exercised over the eighteenth century. Jean d'Alembert, the one major mathematician of the period who remained skeptical of the more grandiose claims of probability theory, found himself caught up in and all but paralyzed by the same association of ideas as he wrote the article "Fortuit" for the *Encyclopédie*. He begins the entry with the Enlightenment's standard dismissal of chance and *le fortuit* as meaningless figments of our ignorance: "a fairly common term in our language and one completely bereft of meaning in nature. . . . We say that an event is fortuitous when its cause is unknown to us."[20] As he continues his analysis, however, the shadow of death and its links to chance and the fortuitous fall more and more heavily on his faith in the proud advance of human knowledge: "Anyone who reflects deeply on how events are related to each other will realize with terror to what extent our lives are fortuitous, and his thoughts will turn toward the idea of death as the single event freeing us from the universal servitude of living things" (2:63).

For d'Alembert as for Buffon, there is, consciously or unconsciously, a link between any meditation on chance, the less than certain, and the gamble of death. The truly fortuitous event, the event outside any causal chain through which we might control it, represents an unacceptable scandal in the same way that the reality of our own death, the ultimate unthinkability of that death, is antithetical to any true living of life. If probability theory was able so effectively to impose the illusion of its having tamed chance, of its having contained and mastered the threateningly uncertain within its mathematical equations, it was because in elaborating that utopia, probability theory turned our eyes away from that most terrifying gamble of all—our own death.

2

Gambling as Social Practice

*Le marchand acquère, l'officier conserve,
le noble dissippe.*
—A bourgeois of Lyon

*But the age of chivalry is gone. That of sophisters,
economists, and calculators, has succeeded; and the
glory of Europe is extinguished forever.*
—EDMUND BURKE, *Reflections on the Revolution in France*

Gambling gets no respect. Historians and literary critics of whatever persuasion have given it at best passing and condescending attention. Yet of all the social practices characterizing eighteenth-century France in its transition from *ancien régime* absolutism to revolution and democracy, few were more ubiquitous than gambling. King and court gambled. Rich and poor gambled. City dweller and peasant gambled. It is perhaps because gambling appears on both sides of the traditional cleavages through which we define the Enlightenment that it becomes all but invisible for those studying one group or another. In spite of the growing scholarly interest in the social and cultural dimensions of everyday life, no study has as yet seriously addressed what was actually at stake around the cards and dice always close at hand in the pockets and drawers of the eighteenth century.

To study gambling in *ancien régime* France is, in one sense, to study a new chapter in the history of the circulation of wealth and the increasingly ubiquitous phenomenon of money. Gambling, especially high-stakes gambling (a concept that waxes and wanes to accommodate every purse), was one of the first and purest forms of the circulation of money. To study gambling is to look at how different social groups related to this circulation of money—how they responded to being redefined, at least within the context of the game, by the cards they drew and the points they threw. For a society whose fundamental understanding of itself was racked by the conflict of divergent responses to the question how who one was related to what one owned, gambling's hyperactive redistribution of wealth cannot be dismissed as the indulgence of insignificantly personal vices. It was, I would contend, the very truth of the Enlightenment that was in play on the period's countless gaming tables.

Gambling seemed to be everywhere. And this in spite of its prohibition by a series of royal and parliamentary edicts that appeared with almost drumroll regularity—no fewer than thirty-two between 1643 and 1777—but whose very repetition testified to their futility. In Paris action could be found in any number of different settings. Because they were ideal for police surveillance and justified as a kind of public safety valve, there were ten authorized *maisons de jeux* in the capital where, much as in today's California poker parlors, gambling was allowed so long as it was on what were considered to be *jeux de commerce* as opposed to *jeux de hasard*—games such as piquet, trictrac, triomphe, and médiateur, in which the skill of the gambler was seen as playing a larger role than the purely chance-driven turning of a card or picking of a number. In fact, the *jeux de commerce* usually served as little more than a front for the far more lucrative *jeux de hasard*—basset, pharaon, biribi, lansquenet, loto—played in the backrooms of the same establishments. Also within the realm of tolerated gambling were the games offered at the two Paris fairs, the Foire Saint-Germain from early February to the eve of Palm Sunday and the Foire Saint-Laurent from late July to late September, a total of roughly four months every year. Various foreign embassies, lucratively exploiting the principle of extraterritoriality, ran games all year long on their premises.[1] By special permission of the king, the duc de Tresmes was allowed as governor of Paris to exploit the Hôtel de Gesvres as a gambling house, and later Madame de Carignan was authorized to open the Hôtel de Soissons for the same purpose.

To these relatively few tolerated gambling operations there must be added the literally hundreds of clandestine *tripots* scattered throughout the city and signaled to the knowing eye by the presence in front of them of *lampions*, lights so ubiquitous that one visitor to Paris observed that they functioned almost as a municipal lighting system: "Flaming pots set the Paris night ablaze."[2] And Paris was hardly alone in its devotion to gambling: even in a provincial town such as Bordeaux more than two hundred clandestine gambling houses were known to the police in the eighteenth century.

If the whole of France gambled with abandon in spite of what the law might say, this was in no small part due to the example set at court. While Mazarin is usually credited with bringing with him from Italy the fashion of playing cards, the real heyday of royal gambling dates from the reign of Louis XIV and the creation of Versailles. His three-hour-long *appartements du roi*, held thrice weekly, were for the sole purpose of gambling. Beginning in 1674, the queen hosted a game in her quarters each night from eight to ten, at which time the king would arrive to take her to supper. Madame de Maintenon, Monsieur, the king's brother, and the duc de Bourgogne, the king's grandson, also regularly organized games for their own and the king's pleasure. During the reign of Louis XV, his daughter Adélaïde organized the king's public game until that privilege passed to the dauphin's new bride. While Louis XVI had little taste for gambling and became decidedly peevish when others discussed their latest win or loss in his presence, the queen, Marie Antoinette, regularly presided over games of dizzyingly high stakes in the Salon d'Hercule.

Intensity as well as regularity characterized gambling

among the nobility from 1660 to the Revolution. The duchesse d'Orléans had a special canapé built so she could lie down during the long sessions she insisted on of her beloved lansquenet. The archbishop of Reims was rumored to have lost forty thousand livres in less than thirty minutes while gambling in a carriage following the king's boar hunt.[3] Madame de Sévigné speaks of the queen's having lost sixty thousand livres before noon one day in 1675. A few years later the king was said to have been quite upset at the news that Madame de Montespan had lost the tidy sum of 4 million livres in one evening of cards. He was relieved to learn that she had retrieved the situation by forcing her lucky companions to play on through the night until she recouped most of her losses.

Gambling at the royal chateaux—Fontainebleau, Saint-Germain, Chambord, and Marly as well as Versailles—set the tone for the nobility living in Paris. Fougeret de Monbron makes the exaggerated but nonetheless significant claim that at least three-quarters of the most respectable Parisian families defrayed the costs of their receptions with revenue from the games with which they entertained their guests.[4] The solicitous host was only too happy to serve as banker for the immensely lucrative games of hoca, biribi, pharaon, and cavagnole often held before as well as after dinner.[5] Satirists claimed that the first question any host was likely to ask before extending a dinner invitation was, Does he gamble? Writing to the raugrave Louise in 1695, Madame, the duchesse d'Orléans, lamented how gambling had killed people's taste for all other social activities: "Is dancing out of fashion everywhere? Here in France, whenever people get together, they want only to play lansquenet. It is the game in vogue here. Young people no longer have any desire to dance."[6]

These scenes, easily supplemented by any number of others drawn from the chroniclers and moralists of the period, eloquently confirm the fact that, as François Bluche put it, gambling was "le vice principal de la cour."[7] But why? What was it about high-stakes gambling that made it so integral a part of the social rituals of the most influential groups within the *ancien régime?* And why, from a different perspective, have historians of the period so consistently neglected any serious consideration of this phenomenon? Is there something about the *ancien régime's* gambling, or about us, that makes such questions so unseemly? Depending on how one looks at it, gambling was a consuming passion or a leisure activity that was part of everyone's life over a long and important period of the French monarchy. Yet, like Bluche, most historians consign the phenomenon of court gambling to the dubious category of "vice" and give it far less consideration than they do the various priapic feats carried out under the banner of a brother vice.

Explanations of gambling's ubiquity have, of course, been offered. Social historians point to the law of primogeniture and its injunction that the first-born son inherit the bulk of any family estate. Such an inheritance structure is seen as contributing to the formation of an ever-expanding corps of noble younger sons who, unable by reason of their station to participate in trade or manufacturing, saw gambling as one of the few avenues open to them for making their fortune.[8] Historians of everyday life under the *ancien régime* have hypothesized that part of gambling's attraction came from its status as one of the few readily available remedies to the crushing boredom of day-to-day life at Versailles. Other historians, following the interpretation most eloquently defended by Saint-Simon, claim that like some latter-day Machiavelli, Louis XIV singlehandedly imposed the fashion of high-stakes gambling as a cunning strategy to ensure the financial ruin of the nobility and thus eliminate any reenactment of the rebellious *frondes* that had traumatized his youth. Georges Mongrédien states, for instance, that "these enormous gambling losses became an occasion of new benefactions for the king and a way of keeping the court under his control."[9] More psychologically oriented historians have opted for the explanation offered by those such as D. M. Downes, who claimed that "those whose status is based on the aleatory principle of heredity will cultivate it at play."[10]

Each of these explanations has the shortcoming of seriously misinterpreting the facts of high-stakes gambling at Versailles. The hypothesis that gambling was the only financially lucrative option available to disinherited younger sons has been discredited by Guy Chaussinand-Nogaret's demonstration that a substantial portion of the nobility was very much involved in trade, manufacturing, and finance.[11] To assume that gambling can be attractive only as an escape from boredom is to adopt uncritically and, as anyone who enjoys gambling surely knows, erroneously a modern moralism quite alien to the nobility of the *ancien régime*. To take Saint-Simon's explanation at face value is to extend to the entire pandemic of gambling in seventeenth- and eighteenth-century France a claim that says far more about Saint-Simon's own obsession with the threats facing a debilitated nobility than it does about gambling as a social practice. To assume that the nobility saw their social status as somehow "aleatory" and were therefore drawn to such epiphanies of chance as gambling is to accept as fact a view that, during the period, was little more than a recurring theme of third estate propaganda. How, the noble would surely retort, could one more necessarily be who one was than by the fact of birth?

The inadequacy of these explanations underlines the fact that in order to understand high-stakes gambling during the *ancien régime,* we must make the difficult effort of adjusting to a value system and a way of thinking substantially different from our own. Robert Mauzi in 1958 and John Dunkley in 1985 have pointed out that in the period 1650–1789 there was a distinct evolution in the rationales offered for the repression of gambling.[12] The first phase, roughly corresponding to the reign of Louis XIV, was characterized by an attitude toward gambling that reflected the intimate union of church and state. Gambling was condemned for explicitly religious reasons, and that condemnation was enforced by civil authority. Gambling was wrong, so the arguments went, because all were placed on earth to merit eternal salvation through devotion to their creator and productive work for their fellows. Gaming and its concern with material wealth were antithetical to these duties. In addition to frustrating the purpose of human existence, gambling sinfully abused and trivialized a divine providence seen as presiding over all earthly events, the turning of every card and the roll of every die. Gambling even for small stakes was wrong, the moralists proclaimed, because the money so wagered could have been far more suitably used as alms for the poor. The tension and frustration of gambling all too frequently made it an occasion for blasphemy and superstition. These strictures, voiced by such religious figures as Frain du Tremblay, Bourdaloue, and Joncourt, were translated by civil authority into the cascade of antigambling laws promulgated between 1643 and 1717.[13]

During the period from the Regency to the Revolution, the religious arguments gave way to a quite different and distinctly sociocentric discourse. Gambling came more and more to be seen as a secular danger, an activity not so much threatening the divine order as promising the financial ruin of gamblers and their families. Because it reduced all players to the common denominator of the money they could wager, gambling also came to be seen as a dangerous corrosive to the sense of social order and rank. Critics of gambling turned their attention more and more to what they saw as the scandal of the crown's actually profiting from such disorder through its tax on playing cards, the hefty fees charged the tolerated *maisons de jeux,* and the revenue produced in the supposedly clean gambling of the newly instituted *loterie royale.* This willful complicity of crown and gambler amounted for its critics to a corruption of the people by the state in the name of profit. The evil of gambling was defined more and more as its unleashing of potentially uncontrollable passions threatening the individual's sovereign exercise of reason. Writers such as Barbeyrac, Caraccioli, and Dusaulx, contributed to the construction of this broad consensus relegating gambling to the category of the antisocial and the irrational.[14]

The eighteenth century saw the movement from a context in which gambling was seen, at least from the nobility's point of view, as a relatively minor deviation from the rigors of proper Christian conduct to a far more virulent and politically charged context in which gambling was indicted as a preeminent evil by those claiming to speak in the name of a purifying and regenerating nature. Jean Dusaulx's *De la passion du jeu* (1779) offers a particularly significant version of this sociocentric approach to gambling. For Dusaulx, the gambler is a monster whose actions defy rational analysis because he has in fact lost any individual character he might properly call his own. Like a reeling derelict, the gambler, lacking will, self-control, and any sense of purpose, becomes an empty space within the triumphant discourse of reason. Even his physical features become icons of this incapacity actually to *be* anything: "What particularly characterizes gamblers is their lack of any character. Their tumultuous and contrary feelings reciprocally destroy each other and leave only confused traces. They have the faces of lost men with no distinct physiognomy."[15] Without rational motive and even without physical features, the modern gambler became an affront to all social value. Consigned as he was to the realm of the unspeakable, his motivations and our understanding of them can be enunciated only by translating them into the madness at their core.

This shift in the attitude toward gambling that occurred in the eighteenth century is important because we remain today very much within its particular ethos of condemnation. Gambling is still defined, albeit in more contemporary language, as a self-destructive madness. Freud's well-known essay "Dostoyevsky and Parricide" uses that author's *The Gambler* and Stefan Zweig's *Twenty-four Hours in a Woman's Life* to argue that the supposedly masturbatory hand movements of the gambler reveal how the noxious pleasures of gambling are rooted in its rekindling of Oedipal fantasies of repressed patricidal omnipotence, which in turn provoke the masochistic self-punishment of deliberately losing. One of the most influential contemporary analysts of gambling, Edmund Bergler, nicely reveals the continuity of current attitudes toward gambling with the sociocentric discourse of the Enlightenment. For Bergler, gambling is the "old childish fantasy of grandeur and megalomania. More important, it activates the latent rebellion against logic, intelligence, moderation, morality, and renunciation. . . . [It is] the one exceptional situation in life in which the reality principle has no advantage over the pleasure principle. There blind chance rules. . . . Since the child has learned these rules [of the reality principle] from his parents and their representatives (teachers, priests, superiors, etc.), his rebellion activates a profound unconscious feeling of guilt."[16] As though poeticizing these earlier strictures, the gambler Clappique in Malraux's *La Condition humaine* defines his passion as "a suicide without death."

I emphasize the continuity between the Enlightenment's condemnations of gambling and our own post-Freudian views of the subject because their similarity lies at the heart of our difficulty in understanding what in fact was happening at Versailles—why king and court gambled as they did and why we judge them as we do. When we speak of gambling today, we remain, even within those discourses we sense as most contemporary and most our own, very much in the wake of the total victory of one view of gambling over another quite different and, for us, all but inconceivable understanding of that phenomenon. The premises sustaining contemporary condemnations of gambling— the supremacy of a reality independent of human volition, the triumph of the rational, the value of productive work, and the necessity of self-control—represent a heritage of the Enlightenment so fundamental to our understanding of the human situation that it has become all but impossible to think outside it.

The challenge before us is to move outside the compellingly obvious: to imagine gambling differently. Meeting that challenge can best be accomplished by a two-staged movement back in time from the Enlightenment. The first stage of this movement involves the relatively minor remove to the sixteenth-century Italy of Castiglione and Cardano. Baldesar Castiglione speaks of gambling in his *Il Cortegiano* (1528), the influential compendium of proper conduct at court that he drew from his long experience in the service of Guidobaldo de Montefeltro, the duke of Urbino. *Il Cortegiano,* soon translated into all the major European languages, was to have a tremendous impact on all who found themselves asking, for one reason or another, how they should act in the presence of king and court. To Gasparo's question in book 2 whether it should be thought a vice on the part of the perfect courtier to gamble at cards and dice, Federico responds with a definite no: "I do not, unless he should do so too constantly and as a result should neglect other more important things, or indeed unless he should play only to win money and to cheat the other player; and, when he lost, should show such grief and vexation as to give proof of being miserly."[17]

Gambling is a social practice within courtly society with which the gentleman must be familiar. But there are ways of gambling that are unacceptable for the true courtier: to play with the primary intention of winning money; to cheat; or, when losing, to act in such a way as to reveal an inordinate attachment to money. Castiglione's position on gambling draws a careful distinction between gambling itself and the appearance of any real concern with the money in play. Gambling must, in other words, be an occasion for the courtier to demonstrate his independence from money as money. The true courtier never plays *only* to win money. If he gambles, it is to demonstrate a prowess superior to that of his adversary. But that superiority must never be secured at the cost of cheating, of defining oneself as morally inferior to the opponent for the sake of gain. Finally, to show anger over a gambling loss is to avow publicly one's dependence on what can never be more than anonymous money. Gambling, Castiglione helps us understand, was seen by the courtier as an activity centered not on money and financial gain but on affirming one's basic ethics and identity. The identity at stake was that of the individual as one who knew, lived by, and incarnated a socialized perfection conceivable only within the context of the court.

Writing fifty years after Castiglione, Gerolamo Cardano is best known as the mathematician who first provided the solution for third-degree equations in his *Ars magna sive de regulis algebraicis* (1545). Twenty years later, in 1565, he published his *De ludo aleae,* which, coming thirty-five years before Galileo's treatise on dice playing and almost a full century before the correspondence between Pascal and Fermat, is often described as the first glimmer of what would come to be known as probability theory. As a scholar, Cardano was concerned mainly with the mathematics of the games he considers. Before beginning that analysis, however, Cardano considers the ethics of gambling, how his subject relates to the realm of moral value. Gambling and understanding how games work constitute a laudable enterprise for the true gentleman. To gamble for gain, however, is quite another affair. In explaining his position, Cardano elaborates an eminently scholastic classification of the various ways one might seek financial gain. Gambling to win money stands, it turns out, near the very bottom of his classification. The most morally acceptable way to earn money, Cardano tells his reader, is through transactions where the paying party is both aware of what is happening and willing to participate. This is the case for fees earned by lawyers and physicians. Below that on the moral scale comes earning money through transactions with people who are aware of what is happening but participate unwillingly. This, for Cardano, is the case of the merchant who sells for more than he has paid what others find themselves obliged to buy. The moral value of winning money at gambling is even lower than selling goods because the astute gambler, also making money from people aware of what they are doing but unwilling to lose, profits from people he knows, while the merchant usually sells to strangers. The only financial gain morally inferior to winning at gambling is that derived from a party who is both unwilling and unaware of what is happening—as is the case with trickery and theft. The conclusion Cardano draws from this elaborate and somewhat muddled exercise in categorization is clear: "Gambling is disgraceful because a man makes gain from his friend against that friend's will."[18] Cardano completes his consideration of the ethics of gambling by agreeing with Aristotle's statement in the *Ethics* that "gamblers, thieves and robbers ply a sordid trade for they traffic in base gain." Finally, Cardano adds, the thief could even be seen as morally superior to the gambler, since the thief at least runs a risk in securing his gain and thus shows some degree of courage.

Castiglione and Cardano insist on a distinction between gambling and gain that was to remain a constant of the courtly ethos on both sides of the Alps for two centuries. Roger Mettam, describing the French aristocracy of the *ancien régime,* points out that there were three tests by which the prestige of a noble was assessed.[19] The first was the social status of the man and his family as defined by genealogical pedigree. In this regard the year 1400 was of particular importance, and Mettam points out that during the personal rule of Louis XIV, over three-quarters of the nonroyal peerages claimed origins that went back to the fourteenth century or earlier. The second test turned on the influence and social power of the properly pedigreed noble: the extent of the clientele beholden to him and the importance of the patrons from whom he might expect protection. The third and most tangible index of prestige was the manner in which the noble lived: "The third test of personal and social prestige was based on the life style of the individual courtier. . . . The aristocratic disdain for money and for the debasing bourgeois world of commerce and trade received practical expression in the lavishness of their daily lives. A high noble lived more spectacularly and wastefully than a lesser one, and the king had to outshine everyone in the splendour of his household, his prodigality and his generosity" (59). Notorious examples of this imperative are well known: Madame de Guéménée owed her shoemaker the sum of 60,000 livres, Madame de Montmorin owed 180,000 livres to her dressmaker, and Madame de Matignon paid her coiffeur 24,000 livres to style her hair differently each day for one year—this during a period when the average daily wage for an unskilled worker was approximately 1 livre.

As such examples demonstrate, the essential trait of the noble's lifestyle was a disdain for any limit on personal prerogative by reason of cost. Not only was extravagance the rule but any sign of personal concern with money was potentially derogating. Mettam points out that "ideas like 'balancing the budget' and 'living within one's means' were bourgeois preoccupations which had no place in the noble ethic. All responsibility for domestic finance was accordingly delegated to household officials, who were simply required to keep the family financially afloat by whatever methods they could devise" (61). If whatever worked was fine, this was in part because the debts incurred in consolidating aristocratic prestige, such as those for shoes, dresses, and coiffeurs, were inevitably owed to people of inferior social status, who could be, and quite often were, treated as such.

There was, however, one all-important exception to the aristocracy's cavalier treatment of debts. It was the duty of a gentleman always to pay his gambling debts, and that before any other kind of debt. One of the most interesting references to the special status of gambling debts occurs in the article "Jouer" in Diderot and d'Alembert's *Encyclopédie*. While this entry consists for the most part of a mathematical illustration of how the new science of probabilities had extended the rule of reason to territories where before one saw only chance, it begins with a statement on the singular status of gambling debts *dans le monde:* "One might ask why gambling debts are so rigorously honored in polite society while the same people often feel little scruple in neglecting far more sacred debts. The answer lies in the fact that in gambling one accepts a man's word in a situation where there is no legal recourse. A trust has been extended to which one must respond. In other circumstances, the person could be compelled by the courts to meet his obligations."[20]

Gambling, in the eyes of the law, held the peculiar legal status of an activity that was *toléré mais non permis.* This meant that as far as the state was concerned, gambling debts had no legal status. To pay such a debt was equivalent, from a legal standpoint, to bestowing a gift: while the giver could not ask for the return of what he had already given, he could not be obliged on the basis of a promise to give more than he in fact chose. As obligations backed only by the value of one's word, gambling debts inevitably obliged the noble. The true aristocrat recognized a gambling debt as binding because in so doing he was not submitting to the dictates of any externally imposed law but acting entirely of his own free choice. To pay one's gambling debts said nothing of the status of the person to whom they were owed, but it said everything of the value of the debtor's freely given word. Gambling in the *ancien régime* existed within what for us is a startling configuration of values. For Castiglione, knowing how to gamble nobly meant knowing how to lose. For Cardano, the ethical value of gambling became negative only when one gambled to win money. In France high-stakes gambling was an important symbolic activity for a nobility obliged to affirm its prestige and its independence of any limiting financial considerations.

For today's readers, descriptions of court gambling at Versailles and the often colossal sums that changed hands there inevitably evoke echoes of Veblen and his analysis of a late-nineteenth-century monied leisure class fixated on the affirmation of its status through various rites of conspicuous consumption. Such an equation of the behavior of the *ancien régime* aristocracy with that of a capitalist plutocracy has, however, the enormous disadvantage of distorting and dehistoricizing the vastly different motivations actually at work within these two groups. For an understanding of the social practices of the eighteenth-century French nobility, we should look not so much forward to the very different reality of American capitalism but backwards to both the real and the fictive image of the Middle Ages within which the ideology of the French aristocracy was grounded. If, that ideology tells us, the noble was noble, it was for one reason alone: his ancestors had, on the field of battle and with their blood, won the recognition of their king. Their titles were grounded first and foremost in feats of arms carried out in a virile past of nation-building under the direction of the king. To be noble was to have demonstrated—personally or vicariously through an ancestor—a willingness to risk one's life in battle beside one's king. The courage to stake one's life on martial prowess was seen as so sure an indication of personal valor that it was hypothesized as a quality transmitted through blood from one generation to the next. This more than anything was the foundational idea of the hereditary nobility.

The reality of the eighteenth-century nobility was, of course, something far more complex. The massive selling of letters of nobility initiated by Louis XIV as well as the ever-growing number of "mésalliances" between the traditional nobility of the sword and the parvenus of the robe placed the claim to noble blood on a basis far more mythical than biological. If the founding urfathers had valiantly shed blood for their king, the same could hardly be said of those who simply bought their way into the ranks of the second estate. It is the existence of so obvious a gap between the explicit ideology of the nobility and its reality that explains the importance to this group of a number of compensatory activities in which the challenge and glory of the battlefield were reproduced and, at least to our eyes, parodied. The most obvious of these substitutes was the duel. Etymologically rooted in the Latin *duellum*, an archaic form of *bellum*, the duel was a kind of mini-war in which life was risked and blood shed. The duel was, however, an ultimately solipsistic gesture directed only at the preservation of one's threatened sense of honor rather than at any real service to the king. The duel was an affirmation of the individual's willingness to risk his life rather than see his honor compromised by some derogating word or action. To call the other out was to limit the future to one of two alternatives: proving one's nobility or dying.

In his recent study of the duel, V. G. Kiernan makes explicit how gambling was defined by the same kind of metaphoric substitution: "A man had to be able to hazard his fortune on a turn of the cards as coolly as his fore-fathers risked their lives on the luck of battle. Card-tables at Versailles, where millions of livres were yearly staked, offered a new tournament ground for blood to show its quality."[21] As one of a number of substitute affirmations of nobility, high-stakes gambling held the appeal not only of proving one's willingness to confront risk with equanimity but also of proclaiming the individual's superiority to the ever more imperious rule of money. La Bruyère alludes in his *Caractères* to how high-stakes gambling all but guaranteed public attention and elevated social standing: "Nothing makes a man more immediately fashionable or raises him higher in public esteem than high-stakes gambling. . . . I would be surprised to see any polished, lively, witty man . . . even begin to compare himself to someone who has just lost eight hundred pistoles at a sitting."[22]

The first stage of the movement back in time I suggested as a way of understanding the significance of gambling for the French aristocracy led to its roots in the Italian Renaissance of Castiglione and Cardano as well as in the formation of chivalric society on the battlefields of medieval Europe. The second stage of that movement into the past involves the almost Rousseauian gesture of a step back to a prehistory of the nation-state available to us only through the work of anthropologists.

In his *Essai sur le don* (1925), Marcel Mauss offered a groundbreaking study of the function of the gift in a number of archaic societies ranging from the Melanesia Islands and the American Northwest to the Hindu Classical period. Mauss's analysis of the gift in those contexts provides one of the best tools for understanding the distinctly antimodern underpinnings of aristocratic gambling in *ancien régime* France. Better put, Mauss's remarks on the function of the gift help us to grasp why and how it is that we have so consistently misread and misunderstood the meaning of aristocratic gambling during the eighteenth century.[23]

Mauss explicitly considers the function of gambling while discussing various tribes of Alaska and British Colombia. Gambling, he points out, was one of a number of practices crucial to a concept of honor according to which individuals fulfilled, through what could be virtually unlimited consumption and destruction, "the duty of returning with interest gifts received in such a way that the creditor becomes the debtor."[24] Throughout his study, Mauss struggles to describe for his readers an economic system based on principles radically different from our own. In modern Western societies, the concept of individual wealth is defined as a personally controlled reservoir drawn from a larger system of exchange encompassing an entire society. One's wealth is what one has been able to accumulate, designate as one's own, and thus control, if not physically at least juridically, within the system as a whole for whatever purpose one wishes.

In the archaic societies Mauss studies, wealth is a concept subservient to prestige. Utterly at odds with a mentality capable of imagining the Swiss bank account, these societies defined prestige, not by how massively one was able to abstract elements from circulation and accumulate a personal reservoir, but by the degree to which the wealthy individual was able to incite, continue, and multiply the intensity of a series of exchanges in which all were involved and by which all were defined. The highest prestige accrued to a giving from which no return was expected, to a surrendering of one's wealth equivalent to its pure destruction: "Sometimes there is no question of receiving return; one destroys simply in order to give the appearance that one has no desire to receive anything back" (35–36). This summit of seemingly gratuitous destruction is important because it cautions us not to equate our contemporary understanding of commerce with the workings of a prestige-based system of exchange: "It is an aristocratic type of commerce characterized by etiquette and generosity; moreover, when it is carried out in a different spirit, for immediate gain, it is viewed with the greatest disdain" (36).

Similarly unconcerned with any personal accumulation of wealth, in fact debased by any such goal, the true *ancien régime* aristocrat gambled not so much to win money as to project and consolidate a socialized image of himself through a singularly rapid giving and receiving of gifts. Mauss's analysis of prestige and the gift helps us to understand how high-stakes gambling at Versailles became one of the primary social practices through which nobles sought to affirm their identity within an individual and group ethos defining them as independent of the ever-increasing power of money. Gambling for high stakes and standing ready to lose "nobly" became an essential trait within the ideal of the "honnête homme." Writing in the mid-seventeenth century, the chevalier de Méré states: "One must always gamble as an honnête homme, and be ready to lose exactly as one might win, such that neither outcome be visible on one's face or in one's way of acting."[25] Almost a century later, in 1746, the abbé Pluche reaffirms the same attitude in his *Le Spectacle de la nature:* "One of the first duties of the gentleman is to gamble heavily, and to know how to lose calmly. The sporting player [le beau joueur] . . . collects what he has won with an air of indifference and pays what he has lost with a smile."[26]

The ambiguous status of this ardently desired but ultimately impossible superiority of the nobility to the force of money can be seen in the way Louis XIV would on occasion pay the gambling debts of a family member or favored courtier. In 1675 he liquidated a debt of 120,000 livres for his brother, Monsieur. The most significant of these gestures occurred, however, in 1700 when the duc de Bourgogne, after much hesitation as to whether he should himself go directly to the king for help or approach him through an intermediary, decided to act himself and asked the king for the sum he needed to settle what had become a particularly pressing gambling debt. The memorialist Dangeau reports the king's unexpected reaction in his entry for May 15, 1700:

> Monseigneur, the duc de Bourgogne, recently asked the king for money. The king gave him more than he has requested and, giving him the money, told him how happy he was that he had approached him directly without asking anyone else to talk to him first. The king insisted that he should always do that, and that he should gamble without worrying, as there would always be money, and because losing should be of no importance to people like them [de nulle importance à des gens comme eux].[27]

The duc's request to the king thus became the occasion of a royal lesson seen as far more important than the sum in question. No problem that involved only money, the king was saying, should be of real significance for persons of their rank. Gambling debts were, more than anything else, an occasion to affirm a superiority to the rule of money, which was, finally, "de nulle importance à des gens comme eux."

This contempt for the anonymous power of money as money is important because it points to the nobility's grounding of its personal identity in a fixed, inherited sense of self that brought with it a freedom of thought and action far greater than that available to those whose social status depended entirely on acquired wealth and a compulsive mimicry of aristocratic conduct. Because everything money could buy was finally only an accouterment to a far more essential sense of self concomitant with birth, the noble of long standing was open to an infinitely greater independence than those who, if deprived of the symbols confirming their wealth, risked losing all sense of their social identity.

As a codification of Louis XIV's new orthodoxy, the esthetic dictates of classicism legislated what persons of taste and breeding were to prefer and why. The audience toward which that pedagogy was directed was not the traditional nobility of the sword (which could be assumed to know quite well what it liked and why) but the growing ranks of the king's newly ennobled and culturally insecure officeholders and functionaries who had only recently been called to the service of the crown. Often totally ignorant of the behavior expected of them in the court's rigidly hierarchical world, they formed a singularly docile audience anxious to learn how they should speak, how they should act, and what they should enjoy. The protocols of gentle station figured forth in the innumerable dictionaries, grammars, hierarchies of genres, criteria of taste, and rules of polite conduct so carefully codified during the reign of Louis XIV were breviaries for a recently elevated bourgeoisie grasping at every assurance that they took their pleasures exactly as they should. The traditional nobility of the sword, sure of who they were, could comfortably and without fear of *déclassement* find their pleasures where and as they wished.

There was during the eighteenth century no such thing as a single nobility. To the contrary, a century of the crown's selling ennobling offices as a way of replenishing the treasury had made of the French aristocracy and its attitude toward wealth a divided and polarized amalgam of distinctly different interests. At one extreme, within what I have called the traditional nobility, was an old guard that refused all contamination by lucrative activity. At the other, as the far more numerous component of the nobility, were those nobles literally made of money who participated avidly in the various financial and commercial activities encouraged by the crown.

Recognizing this cleavage within the second estate, its status as a volatile mixture of two antithetical world-views, is crucial to understanding the significance of high-stakes gambling as a social practice during the Enlightenment. On the one hand, there was within the traditional nobility a continuing allegiance to the practice of gambling as a prestige-conferring secular oblation. On the other, there was on the part of the newly ennobled an at least implicit ethos of economic calculation equating worth with individual wealth. The nobility present at Versailles, itself a mixture of members of the oldest families serving as personal officers to the king and of the recently elevated serving as administrators to the crown, was a highly conflicted subset entirely representative of the second estate as a whole. Existing alongside each other, yet in all but total contrast to each other, the diverse components of this expanded nobility achieved little more than a truce marked by a progressively more strident polarization. For the traditional nobility as well as the parvenus, to be truly noble came more and more to depend on affirming one's difference from that sinisterly similar group of impostors just across the invisible divide.

The fundamental oppositions within this ideological struggle are clear. At the summit was a nobility whose sense of self was based on personal ancestry, on an inherited title held over time, and on its identification with a geographically specific estate providing the individual's name and social identity. For this group, up until the time of its extinction, money, the token of mobile wealth independent of its holder, was regarded as a means, a pure instrument useful only for the duty of "living nobly" and

49

of no real value in itself. To take money seriously was to debase oneself, to subordinate one's value as the biological continuation of a dynasty to the pseudo-value of ultimately meaningless pieces of metal prized only because of the cupidity of others unlike oneself. From this point of view, the noble was noble precisely because he was beyond the power of money to make him more or less than what he was by the unalterable fact of birth. It was in terms of this ideology that the traditional French nobility sustained, far longer than any other European variant, a contempt for all involvement in trade, banking, and industry as activities sullied by their obvious involvement with the lucrative movement of money.[28]

Seen from this perspective, the practice of high-stakes gambling became a token of class affiliation, an affirmation of the individual's superiority to any change of fortune consisting solely in a gain or loss of money. The higher the stakes, the more noble the superiority to money they expressed. For us, and it is here that Mauss's analysis of the gift in archaic societies proves so helpful, any intuitive identification with this position is impossible. Universally defined by and through money, the contemporary imagination is obliged, even as it tries to imagine some real independence from the rule of money, to remain within its framework. Freedom from the rule of money appears today as a privilege exclusively reserved to the immensely wealthy. As though any coherent suspicion of money's problematic status, of its being itself the cause of the very ills it claims to cure, had become unthinkable, the power of money has cleared all opponents from the field and occupies alone the only apparently antithetical positions of all that is worst (when there is not enough of it) and of all that is best (if only there were enough of it).

At the same time that the traditional nobility practiced high-stakes gambling as an affirmation of its superiority to money, a complex change was taking place within the ideology of the other group making up the uneasy amalgam of the second estate. The recently ennobled bourgeois was by definition someone who had set himself apart from and above the other members of the third estate through a particularly successful manipulation and accumulation of money. Confronted with this man of money, the traditional nobility expressed only revulsion. The ennobled bourgeois, when he raised his eyes from the circulation of money, discovered that no matter what he possessed and no matter what he could purchase, he remained, precisely because he depended on money, an object of thinly disguised contempt for that segment of the nobility whose legitimacy was infinitely more obvious than his own. If the *anoblis* were to overcome the stigma of money and accede to a higher legitimacy, they were obliged, as they consistently did, not only to purchase a title providing them with a *nom à particule* but to adopt as their own a lavishness antithetical to the careful management of wealth on which their social ascension had been based.

The eighteenth-century French nobility had become a confluence of impossibilities, a juxtaposition of mutually sustaining contradictions. For the traditional nobility, the contradictions were obvious. High-stakes gambling and its potential for colossal losses might allow the momentary affirmation of the self as beyond the power of money, but the results of that loss had ultimately to be lived out in a world where the sway of money was already irresistible.

Our understanding of the ambiguous appeal of high-stakes gambling to the traditional nobility has been compromised by the too rapid assumption that in this practice they were somehow victims of their king. All the most powerful nobles, the argument goes, were severed from real power by their residence at Versailles, where, whipped on by the king, they gave themselves over to gambling so completely and in so unreal a context that they blithely diced away the economic basis of any possible independence from the central monarch. According to this view, Louis XIV is congratulated for tactics of statecraft more appropriate to a Las Vegas entrepreneur.[29] What this argument chooses to ignore is an aristocratic ethos of gambling that was far more certainly shared by Louis XIV than it was created *ex nihilo* to serve some sinister purpose. The nobles gambled as they did because they were nobles, not because they were duped by their king.

If this view of the king's role has nonetheless achieved considerable currency, it is in large part because its adoption after the fact by important spokesmen for the traditional nobility provided the only palatable alternative to a vision of themselves as financial lemmings in a world where the power of money had grown progressively more absolute. Some other explanation had to be found. And it was Saint-Simon, more than anyone else, who pointed his finger and leveled the accusation. For him the culprit was not so much Louis XIV himself as Mazarin, the incarnation of the corrupted and corrupting foreigner who had even gone so far, during the regency of Anne of Austria, as to prolong artificially the king's childhood by addicting him to one puerile card game after another. Writing many years after the events described, Saint-Simon lays the blame squarely at the feet of Mazarin: "It [le gros jeu] was one of the sources he [Mazarin] drew copiously from, and one of the best ways of ruining a nobility he hated and held in contempt, just as he did the entire French nation, of which he wanted to destroy all that was great in itself. Others have labored in the same direction since his death, arriving at that perfect success which we see today and which foretells with certainty the end and imminent dissolution of our monarchy."[30] The real evil of such gambling for Saint-Simon lay in the avarice it inspired, not so much as a moral failing of the individual, but as a socially destructive threat to due respect for rank and privilege. To gamble avariciously, to gamble for what might be won, meant that one welcomed to the gaming table as one's equal those whose only qualification was a full purse.

To Saint-Simon's aristocratic eye, one man more than any other came to incarnate the noxious effects of this promiscuous social intercourse: Philippe de Courcillon, ultimately the marquis de Dangeau. Not only was Dangeau born a Huguenot, Saint-Simon points out, but his nobility was "fort courte" (16:73). Perhaps because Dangeau was a rival chronicler of Louis XIV's court, Saint-Simon offered an extended portrait of him upon his death in 1720. Dangeau represented for Saint-Simon the perfect example of what was to be expected from the recently ennobled. First admitted to court for his skill at gambling, he began his career by using the Spanish he had learned as a soldier to charm the king's mother and his new bride. Dangeau won such large sums from the two of them while playing reversi that Colbert complained of the situation to Louis XIV. Having decided to investigate firsthand, the king watched the three play while hidden behind a drapery. Not only did this convince him that Dangeau was not cheating but he was so impressed with the quality of the man's play that he invited him to join his own game.

From all accounts, Dangeau was a singularly astute gambler who won the equivalent of several fortunes during his time at court. Madame de Sévigné speaks with admiration of how she watched him win two hundred thousand livres during one ten-day period and then another three hundred thousand the following month. Dangeau was one of the few big winners at court who was never accused of cheating. If Dangeau was such a successful gambler, Saint-Simon was quick to point out, it was because he was both the antithesis and the nemesis of the truly noble style of play that should characterize the aristocratic gambler. Dangeau's consistent winnings depended not on the display of any singular courage in the face of risk and a worthy adversary but on the most venal and thoroughly bourgeois calculations as to how, regardless of the quality of his adversaries, he might always win. Dangeau's manner at the gaming tables was, as Saint-Simon saw it, one of base and steady self-interest: "He applied himself to acquiring a perfect knowledge of all the games then played . . . as well as to learning their intricacies and the probabilities for every card, all of which he mastered to the point of rarely making a mistake . . . and of being able to calculate carefully and bet heavily on the cards he estimated would win" (16:74). In his *Eloge de Dangeau*, Fontenelle confirms these same traits while giving them a far more positive coloration: "He had a supreme feel for gambling . . . he had penetrated its entire algebra, that infinity of relations between numbers which reigns within its various games, as well as all the delicate and imperceptible combinations of which they are composed, and which are often intermeshed with such complexity that they resist even the most subtle analyses. . . . He applied theories only he could understand and solved problems only he could pose."[31]

Once established by way of the gaming room, Dangeau began a brilliant career that, for Saint-Simon, was perfectly consonant with his origins: "He never uttered a word against anyone, he was mild and accommodating . . . an obliging admirer of trivia so long as that trivia came from the king or from those in power and favor" (16:74). Always anxious to anticipate the royal will, Dangeau was for Saint-Simon a man who became everything his money and his sycophancy could buy: "His money began to make of him an intimate of the king, a governor of Touraine, and a regular guest at the daily games organized by the king and Madame de Montespan" (16:75). It is not surprising that when it came to summing up, Saint-Simon should see him as "a large and well-built man . . . he promised exactly what he delivered, a dullness that could make one vomit" (16:74).

Far from being innocuously grotesque, Dangeau came to represent for Saint-Simon the parvenu's dangerous combination of an envy and recrimination always ready to disparage whatever he himself could not achieve. With the king's complicity, Dangeau had risen far higher than his merits, but this did not stop him from becoming the implacable enemy of those one rung above the highest point of his ascension: "Dangeau never got over the fact that he had been unsuccessful in all his ploys to have himself named a duke. He developed an acute hatred for that honor to which he had been unable to accede. That was his way of compensating himself" (16:79).

For Saint-Simon, the real scandal of a career like Dangeau's lay not so much in his having become one of the king's intimates and his willingly denigrating betters he could never hope to understand as in the fact that so many other ducs, Saint-Simon's peers, had helped create this situation by their willingness to welcome as their equal at the gaming table anyone with the money to play. In so doing they had collaborated in a disregard for rank and station that was at the heart of what Saint-Simon saw as the ultimate corruption of the traditional nobility. Their avarice had made them the unwitting accomplices of a royal policy of unmerited advancement threatening to destroy the nobility and everything it stood for.

Dangeau's career, built on pitting his careful study of probabilities against aristocratic opponents for whom such an approach to gambling was unthinkable, became a perfect symbol of the dilemma facing the traditional nobility: the high-stakes gambling through which they sought to affirm their superiority to the rule of money only destroyed their independence and consolidated their devolution to a level on which, finally, everything could be bought.

Alongside the traditional nobility for whom Saint-Simon was the most eloquent spokesman was the other group, almost two-thirds of the whole, whose titles, dating back no further than 1600, had been purchased from the crown as the last step in their ascension from the third estate. Law, trade, finance, and manufacturing were the lucrative avenues through which a sufficient fortune could be amassed to gain entry into the nobility. In buying their titles, these wealthy bourgeois purchased the privilege of joining a group whose explicit value system recognized no merit in what had been the arena of their greatest success.

Given that itinerary, it is not surprising that gambling and the gambler, the circulation of money and those participating in it, became the scapegoat of everything this ennobled bourgeoisie, acutely uneasy about the real source of its power, chose to deny, condemn, and repress. It is this obsession with erasing their own shameful origins in money that explains why gambling became for the ascendant bourgeoisie a scandalous evil marked by a moral value totally unlike that given it by the traditional nobility. The ennobled bourgeois, all too aware of the value of the money being wagered, used his strident denunciation of that pure circulation of money to affirm his newly acquired contempt for so plebeian an appetite for gain.

Given the profound conflict of attitudes converging on the social practice of gambling, it is not surprising that the moralizing strictures of the *anoblis* should come to play a crucial role in the developing ideology of the Enlightenment fostered by a bourgeoisie soon to be triumphant. The formation of any community, Michel Foucault tells us, depends on what he calls its "archeology of alienation"—the way it designates a particular configuration of thoughts, words, and practices as antithetical to itself, as constituting an abhorrent other reinforcing the values of the self.[32] To be most effective, such alienation fastens not on some totally foreign otherness but on something very much a part of the self, such that its denunciation will all the more effectively mobilize the community's sense of change and achieved moral superiority. Alienation is a process of scapegoating, the denunciation of some part of the self, now labeled as other, so that the group's dubious integrity might be redefined and consolidated.

The ever more vociferous condemnation of gambling by the ascendant bourgeoisie, liberal and conservative, *philosophe* and *dévote*, brought with it a number of distinct advantages. It assumed that there existed an essential difference between gambling as a self-interested manipulation of money and those various other manipulations of money through which the bourgeoisie had acquired its wealth. It allowed those whose social status depended entirely on money to adopt a posture of moral repugnance toward its movement in the purest form. It carefully exploited the popular association of high-stakes gambling with the practices of the traditional aristocracy to appropriate to itself the moral high ground in any discussion of the subject.

The most important advantage of the denunciation of gambling for the bourgeoisie related, however, not so much to the high-stakes gambling of the aristocracy as to the equally pandemic gambling of the urban poor. Condemning gambling as a social evil guaranteed its enlightened castigators both the right and the duty to elaborate what would become a veritable arsenal of educative and repressive measures aimed at uplifting the deficient moral sensitivities of the poor. In terms of its historical importance, especially as regards the coming of the Revolution and its aftermath, it was this last advantage, the bourgeoisie's self-appointed mission of reforming the depraved poor, that was to assume the greatest significance. As the outcome of their struggle against the nobility became obvious, the crucial conflict for the bourgeoisie as a class became that opposing it to a more numerous and ever more explosive urban proletariat. Within that conflict, gambling as a social practice once again had a major role to play. In order to understand its importance, we must look at what was distinctive about the way the poor gambled. While the card, roulette, and dice games favored by the aristocracy were certainly known to the poor, one form of gambling, immensely popular during the eighteenth century, was immediately accessible to all but the totally impoverished and presented particularly fertile ground for the development of bourgeois moralities. The lottery, unlike the face-to-face and one-on-one jousts of the games played at Versailles, had the further attraction of being eminently user-friendly. Involving no confrontation or test of individual

57

fortitude, it produced winners who collected only what others had freely spent on their losing tickets.

The lottery was first introduced into France by François I, who, during his Italian campaign, had been singularly impressed by the substantial and all but painless revenue it produced for its organizers. In May 1539 the Edict of Châteauregnard officially authorized a form of lottery called *blanque,* after the blank losing tickets that made up the great majority of those sold. The right to exploit blanque was sold to the king's friend Jean Laurent for the modest annual fee of two thousand livres. While this early form of state-sanctioned lottery never really took hold and was reauthorized only sporadically, the early eighteenth century saw the growth of a substantial number of such lotteries to raise money for worthy causes. Between 1714 and 1729 more than half the churches of Paris were renovated with money generated by parish lotteries. By mid-century a number of more broadly subscribed lotteries with far larger prizes were authorized to support various public charities. The Loterie des Enfants Trouvés was first established in 1754, and the Loterie de la Pitié in 1762. It was, however, the Loterie de l'École Militaire, established in 1757 under the control of none other than Casanova of Seingalt, that achieved the greatest popular success and was to serve as the model for both the Loterie Royale and the Loterie Nationale. Using his friendship with the abbé de Bernis, Casanova secured an introduction to Choiseul, who in turn referred him to the contrôleur général des finances, by whom he was granted permission to implement his plan for a nationwide lottery on the condition that it generate 20 million livres for the École Militaire.

Abandoning the uninvolving format of a small number of winning tickets mixed in with a large number of blanks, Casanova adopted the system developed in 1610 by Benedetto Gentile for the Genoa lottery. Much as in contemporary lotto, but with far worse odds for the player, the monthly drawing was done by a blindfolded child, who chose from a revolving cylinder called *la roue de fortune* five winning numbers from a total field of ninety. Different kinds of bets were possible: the *extrait simple* was a bet on one number, which thus had five chances in ninety to win; the *extrait déterminé* was a bet not only on a particular number's being chosen but on which of the five draws would produce it. The *ambe* was a bet on two winning numbers, the *terne* on three, and the *quaterne* and *quine* on four and five. Payoffs varied from fifteen times the sum bet for an *extrait simple* to fifty-two hundred times the bet for a *terne* and up to 1 million times the bet for a *quine*. As seductive as so large a payoff might seem, the odds massively favored the organizers. The probability, for instance, of winning the *terne,* which paid fifty-two hundred to one, was in fact one in 117,480.[33]

No matter how prohibitive the odds, these new lotteries owed their overwhelming success to the fact that they provided the poor, on a monthly and state-sanctioned basis, some hope of financial and social advancement. Given the rigidity for the lower classes of the prevailing political and economic orders, the dream of riches from the lottery was in fact little more unrealistic than the prescribed regimens of hard work and personal economy. Rightly criticizing even as astute a student of gambling as Roger Caillois for his equating gambling with an entirely passive surrendering of self to the powers of chance, Lorraine Daston makes the point that

despite the ideology of the meritocracy that blossomed in the eighteenth century . . . the reality was quite different for the mass of people. They were imprisoned within a static social and economic order that no amount of talent, resolution, patience, and audacity could unlock. . . . The only hope of moving up in the world was suddenly to acquire a vast sum of money, and practically the only hope of such a windfall in a nonmeritocratic society was to buy a lottery ticket. Where industry and talent counted for little, buying a lottery ticket might have been the one escape from passivity.[34]

The moralists of the period condemned the lottery for what they saw as its cynical exploitation of the hope and credulity of the masses. The popular preference for the high-payoff but near-impossible longshots of the *quaterne* and *quine* proved, to the eyes of those critics, that the state was culpably profiting from an ignorance it should instead be doing all it could to limit and correct. For such critics, the lottery amounted to the premeditated robbery of the people by the state. In 1793, on the eve of the Loterie Royale's four-year suspension before it would be reborn as the Loterie Nationale, one deputy described it as "a scourge invented by despotism to silence the people in their misery, deluding them with hopes that only aggravated their sufferings."[35]

As though bent on providing equally somber interpretations for all possible outcomes of the lottery, these moralists insisted that even the rare winners, moving from poverty to wealth in the time it took to draw the five numbers, represented an evil every bit as pernicious as the exploitation of the losers. The very possibility of a million-to-one winner recalled all the painful memories of the Regency's *affaire de Law*, when, as the popular imagination remembered it, lords and lackeys played musical chairs to the tune of the Compagnie des Indes stock prices. For the bourgeoisie, the spectacle of so rapid a social promotion amounted to a scandalous undermining of the whole equation of wealth and merit at the center of their ever more triumphant ideology. Lottery millionaires, as rare as they might be, had the profoundly disquieting effect of making the possession of wealth appear no less arbitrary than birth—and this in a context where the denunciation of all arbitrary bases of social preeminence was among the most potent weapons in the arsenal of bourgeois ideology. It was to talent, hard work, and right thinking that wealth should accrue as their tangible sign, reward, and proof. If money had a morally correct function in the society dreamed by these ideologues, it was that of consolidating the triumph of beneficent social virtues over both the abused privilege of a declining aristocracy and the suicidal infatuation with instant wealth of a deluded poor.

Because the odds meant that losing seemed always to follow the dream of winning, the very mechanics of the lottery surreptitiously justified the social therapeutics through which the defenders of true merit sought to address the people's sad predilection for gambling. The lottery, which seemed at first to challenge the new equation of wealth with merit, served ultimately to reinforce the pseudo-consensus of rich and poor, moralist and unlucky punter, around the supreme value of bourgeois rationality.

The greatest evil of gambling, one threatening all regardless of their station, was now defined as its unleashing of uncontrollable passions. To gamble was to risk losing all self-control, to create a situation in which one literally did not know what one would do next. Trying to analyze gambling's power to inspire such disarray in otherwise rational individuals, Barbeyrac hypothesized that gambling should be understood not as a single passion but as a monstrously self-perpetuating synthesis of antithetical passions—desire and fear, hope and disappointment, joy and regret, anger and hatred: "It is that very trait that makes the passion for gambling so constant. The variety and the vicissitudes of its movements forestall disgust while providing it with a perpetual sustenance over which time holds no sway."[36] To gamble was to render the self equally as unpredictable as the cards and numbers on which one bet. Absorbed entirely within the impassioned present of the wager, the gambler lost all sense of past and future. Abstracted from the prevailing laws of cause and effect, beyond prudence, uninterested in foresight, the gambler became a figure of solipsistic idiosyncrasy closed to everything beyond the immediate present. That state, measured against the calm ideal of a rationality shared by all, could only be a self-inflicted madness which men of reason must refuse, condemn, and extirpate from themselves and all around them.

Mauss's study of the gift is useful in analyzing *ancien régime* gambling because it helps us avoid imposing on that subject a set of concepts and values that were themselves generated by the emerging bourgeoisie as weapons in their campaign both to discredit the ethos of the traditional nobility and to affirm their right to a therapeutic control of the poor. The all but universal condemnation of gambling now subscribed to with surprisingly equal enthusiasm by the voices of the social sciences and of common sense forecloses any real understanding of what that practice represented in the context of the eighteenth century.

Mauss's analysis is based on a muted but real conviction that in losing contact with the archaic function of the gift and gambling, mankind has lost something important. Speaking of the Greek and Roman civilizations as far closer to our own than the Tlingit or Kwakiutl, Mauss asks, "Did not these [the Greek and Roman] civilizations pass through a previous phase in which their thought was less cold and calculating?" (46). Mauss's nostalgia for some alternative to cold calculation flows from his profound sadness at how an obsession with the accumulation of wealth has impoverished us: "It is only our Western societies that quite recently turned man into an economic animal. But we are not yet all animals of the same species. . . . *Homo economicus* is not behind us but before us, like the moral man, the man of duty, the scientific man and the reasonable man. For a long time man was something quite different; and it is not so long now since he became a machine—a calculating machine" (74). For Mauss, the approaching universality of economic man represents a dangerous compromising of a more fundamental solidarity between all members of a society, rich and poor, that must be at the heart of every true community. What seemed clear to Mauss as he wrote in 1925 was that this progressively more exclusive concern with the accumulation of wealth had already transformed man into a "machine—a calculating machine." But this was, Mauss insists, a recent change, one that occurred "not so long ago."

But when? and how? In *The Emergence of Probability,* Ian Hacking tries to understand how there occurred a similar change in the way humankind understood their relation to the world around them. In examining what he calls "mathematical expectation," Hacking points out that this concept had no precedent within the European consciousness before the decade of the 1650s, when Pascal, Fermat, and Huygens were developing the science of probability.[37] Mathematical expectation means for Hacking the idea of the average payoff one might expect over the long run from a series of similar wagers. Hacking offers the example of a person betting that he can draw a red marble from an urn in which he knows there are ten red and forty white marbles. In that situation the "expectation" of winning would be the relation between the number of winning and losing draws—one to four.

The real question for Hacking is why before 1650 we find in the mathematical literature no parallel to what now seems to us an exercise in the obvious. Paccioli, Cardano, and Galileo had analyzed games of chance well before 1650, but none of them had developed the concept of expectation. This, for Hacking, is related to the fact that there is likewise no sign within that literature of what we today call the average: "The very concept of averaging is a new one and before 1650 most people could not observe an average because they did not take averages. Certainly a gambler could notice that one strategy is in Galileo's words 'more advantageous' than another but there is a gap between this and a quantitative knowledge of mathematical expectation" (92). This absence of the average is an important indication that for the pre-Enlightenment mind, it was far from obvious that any individual play or player should be seen as sufficiently similar to all others that they be summed to one whole that, when divided by the number of cases, would yield our notion of the average.

If, in the analyses of gambling prior to probability theory, the notion of the average did not exist, it was because the sense of the "player" within the aristocratic ethos of gambling remained individualized to such an extent that the idea of summing distinct persons into a common sum from which an average might emerge was quite simply unthinkable. The aristocratic gaming table was never imagined as the site of a confrontation between the player and the game as a structure of abstract mathematical expectations. To the contrary, gambling was the always personalized and individual conflict between each specific person and his opponents. The sense of the other as a significant and worthy adversary would have ceased to exist were he to be subsumed into the faceless anonymity of an average applying only to the impersonal structure of the game.

It was Dangeau, we recall, who struck his contemporaries as the champion of this new awareness of the average. His winnings, Fontenelle and Madame de Sévigné told us, were the fruit of his careful study of the averages and probabilities governing the games he played. It is not surprising that Saint-Simon should have sensed that in the person of this always victorious parvenu he was witnessing the end of the aristocratic order. It was Dangeau's method, his willingness to reduce himself and his opponents to faceless permutations of a mathematical structure, that signaled the coming universal victory of the scientific man, the average man, and the economic man.

We saw in chapter 1 how probability theory tamed chance by excluding it from its models. Rather than confront the inexplicable specificity of the turning card or rolling die, probability theory chose to analyze the seductively complex paradigm of all possible outcomes. Never admitting that it had changed the subject, probability theory substituted the impersonality of the mathematical model for the unique present of the chance event. In the same way that the law of large numbers never speaks to the specific case, the concept of the average holds the promise of a false superiority to the wager as a redefining event. The rule of the average, like the science of probability, is the talisman of the objective and unmoved analyst. When once the players forget themselves as individuals subject to the unpredictable present of the wager and instead imagine themselves as interchangeable instances of the game's mathematical structure, the average can and will tell them everything they need to know.

In their attempt to understand our contemporary fetishizing of mathematics, Philip Davis and Reuben Hersh point to the all but sacred status now accorded to what we call the 'stochastic'. The word comes from the Greek *stochos*, meaning "to guess or to aim at." The 1971 edition of the *Oxford English Dictionary*, itself woefully off the mark as to where scientific fashion would take the word over the next twenty years, lists as its single meaning "that which pertains to conjecture" and gives as its most contemporary occurrence a 1720 quote from Jonathan Swift in which he describes the physician as "the master of the stochastic art." Since the writing of that entry, 'stochastic' has in fact come to occupy within almost all discourses pretending to scientific status the entire semantic field once divided among such terms as 'random', 'chance', and 'chaotic'. The term's inflation should not surprise us, since as Davis and Hersh make clear, what we now refer to as the stochastic occupies a place in our lives far greater than that ever granted the random, the chancy, or the chaotic: "The stochastization of the world so permeates our thinking and our behavior that it can be said to be one of the characteristic features of modern life. Our insurance companies, our pension and social security plans, are postulated on notions of randomness. Polling, sampling, election predictions, and scholastic testing are based on stochastic notions, and these are vast enterprises."[38] The current sense of the term 'stochastic' is fascinating for the ambiguity of its connotations. On the one hand, it implies that chance and the random do exist, that there are important areas of our lives that escape the laws of any precise determinism. On the other, the stochastic carries with it the implication that the chance and randomness thus recognized are at the same time perfectly amenable to a mathematical analysis, which will finally render that indeterminacy no more threatening in any real sense than are phenomena governed by predictable sequences of cause and effect. The stochastic may refer to chance and chaos, but it is to chance mastered and chaos eliminated.

Davis and Hersh ask us to reflect on the price we pay for having sacralized mathematics and abolished even the most minute space for the specificity of the individual case. Writing in 1986, they help us to understand that the imperial and mutually reinforcing pieties of Enlightenment morality and Enlightenment mathematics have not entirely eliminated the possibility that the lost ideal hinted at in Mauss's essay and still at work in the aristocratic ethos of gambling can speak to us even today: "This tale is an attempt to come to an understanding of a destochastized way of life, a way that says: I will risk all. I may gain all, I may lose all, but I won't join the crowd and average out. The stochastic view has so engulfed us that we would feel absolutely unprotected and naked to the world if we were compelled to come out from behind our averages. Probability is a net that supports us and a cage that confines us" (31).

3

Law's System and the Gamble Refused

*The gambling known as business looks with austere
disfavor upon the business known as gambling.*
—AMBROSE BIERCE, *The Devil's Dictionary*

The French Enlightenment began with the biggest and
most devastating state-supported gamble Europe had ever
seen. During almost three years its long roll of the dice
touched every class and region of France, breaking down
even the stubborn division between Paris and the provinces
as it redefined the country's relations to other states and
her own colonies. This breathtakingly convulsive gamble
was presided over by a foreigner, a Scotsman, whose name
even today the French insist on mispronouncing as *l'as*,
'the ace'.[1]

John Law arrived in Paris with a personal fortune of
one hundred thousand livres won at the gaming tables of
Genoa, Venice, Florence, and Amsterdam. His System,
and the Mississippi Company on which it was built,[2] consti-
tuted the single most important economic event in eighteenth-century France prior to the upheavals of the Revolution. Spread out over three years, but in full force only
from mid-1719 to mid-1720, the System's turmoil moved
so quickly and so dizzingly that once the regent withdrew
his support from what in fact was nothing less than a corporate takeover of the entire French state, it fell apart
overnight. France spent the rest of the century doing all
it could to forget that the System had ever existed. Its
traumatized rulers insisted that the only way to conjure
away its memory was to return to the same disastrous fi-

nancial practices that had originally created the economic and social context in which Law's System became possible.

The story of John Law and the Mississippi Company is crucial to understanding the Enlightenment's attitude toward chance. We saw in chapter 2 how the traditional nobility's attitude toward chance manifested itself in high-stakes gambling as an ultimately self-defeating affirmation of their superiority to the growing rule of money and the power of a financial and commercial class by which they felt themselves increasingly challenged. Their sublime disregard for the value of money was a forced and suicidal reaffirmation of their more and more imaginary status as free and autonomous individuals. The nobility's contempt for money was buttressed by an obsessive reverence for land as the one true value passing from generation to generation and defining the status of its owner. The true noble continued a family designated by a name referring to a place. That name equated the individual with the land as a tangible, productive property infinitely more real than the play of coins and notes generating the power of the ascendant bourgeoisie.

From the noble's point of view, the truly diabolic force of Law's System lay in its power to destroy any distinction between land and money, between real property and credit. Paradoxically, Law first secured the regent's support for his plan thanks to the support of such resolutely conservative figures as the duc de Saint-Simon. Like so many of Philippe d'Orléans's counselors, Saint-Simon was seduced by Law's promise to initiate the realm's economic rebirth by issuing notes backed not by the gold and silver of the merchant class (a practice already operating in Holland) but by land—by what the nobility saw as the true touchstone of economic wealth and order. During the System's rise, Compagnie des Indes stocks, by then interchangeable with Law's endless issues of notes, were sold as financial instruments backed by the full value and promise of the crown colonies in Louisiana and throughout New France.

Law's land-based credit system, a plan he had first submitted to Louis XIV as early as 1705 and subsequently to both the emperor in Vienna and Victor-Emmanuel in the Piedmont, held an irresistible charm for a nobility that saw the regency following Louis XIV's death as their long-awaited opportunity to reclaim control of the state. Law's refusal to equate his paper money with gold and his insistence on defining it through land was music to the half-understanding ears of a conservative nobility whose wealth consisted all but entirely of land. They could only be delighted by this apparent attack on their upstart rivals' pernicious equation of wealth with the grubby specie of merchants and financiers.

Credit, both as a concept and as an array of specific financial instruments, was central to the dynamics of the eighteenth century. Its explorations, colonies, and wars could never have occurred as they did without the credit structures that sustained them. No matter how simple or complex the financial instruments involved, the phenomenon of credit was rooted in its derivation from the Latin *credere* 'to believe'. Credit had everything to do with what people believed. But the kind of belief it involved was quite different from what that term had come to imply within the Western philosophical tradition. Credit had nothing to do with religious belief, with the conflicting belief systems that had racked France and Europe over the two previous centuries. Credit bore no relation to creed—although largely as a result of France's post-System financial conservatism European banking did take on a decidedly Protestant as opposed to Catholic hue.

Credit had to do, not with any dogma anchored in the past, but with a belief in the future, a belief in what one thought would happen but of which one could never be certain. Anticipating an uncertain future, credit was defined by the twin emotions hope and fear. It had everything to do with the way a specific financial decision brought one closer either to what was hoped for or to what was feared. Credit concerned not what existed in the present but what was still to come in a future to be played out in the purely secular world of human enterprise. In spite of its quantifiable economic reality, credit stood squarely in the realm of imagination and fantasy, of what one suspected, wished for, or dreaded. As the expression of an opinion about the future, it was an object of passion rather than of knowledge. The eighteenth century, with its creation of stock companies and their attendant acolytes of optimistic bulls and pessimistic bears, translated the metaphysics of hope and fear at the heart of credit into specific financial institutions and instruments that ultimately redefined the world. The Mississippi Company and the other European stock companies devoted to colonial development initiated a form of credit speculation that made accessible to all what were the brightest and most tangible hopes for some part of the New World's fabled riches. By the beginning of the eighteenth century, however, it had also become clear that the giddy hopes for colonial riches were inextricably linked to the fear of ever more costly wars between the metropolitan powers both at sea and along the frontiers of their often adjacent possessions. As part of the constant jockeying for military and economic advantage among the European states, colonial wars had immediate and strong effects on the credit markets. News of even a minor victory or defeat could send the price of a particular stock soaring or plummeting.

The colonial struggles and their symbiotic relation to national credit markets redefined the reality of warfare as it passed from an aristocratic to a commercial context. The field of battle, we remember, was for the traditional nobility the *champ d'honneur* on which their disinterested risking of life under the appreciative eye of the king founded their right to social preeminence. Warfare in the colonies involved something entirely different. Reports on its usually ambiguous and inconclusive skirmishes were watched most closely not by the king but by credit speculators, whose

profits and losses depended on how aptly their purchases
and sales of stocks had anticipated the good and ill fortune
of those distant conflicts. Battle, no longer the exclusive
concern of the nobility, became instead the rolling dice on
which astute speculators daily staked their fortunes.

In his study of land and trade in England during this
period, J. G. A. Pocock argues that commercial credit became the eighteenth century's equivalent of Renaissance
fortuna, of chance as it was at work in human affairs:
"Credit typifies the instability of secular things, brought
about by the interactions of particular human wills, appe-
tites and passions. . . . [Credit is] not simply the wheel of
fortune running eccentrically about its unmoving axis . . .
it is part of a huge new force in human affairs, creating
new modes of war and prosperity, a new balance of power
in Europe, a new conquest of the planet."[3] Although referring to England, Pocock's description is perfectly applica-
ble to the France of Law's ascendancy from 1717 to 1720.
During the rise and fall of the Mississippi Company, the
arena of ennobling chance was no longer the battlefield
but the rue Quincampoix, the nerve center of credit speculation. The real gambler was not so much the warrior risking his life in the hazards of battle but the stockjobber
playing everything for the maximum profit. For England,
the situation Pocock describes would develop throughout
the century and provide the economic foundation of the
industrial revolution. For France, this new understanding
of chance's workings was a brief interlude limited to the
three years of the System's triumph. Rather than consolidating itself, this unnerving experience of a frighteningly
different world set off a reaction against everything it
stood for on the part of the old as well as the new elites,
the traditional nobility as well as the monied bourgeoisie.
France's first and colossally explosive experience of credit's
boom-and-bust cycle led the nobility and the physiocrats
to seek refuge in the most strident allegiance to land alone
as the one true basis of economic wealth. Credit was denounced as a figment of the imagination, a fantasy based

only on opinion and forever subject to the capricious rising and falling of human fear and greed. Wealth in land, on the contrary, was calm, real, and natural. To be rich in land was to anchor one's identity in something that would always be there, firm under foot, as the stable foundation of all that might transpire upon it. Credit was the evanescent illusion of wealth, ready to be obliterated by the next roll of the world's dice, by the next battle lost on some distant shore. Credit conferred only a frantic and desperate identity subject to all the vicissitudes of the moment.

The opposition between innervating credit and ennobling land left as a legacy of Law's debacle mirrored and consolidated a number of parallel oppositions making up the ideology of nobility: their choice of an honor based in name and land over a self-interest grounded in money, of unswerving virtue over fluctuating passion, of the enduring over the momentary. None of these oppositions was entirely new. Most were deeply rooted in Renaissance and medieval traditions. What was new, however, was the stridency of their affirmation and the way they would hobble France's economic development for almost three-quarters of a century.

There is something immensely sad about the story of John Law, his System, and its effects on France. A gamble so huge that nothing like it had been attempted before, it could very well have succeeded. Looking back on it from the 1990s with our experience of Keynesian theory, supply-side economics, mortgage debt, and junk bonds, we know there was no intrinsic reason why it was doomed to failure. If anything, it too abruptly anticipated an understanding of economic structures that would take more than two centuries to gain general currency. As an audacious gamble, the System lost the game not because it held the wrong cards but because it was bluffed out. Law's indispensable partner, the regent, finally folded what could have been the winning hand when the coalition of Law's enemies raised the political stakes to a level where he dared not follow.

The story of Law's experiment properly begins with the near coup d'état of September 2, 1715, when an alliance of nobles and parliamentarians set on undoing Louis XIV's centralization of power ignored the dead king's last will and installed Philippe, the duc d'Orléans, as regent. This was a mortal blow to the pro-Spanish and pro-Roman positions of a court centered on the Bourbon alliance of Madame de Maintenon, the *dévôts,* and the royal bastards. The coming to power of Philippe d'Orléans brought with it a momentous reshaping of France's alliances away from Spain and toward England. This shift from Catholic to Protestant and from agrarian to mercantile had, however, to be handled with the utmost discretion and subterfuge if it was not to flounder on what was sure to be widespread opposition to so clear a break with tradition. If for no other reason, tact and diplomacy were mandated by the impoverished and bloodless state of crown finances after more than two decades of ruinous foreign wars, ever less efficient and more onerous taxation practices, and massive borrowing. At the time of Louis XIV's death in 1715, crown debt stood at approximately 3 *billion* livres, with roughly two-thirds in the form of annuities and one-third in floating debt. The annual deficit for the single year before the king's death was almost 77 million livres.[4] These figures indicate that even if we take inflation into account, royal debt had risen in 1715 to a higher level than it would in 1788 when it forced the convening of the Estates General on the eve of the Revolution. This disastrous financial situation had only been aggravated by the two devaluations of the coinage imposed by Louis XIV's contrôleur des finances, Desmarets, in 1713 and 1715, which led to massive hoarding and the near-total disappearance of money from the marketplace.

Faced with imminent economic collapse, some suggested that the regent adopt the traditional remedy of declaring bankruptcy, of disavowing all the debts of his royal predecessor. What might have been possible before the monarchy had become dependent on its credit standing with the commercial and lending sectors both at home and abroad was now rejected as suicidal. The other expedient—of issuing still more debt instruments on top of all those inherited from the past—was of limited benefit and ultimately self-defeating. Crown notes issued in April 1716 were quickly discounted at 37 percent and soon after by as much as 60 percent. Somewhat spectacularly, the new regent did establish a special tribunal, a Chambre de justice charged with investigating the financial affairs of every individual who had been involved with crown funds over the last quarter-century, from 1689 to the date of the Chambre's establishment. This massive exercise in ferreting out profiteers (as well as in political intimidation) eventually fined over four thousand individuals for various amounts adding up to roughly 220 million livres. While moral obligations and political scores may have been settled, the Chambre de justice finally brought scarcely 100 million livres into the treasury—hardly enough to make a difference. The Chambre did, however, impose some of its heaviest fines on the small group of influential financiers who, five years later, would preside over the liquidation of Law's System, a scheme that by that date was to have successfully absorbed the whole of the massive debt the regent so quixotically labored to reduce. The Pâris brothers were fined a total of 1,216,000 livres, and Antoine Crozat, the holder of the Louisiana concession that was to become Law's centerpiece, was fined the astounding sum of 6,600,000 livres.

Against this backdrop of the near-total exhaustion of royal finances there emerged on the scene a man who had been born into a family of Edinburgh goldsmiths in 1671 and who had precipitously left England at the age of twenty-three to escape a prison sentence for having killed one Edward Wilson in a duel over a woman. It had certainly not been a case of murder, but Wilson's family was well connected at court. Law supported himself during the more than twenty years between his exile from England in

1694 and his rise to power in Paris through his skill as a gambler. In his lively study of Law and his System, Edgar Faure is deeply troubled by what he sees as a contradiction between the positive quality of Law's economic genius and his life-long love of high-stakes gambling.[5] There can be, as Faure sees it, no reconciliation between the inventor of a system showcasing the values of economy, work, and investment and the devoté of chance: "Struggling to invent a currency that would encourage economic expansion is a sign of considerable devotion to public welfare, a community spirit. . . . The typical attitude of the gambler hardly reveals the same tendencies. The gambler is not a man for projects on the grand scale but a man for the present moment. He lives not for others in the future but for himself right now. He is a committed individualist, intellectually a loner. Gambling goes beyond egotism, it is a form of solipsism" (15).

Faure concludes that there was a kind of moral schizophrenia on Law's part, a split that he later finds useful in explaining the far greater paradox of his enormous success and ignominious failure. For Faure, Law is marked by "a profoundly split personality, a split which runs like a fault-line through the whole of his enterprise" (15). What Faure refuses to recognize in this least satisfying side of his analysis is the profound compatibility between Law the gambler's disregard for money as money and Law the economic theorist's fundamental hypothesis that money is never an end in itself, but a tool for motivating individuals and fostering desired activities. The gambler and the economist in fact share a single vision of the world as an array of interlocking but indeterminate structures. They see the world as an integrated system where each element is dependent on the play of all others. Money in circulation, be it on the green felt or in the economy, opens up opportunities for manipulation that would be nonexistent were one's understanding of the system as a whole to be impeded by any fetishistic concern with money as its most visible element. The gambler and the economist share the knowledge that the multitude's obsession with money gives it no value in itself, but makes it extremely useful as a means for determining how others will act. Rather than fixating on any single value, the gambler and economist set out to orchestrate a system.

In proposing his plans to the regent, Law was unencumbered by false modesty. The good he would accomplish for the kingdom of France would far surpass all those benefits the whole of Europe had derived from the discovery of the New World: "But the Banque is neither the only nor the greatest of my ideas. I will produce an enterprise that will astound the whole of Europe by the changes it effects in favor of France, changes more momentous than those brought by the discovery of the Indies."[6] His System would not only solve the credit problems of the moment but also bring about a rebirth of agriculture, manufacturing, and commerce. It would eliminate the need for onerous taxation, and a grateful population would multiply its numbers as the realm's most precious resource.

Given the scope of its ambitions and the speed of its implementation, Law's System defies easy description and clear-cut conclusions. For those who lost from investing in it, a judgment was easy: Law was the devil, and his works were nothing less than evil incarnate. For historians, the task is more difficult. Even as astute and sympathetic a critic as Faure justifies the absence in his seven-hundred-page study of any final conclusion on the value of Law and his System by classifying him and it within the category of the schizophrenic. Herbert Lüthy, the careful and sober historian of early modern banking practices in Europe, prefaces his own analysis of the period with a caveat, a warning to his reader that what he is about to describe is so shot through with folly, frenzy, and chance that logical analysis is impossible:

> One feels an enormous discomfort at trying to reduce the complex tangle of events characterizing this unhinged pe-

riod to a few clear sentences or even to a few well-defined chapter headings. Then more than ever financial history was inextricably linked to political history within a perpetual palace revolution driven by a frenzy of gambling, intrigue, and unbridled passion. Fortunes, as though by the stroke of some magic wand, were made and lost overnight. The most daring players, often of dubious origin, entered and left center stage on the whim of speculation, favor, and disgrace.[7]

The keystone of Law's System was the creation of a paper currency, banknotes based on land, which were to gain public confidence through their expansive effects on the economy as a whole. The first step in that direction became possible on May 2, 1716, when Law was authorized by the regent to open his Banque Générale. This private enterprise was not the Banque de France he had argued for, but it was a beginning. The Banque Générale was to have two essential functions: it would offer shares to the general public for a total value of 6 million livres and, on the basis of that capital, issue banknotes serving as currency. In order to gain control of the crown's outstanding debt, it was stipulated that three-quarters of the stock purchases must be paid in royal debt notes, and one quarter in gold. The crucial problem facing the Banque Générale was to give value to its banknotes, to convince holders that they need not redeem them immediately for specie. This challenge was met by Law's astute decision to do the opposite of past practice. Whereas private banknotes had never before been accepted in payment of taxes, Law convinced the regent to issue an edict in April 1717 declaring that all the *recettes royales,* the independent collection points for crown taxes throughout the country, would accept these notes in payment of taxes. The edict further stipulated that those offices, rather than shipping gold and silver to Paris, must make all payments to the crown in the form of those banknotes. This not only eliminated the slow and dangerous practice of moving large quantities of specie on a still primitive road and river system but also created an immediate demand for and public confidence in the banknotes. The value of the Banque Générale stock was further consolidated by the declaration of a dividend of 8 percent at the end of 1716 and of 12 percent for 1717.

The next step in the creation of the System came in August 1717. Antoine Crozat, the holder of the Louisiana concession, had been, we remember, fined more than 6 million livres by the regent's Chambre de justice. In lieu of payment, Crozat returned the Louisiana concession to the crown, which in turn granted it to Law along with an authorization to float stock in his newly formed Compagnie d'Occident to develop and exploit the colony under a twenty-five-year concession. One hundred million livres in stock were sold, and as had been the case for the Banque Générale stock, shares had to be purchased with the existing royal debt instruments that so burdened the treasury. The combination of Law's obvious political clout and the public's dreams of the immense potential wealth associated with the New World colonies assured that the entire initial stock offering was sold by 1718.

December of that year brought the two final steps in the consolidation of the System. All the shares of the Banque Générale were bought out by the regent, who transformed it from a private bank into the newly christened Banque Royale. The Compagnie d'Occident, on the basis of a series of stock issues at increasing prices, became the fabled Compagnie des Indes. This new stock company was, however, much more than the Compagnie d'Occident had ever been. In addition to the exploitation of Louisiana, it took over the previously private concessions of the Senegal, East Indies, China, and South Sea companies. It assumed all the functions of the royal mint and controlled the issuing of currency. It wrested from the powerful corps of tax farmers and *recettes royales* all responsibility for collecting taxes and paying crown expenditures. In sum, the Compagnie des Indes became the corporate vehicle through which the whole of France and its colonies became one integrated trading company. The Compagnie des Indes was built on an initial stock offering of six hundred thousand shares, of which two hundred thousand were offered for sale to the public at five hundred livres per share, thus raising 100 million livres. The other four hundred thousand shares were held by the regent. Within a year, a share purchased for five hundred livres would be selling at over twenty times that amount.

The apogee of Law's System came between mid-1719 and mid-1720. It was signaled by Law's being named contrôleur général des finances in January 1720 and by the merging of the Banque Royale and the Compagnie des Indes in the following month. Under an enormous surface complexity, the System prospered according to the basic mechanism supporting any boom cycle. One of the clearest contemporary descriptions of the dynamics of money and confidence behind the System's rise can be found in Adam Anderson's eighteenth-century description of stock speculation:

> A, having one hundred pounds stock in trade, though pretty much in debt, gives it out to be worth three hundred pounds, on account of many privileges and advantages to which he is entitled. B, relying on A's great wisdom and integrity, sues to be admitted partner on those terms, and accordingly buys three hundred pounds into the partnership. The trade being afterwards given out or discovered to be very improving, C comes in at five hundred pounds; and afterwards D, at one thousand one hundred pounds. And the capital is then completed to two thousand pounds. If the partnership had gone no further than A and B, then A had got and B had lost one hundred pounds. If it had stopped at C, then A had got and C had lost two hundred pounds; and B had been as he was before: but D also coming in, A gains four hundred pounds, and B two hundred pounds; and C neither gains nor loses: but D loses six hundred pounds. Indeed, if A could show that the said capital was intrinsically worth four thousand four hundred pounds, there would be no harm done to D; and B and C would have been obliged to him. But if the capital at first was worth but one hundred pounds, and increased only by

the subsequent partnerships, it must then be acknowledged, that B and C have been imposed on in their turns,
and that unfortunate thoughtless D paid the piper.[8]

Anderson's description of the basic mechanism behind
even the most elaborate stock company is particularly valuable because he underlines the all-important role of investor confidence. In those terms, the second half of 1719
saw what could be described as an enormous outburst of
investor confidence in the various stock issues of the Compagnie des Indes. Confidence is, of course, a euphemism
here for the panic felt by those who were not invested in
what could be the monthly if not weekly doubling of the
stocks' value. Those who had refrained from converting
whatever land and other property they held into the ever-
soaring stock could only see themselves as self-impover-
ished fools.

The System had two major effects on the royal treasury.
On the one hand, Law's originally modest hope of ab-
sorbing the royal debt from the reign of Louis XIV within
twenty-five years had now been accomplished in a fraction
of that time. On the other, the regent was free to redeem
all or part of his four hundred thousand Compagnie des
Indes shares for banknotes to be used for crown expenditures, as he in fact did in early 1720. At the then prevailing
price of nine thousand livres per share, his conversion of
one hundred thousand shares (one fourth of his actual
holdings) raised the tidy sum of 900 million livres—and
that without a sou's worth of taxation or debt.[9] This kind
of transaction between Law and the regent consecrated the
complete merging of Compagnie des Indes stock and
Law's banknotes—an equation that was a precondition to
the rise as well as the fall of the entire System.

Law was able to effect, through a continual issuing of
stock series as well as the banknotes to purchase them, a
generalized resuscitation of the French economy at the cost
of considerable inflation. This should not, however, be
seen as an exercise in rank illusionism. In today's terms,

Law's System was a daring application of expansionist monetary policy to an economy characterized by substantial unemployed resources. The lethargy of the last years of Louis XIV's reign had left France with vast sectors of unemployed resources capable of real increases in productivity once they were activated by these massive influxes of additional money. From 1718 to 1720 the Banque Royale issued more than 3 billion livres in banknotes.

The System's downfall came not as a result of any internal contradiction or personal malfeasance but because the universal and frenetic hopes for still further profits on which its rapid rise had been built were doomed to collapse once stock prices began to move in the opposite direction. As late as only a week before the turnaround, informed investors (whose money was streaming into Paris from all corners of Europe) could legitimately conclude that Compagnie des Indes stock still offered the best available investment opportunity. In that volatile climate, Law's enemies, the clique of wealthy financiers who had been cut out of the game by his successes on every front, were preparing to act. The Pâris brothers, earlier fined for malfeasance in royal tax farming, convinced both the duc de Bourbon and the prince de Conti to demand immediate repayment in gold for their considerable stock holdings. News of that event was enough to trigger the much-feared ride down on the roller-coaster. One of the great paradoxes of Law's System was the fact that as the Banque Royale adopted a policy of increasing the money supply in order to create an ever greater demand for stocks, it was this manipulated drop in stock prices that initiated the period of greatest inflation. Law only complicated the task of regaining investor confidence when he tried to stop the public stampede away from stocks and banknotes by outlawing individual ownership of gold and silver and legislating that the payment of all but the smallest transactions should be carried out in banknotes. Riots and deaths became daily experiences in the midst of the frantic melees of investors clamoring to convert their stocks at the Compagnie's office. The share price soon began to plummet, and Law was forced to flee France for his life on December 14, 1720.

The System's formal demise came with the government-supervised liquidation, or *visa,* presided over by none other than the same Pâris brothers who had patiently plotted Law's downfall. As the now triumphant *revenants* of the old order of financiers and tax collectors, they represented the regent's only alternative to complete chaos. The *visa* was a case-by-case review of the financial situation of all the holders of the now nearly worthless 3 billion livres in credit instruments issued by the System. Its avowed purpose was to punish pure speculators while offering some compensation to honest investors. The problem, of course, was that the System had erased any distinction between those two categories. On the basis of political connections more than financial rectitude, the 3 billion was reduced to 1.7 billion held by slightly more than five hundred thousand apparently worthy investors who were indemnified with new crown bonds paying 2 percent interest.

Although the System ended in disaster, its effects were by no means entirely negative. For the brief period of his ascendancy, Law had become the first non-monarch to control every aspect of a major European power's fiscal and monetary policy. He acquired that position on the basis of a plan promising prosperity, economic growth, and relief from abusive taxation to all classes in French society—a program that later inspired Louis Blanc to refer to him as "the first modern socialist." For others, Law had anticipated in practice what Keynes would only two centuries later offer as a "general theory." The System and its focal point in the Compagnie des Indes rejuvenated France's maritime fleet and colonial commerce. It initiated a sustained development of France's Atlantic ports and of her entire colonial system. Closer to home, the inflationary spiral of its endgame had the highly positive effect of freeing countless individuals from crushing debt burdens often dating back to the time of Colbert and on which interest payments had equaled the principal two or more times over while never diminishing it. Montesquieu, in a sardonic commentary on the System in *Les Lettres persanes,* lampooned the dubious outrage of many moneylenders: " 'Whom can a man trust today?' he cried. 'There is one traitor I was so sure was my friend that I lent him money. And now he has paid me back! What horrible dishonesty! Say what he will, for me he will always be dishonored.' "[10] The steep rise in grain prices that accompanied the System benefited, even after inflation, an agricultural sector that had been systematically impoverished during the last decades of Louis XIV's reign. Urban workers, artisans, and shopkeepers, France's entire production and retail sectors, clearly profited from the increased demand for a broad spectrum of goods and services fueled by the System's influx of buying power. Real wage levels rose for the first time in thirty years. Meat consumption in France doubled during the period, and wine consumption increased by a third. Speaking of the Languedoc, Emmanuel Le Roy Ladurie goes so far as to describe Law's System as an *ancien régime* New Deal, an escape from crippling indebtedness coupled with a state-financed expansion that, in spite of its failure, set the stage for the forty-year period of growth and prosperity from 1720 to 1760.[11]

The puzzling amalgam of the System's positive and negative effects, its ending in disaster yet its indisputable contribution to a subsequent prosperity, points to a paradox that Law himself never fully assumed and that cost him dearly. In a very real sense, the same factors that made the System possible also predetermined its calamitous end. As an abstract economic model, Law's System was flawless. It did in fact work, and there was no intrinsic reason it could not have continued to produce the many benefits Law promised in his numerous arguments to the regent. The problem came in moving from theoretical model to the real world of actual practice and established interests. No part of the System, not even the formation of the Banque

Générale, could have been put in place without triggering a crescendo of opposition from those who stood to lose from this new way of doing things. The established interests against which Law had to define himself were far from powerless; they represented everything that was left of the old order against which the regent had to struggle. Law's plan for an economic renaissance based on credit needed not only internal coherence but the political backing of the regent. The very essence of credit is, however, the freely granted belief of the investor. Belief and credit can be abused, deluded, and manipulated, but they cannot be forced. Coerced belief is not belief at all, but the sullen hypocrisy of compliance. As a theory, Law's System presupposed a liberal economy in which individuals were free to make the choices they felt would maximize their individual wealth. The dilemma Law faced as his enemies stiffened their opposition stemmed from the fact that the only effective way to counter their resistance was to assume coercive powers. But asserting those powers simultaneously destroyed the freely made choices on which everything had to be based. Becoming contrôleur général des finances in January 1720 may have been a stunning political riposte to his enemies, but it effectively ended the free play of credit necessary for the System to work. Once again, it was Montesquieu who best captured the absurdity of the position into which Law had maneuvered himself. His "Fragment of an Ancient Mythologist" in letter 142 of *Les Lettres persanes* provocatively isolates the contradiction of a forced imagination, of commanding what people might dream: "People of Betique, do you want to be rich? Imagine that I am very rich, and yourselves too. Convince yourselves each morning that your fortunes have doubled overnight. Then get up and, if you have creditors, pay them with what you have imagined and tell them to imagine in turn" (308). When, after a crisis of popular confidence, that recipe no longer works, the master's tone becomes one of self-defeating menace: "People of Betique, I advised you to use your imagination and now I see you have not. Well then! I now order you to do so" (308).

The futility of the forced imagination was not the only paradox to emerge from the experience of the System. In the final pages of his study of Law, Faure sounds a distinctly cautionary note as he sums up the legacy of this man he so clearly admires:

> The demented adventure of the rue Quincampoix affected not only those who lived it, were a part of it, or observed it from a distance. Its flash and crash spread far out over time and space. People had now discovered that there were mysterious ways of becoming rich, of bettering one's situation, of gambling, speculating, and profiteering. It forced a wedge between legality and morality. It was simultaneously instructive and corrosive, liberating and immoral. (614)

If Law's three-year experiment holds a significance extending beyond the limits of its tenure, it is because it initiated a far more important crisis of belief. The experience of the System not only jeopardized the belief at the heart of credit and investor confidence but also called into question for the first time on so large a scale the belief at the core of all social stability that wealth somehow stood apart from the volatile, mysterious play of pure chance. It was the breaking down of a previously unchallenged frontier between legitimate wealth and pure speculation that made the experience of the Mississippi Bubble as dangerous as it was exhilarating.

Law's System was both an epiphany and a transformation of what chance would come to mean for the eighteenth century. Looking back from the 1750s, Ange Goudar points out in his treatise on how to protect oneself from "Greeks"—the eighteenth-century term for card cheats—that the truly golden age of gambling in France was that happy period of the Mississippi adventure when

making a bet was indistinguishable from prudent investment: "Seeing their fortunes double or triple in a single
day, the Mississippians gambled with abandon. Gambling
losses were not really considered as such, but only as de-
ductions from their immense profits on the other side."[12]
During its brief reign, Law's System transformed France
into an enormous casino where all were obliged to risk
their fortunes on the winning combination.

Buying Compagnie des Indes stock and gambling presupposed a new and deeply disruptive temporality of
wealth. Fueled by an anticipation of profits to come, anchored in an ardently desired but only potential future,
gambling and investing stood in stark contrast to a conception of wealth based on land and a title inherited from the
past. Law's System, rather than appealing to any continuity
with the past, offered the promise of an unlimited future.
That choice of future over past is nowhere better illustrated than in the System's new understanding of the nature of money. The traditional economists of Law's day
insisted that every credit instrument, every banknote, retained its value only to the extent that it was backed by and
rooted in the past of the issuing authority's actual holdings
in gold or silver. Law reversed that temporality. First there
would be money and then, as a result of its circulation,
there would be gold and silver. The bounty of the New
World's mines would flow back to France as a result of
the exploitation generated by the banknotes financing the
endeavor. Instead of gold's giving birth to money, the dynamics of an increased money supply would produce gold
and silver in a quantity far surpassing the value of the
banknotes initiating the process.

If, Law was convinced, money held this power to fashion
a future far richer than any past on which it might be
based, it was because as the common denominator of all
wealth, money was an object of universal desire: "Money
is the principal object of men's cupidity. It is the surest
and most direct means of satisfying their needs and their
desires. All aspire to its possession in view of so using it"

86

(3:408). As an object of universal cupidity, money could determine, as a function of its quantity and velocity, the value of everything else: "It is its usage that gives value to all other goods. When there is only a small quantity of money in circulation, its value is high, and that of all other goods low. Credit is the remedy for so prejudicial a situation. Once it is introduced, the price of money decreases and that of all other goods increases" (3:408). These passages from Law's apologia, the *Histoire des finances pendant la Régence,* which he compulsively wrote and rewrote from exile after the collapse of the System, underline one of the most radical aspects of his theory. Money, no longer a lifeless moon only reflecting the true light of gold, was recognized as a demiurgic force thriving on its own movement. The velocity of money was everything. For Law, the entire history of civilized societies was marked by a tenacious misunderstanding of that truth. Because money was a measure of all other goods, people mistakenly assumed that to be rich was to amass the largest possible stock of that commodity. To the contrary, Law insisted, it is only as money moves from hand to hand that it exercises its most important power of increasing the value of everything it touches.

Unlike immobile land, money initiates a universal dynamism setting everything in play. Law, as he expounded this new vision, wrote as the poet laureate of money and credit. His every mention of those subjects triggered a search for the most grandiloquent metaphor expressing the urgency of his message. The System becomes a rolling wave engulfing and giving new life to everything in its path: "This System will engulf the entire body of the state, the land and its produce, real estate, roads, rivers, the two seas, navigation, in a word everything everywhere. It will encourage work, industry, and human inventiveness. It will set everything in motion" (3:397). Like the rising of a miraculous sun, "this prodigious phenomenon has attracted the scrutiny of the entire universe, but it has been so dazzling, so rapid, and so all-encompassing that few have been able to behold it clearly or understand its principles" (3:398). Law is most eloquent when he contrasts a world paralyzed by hoarded gold to the thaumaturgic liberation of credit:

> I then see before me all work stopped, the value of true riches annihilated, and misery taking the place of abundance. I see men who were once rich in their work, their industry, and their possessions reduced to poverty and enslaved to those who have money. But should someone once dare to introduce credit and make it the equivalent of money, men's work, industry, and commerce will be reborn with even greater force than before. The money that was captive and ensnared all other things will be set free and, joining credit, fortify it. Everything will regain life and value. (3:414–15)

Credit, for Law, is pure synergy. Its effects far surpass the simple sum of the elements present at its inception. The dynamics of credit demand a new semiology of value. Real value never accrues as the simple addition of static signifieds summed together. True value flows from the free play of reciprocally self-defining signifiers, whose ultimate worth depends not on whatever signified they might reflect but on the energy they communicate to all they touch. An early and unrecognized champion of signifier over signified, Law and his System represented the scandal of an understanding of value that could only outrage the defenders of an established order based on the twin foundations of land and gold as ideally immutable signifieds. Saint-Simon and his peers may have given their support to Law in the early days because his plan to issue notes based on land rather than gold seemed to consolidate the triumph of land-based stability. In fact, as Law well knew but discreetly refrained from saying, those notes would volatilize both land and gold.

In book 22 of *L'Esprit des lois*, Montesquieu, still obsessed by the experience of Law's System that he had made so important a part of *Les Lettres persanes*, constructs his analysis of a proper monetary policy as a direct refutation of Law's System. Credit instruments for Montesquieu must never be more than portable gold and silver. "Paper," as he calls it, always initiates a potentially dangerous redoubling of representation that it is the state's duty to control: "Money is a sign which represents the value of all merchandise. . . . As specie is the sign of the value of merchandise, paper money is the sign of the value of specie. And, when it is solid, it represents it in such a manner that, as concerns its effect, there is no difference."[13] Montesquieu's "there is no difference" is a theme he will sound again and again: credit and paper are simply other forms of money, nonmetallic money. Montesquieu's memory of the System and its effects are at work in every position he takes on this subject. Rather than speak directly of the System, Montesquieu equates it with what he sees as its equivalent: the arrival in Spain and Europe of massive quantities of gold and silver after the discovery of the New World. Like the System, the mines of the New World led to inflation, to a generalized rise in the prices of commodities bereft of any real enrichment:

> If Europe has drawn such great benefits from the America trade, one would naturally assume that Spain has derived even more. She extracted from that newly discovered world so prodigious a quantity of gold and silver that the entire stock of money previously known did not even compare to it. But (as one would never have suspected), poverty led to her all but universal misfortune. . . . Gold and silver are a representative and fictitious wealth. . . . The more they multiply, the more they lose their value because they represent fewer things. . . . The specie of Europe quickly doubled, but the real profit for Spain decreased by half since she held, each year, only the same quantity of a metal whose real value had now been cut in half. When, over twice that time, her supply of specie again doubled, her profit was again cut in half. (2:66–68)

For Montesquieu, neither money nor credit effect any real improvement of the economies they enter. Their effect on the wealth of those whose commerce they facilitate is arithmetically and dismally proportionate: double the metal, and the price of all it buys will also double; double it again, and prices will follow with a net gain of zero.

Montesquieu's opposition to Law stems from his conviction that even the possibility of a healthy economy disappears once governments resort to arbitrary monetary systems, to systems involving a *monnaie idéale* such as the livre rather than the *monnaie réelle* of a fixed coinage. While the word *livre* once designated the value of an actual pound of silver, *les peuples policés* soon found their economies functioning not in terms of any such "real" standard but in terms of an ideal money, an arbitrary metaphor imposed only by force. Rather than having anything near the value of a pound of silver, what came to be called the livre was an arbitrary symbol representing the sum it did only because the government so decreed it. Ideal monies bring with them a potential for manipulation that every healthy economy must resist: "To eliminate the source of such abuses, all countries wishing to encourage commerce should establish a law that only *monnaies réelles* be used and that nothing be done which might make them *idéales*" (2:74). Within Montesquieu's preferred semiology of value, not only must money and goods exist as reciprocal signs of each other—"In the same way that money is the sign of a thing and represents it, so also each thing is a sign of money and represents it. A state is prosperous to the extent that, in one direction, money correctly represents all things, and, in the other, that each thing correctly represents money, such that each is the sign of the other" (2:72)—but money, as the universal sign, must be safe from fluctuation: "Nothing should be more protected from change than that which serves as the common measure of all things. Trade is uncertain in itself; and it is a great evil to add a new uncertainty to one already inherent in the activity" (2:75).

If Law so willingly departed from the tradition Montesquieu continues to defend more than a quarter-century later, it was because he felt that such monetary conservatism condemned society to economic sclerosis. As Law saw it, Montesquieu's position might appear convincing in a simple and straightforward kind of way, but its apparent rationality and clear identification of causes and effects served finally to justify and perpetuate a deadened, lifeless economy imprisoned within debt and usury. The energy and expansion Law promised could only occur when those vast sectors of the economy paralyzed by debt had been set free. When Law describes the situation in France before the System, he claims that "a small portion of the people lived on wealth drawn from loans made to others whom they ruined" (3:398). The figure of the usurer becomes for Law the symbol of "l'homme corrompu" whom the Old Regime so mistakenly sought to reward and protect. The moneylender, adamantly opposed to any inflationary movement that would facilitate the actual liquidation of debts, became for Law the forever unsatisfied despot whose pleasure finally depended not on what he himself might enjoy but on the intensity of the deprivation he beheld everywhere around him: "It is not enough for the corrupt man to be rich along with his fellows. A widespread wealth, which he participates in, pleases him very little. He must have special privileges. To be satisfied, he alone must be rich while all others are in poverty" (3:408).

Looking back on his System from exile, Law did not hesitate to identify, with a good deal of irony, those who were its true "losers": "Many lost with the repayment of debts that came as the general economic situation changed in such a way that no one needed to borrow and all were able to repay their creditors. And that is what has been called a great disorder, a great calamity for the state. . . . All the evils brought about by the System finally come down to having diminished the wealth of high-interest moneylenders and *rentiers*" (3:399–400). For Law, all the things the powers of the day now pointed to as the System's greatest evils were, to any with eyes to see, its greatest accomplishments. Singlehanded and armed only with his System, he had joined battle with the vast network of financial interests holding king and kingdom in thrall.

The *visa* of 1721 undid, as Law saw it, all the good he had accomplished. The Pâris brothers, true to the forces they represented, used it to make the usurer's dream come true: "Its ruin spread everywhere. It destroyed liberty. It offended everyone individually. It ferreted out family secrets. It extorted from all stations and all professions an accounting of their wealth" (3:395). For Law, this now universal surveillance was the logical extension of the twin strangleholds of taxation and indebtedness with which the cabal of moneylenders had so disastrously ruled before the victory of his System.

In place of a paralyzed economic order of debt, Law had tried to institute a free-flowing and unbridled expansion in which an ever-increasing credit supply would free all from the shackles of debt by allowing them to advance as far as their skill and wits could carry them. More than anything else, Law's System represented a change in the mentality of power. For Law, the continual mistake of the monarchy under Louis XIV lay in its assumption that the crown's wealth could increase only to the extent that it deprived its subjects of some part of their own within a zero-sum game, where for every winner there had to be an equivalent loser. Ever more crushing royal taxation presupposed a model that had to be rethought: "The ministers who have been controlling fiscal policy for the last thirty years never understood the nature of credit nor its effects. Their only goal was to extract the people's money. Every means seemed fine to them, and they never gave the slightest thought to the fundamental damage they were doing. They labored to give the money they so desperately needed a pernicious value that in fact stifled it. They deprived the country, industry, and commerce of a force that could always have furnished them with money" (3:300–301). The monarchy, as Law saw it, had so long allowed itself to be manipulated by moneylenders that it had finally become their image and auxiliary. Usurers and kings, together at the center of the same web, drew their sustenance from a languishing prey that could only expire under the unrelenting rhythm of always greater impositions.

In contrast to this arachnoid model, Law proposed an economy in which ample credit would orchestrate the free and synergetic play of all talents and capacities throughout the realm. There is a genuinely populist side to Law's theory, and playing on current economic metaphor, the System could be described as relying on a "trickle-up" effect: once all the peasants, craftsmen, workers, and merchants had been freed from debt and given the means for self-enrichment, their collective efforts would create a generalized economic effervescence, setting everything in motion. In this new climate of prosperity, countless new skills would be exercised, and enterprises founded. Individuals with a better idea how some need might be met would have only to issue stock allowing them to raise the money to implement and profit from their ideas. Wise investors would always be in search of just such individuals and anxious to make their funds available. Everyone's activity would enrich everyone, and a universal plenty of ever-rising stock prices would knit society together into one exuberant whole, ending the vampirish extortions of taxation, debt, and interest. The king would finance crown expenditures from his revenue as the realm's First Shareholder. His power would mirror the ever-expanding prosperity of his people as he profited from the kind of stock conversion through which the regent had been able to raise 900 million livres through the sale of only a part of his Compagnie des Indes shares.

Law argued well after the System's fall that the supposed disaster in which it ended could easily have been avoided. If so many were hurt by the credit instruments he had introduced, it was only because their expansive movement had been so abruptly halted: "They [the System's stocks and notes] spread out and penetrated the entire kingdom. They did good for all those through whose hands they passed and hurt only those who held them in the end" (3:400). Even in terms of that sad end, Law went on to claim, it can hardly be said that he did more harm than good. For every one person hurt, the velocity of the System's credit instruments had ensured that there were dozens, if not hundreds, who had been helped: "If a note passed through 200 different hands, it helped each of them and certainly did no harm to anyone. If if happened to become valueless in the last hand, it hurt only one person after having helped 199" (3:416).

Whether Law was right or wrong, his arguments in defense of the System underline its status as an immense gamble whose gains and thrills became so invigorating that the only real evil became that of ending the game, of denouncing it as false in the name of some supposed truth. The power and threat of Law's gamble lay in the fact that its pleasures and rewards were so intense that, if only for a year, it called into question the whole series of exclusions through which such gambles had been vilified by a dominant ideology identifying its own interests with a fidelity to duty, reason, and reality. The real threat of the System can be seen in the satirical legend accompanying a popular woodcut of the period entitled "Monument consacré à la posterité en mémoire de la folie incroyable de la XXe année du XVIIIe siècle" (see fig. 1):

Qui le croira? qui l'eût jamais pensé?
Qu'en un siècle si sage un Sistème insensé
Fit du Commerce un jeu de la Fortune
Et que ce jeu pernicieux
Ensorcelant jeunes et vieux
Remplit tous les esprits d'une yvresse commune?

(Who will believe it? Who could ever have imagined it?
That in an age so wise an insane System
Should make of Trade a game of Fortune
And that this pernicious game

Fig. 1. Fortune led by Folly. B. Picard. Courtesy of
Bibliothèque Nationale, Paris.

Bewitching young and old
Should fill all minds with a shared inebriation?)

Law's System was denounced as a colossal gamble leading an entire nation into a collective inebriation. But it was
a gamble of a different nature and with different stakes
than the wagering at Versailles and among the nobility that
ran as an unbroken tradition throughout the century. To
gamble on Law's System was to gamble on *agiotage,* a term
coined at the end of the seventeenth century as a pejorative
synonym for the more neutral *agio,* borrowed from the
Italian. Both terms originally designated profits made

95

from buying and selling crown debt certificates at fluctuating prices and were quickly applied to the new practice of stock trading as it grew in importance. *Agiotage* was a disapproving term for what today we soberly call capital gains. Law's System, while it lasted, made its players rich because the constantly rising price of the Compagnie des Indes stock provided immense capital gains. What made the System unique was the rapidity of the stocks' rise and the intensity of speculation as not only France but the whole of Europe hurried to find its place on the mounting spiral.

The Compagnie's stocks were a gamble, and buying them was a bet. Unlike what was happening around the gaming tables of Versailles, this gambling was not an affirmation of individual valor or courage but an absorption of the individual within the larger community of all buyers and sellers, of all the investors and profit takers. Purchasing Compagnie des Indes stock never took place as the potentially valorous defiance by an undaunted individual of the fickleness of chance incarnated in a turning card or rolling die. This new gamble demanded not individual bravery but the speculators' constant attention to what others exactly like themselves were doing. The gamble of stock speculation meant weighing courses of action whose ultimate profitability depended, not on what the investor might do as an individual, but on how his choice related to everyone else's. To buy was to bet that others were on the brink of betting the same way and that the stock prices would rise. To sell was to bet that others were on the brink of selling and that stock prices would fall. Stock speculation had become, without anyone formally proclaiming it, the basis of a new and unsuspected social contract—a pact of mutual and self-serving cupidity whose effects were to form precisely the evil against which Rousseau would write when, nearly a half-century later, he proposed his own version of the social contract as a unanimous renunciation of self-interest in favor of the common good.

The investor gambles not on himself as an individual

but on himself as part of that same large number that was to play so crucial a role in the development of probability theory and statistics. Without that multitude of other buyers and sellers acting on motivations similar to his own, the speculator's bet would be meaningless, and there would be no arena for his gamble. Buying and selling Compagnie des Indes stock anticipated a way of thinking that would be fully articulated only a century later. The stock speculator saw himself, not as an individual, but as part of a diffuse, aggregative, and, to use a nineteenth-century term, statistical mass. Buying and selling stock had no meaning in itself but expressed the speculator's conviction as to what the vast majority of others, the market, was about to do. The speculator not only accepted but derived pleasure and profit from the way his actions related to and were defined by those of all around him. To stake a fortune on the next card was to accept a reward or ruin that depended exclusively on the individual's free choice and the card that turned up next. To buy or sell stock was to bet on what everyone else was about to do. Stock speculation was the epiphany of that radically decentered individuality for which the only center was the periphery of a conglomerate other.

What happened to John Law as he lived the rise and fall of the System tells us a great deal about the stakes of this new speculation and how it differed from aristocratic gambling. Law may have lost his real bet during his lifetime, but he has won it many times over in the subsequent development of monetary and economic theory. His bet had nothing to do with personal gain. It was common knowledge that he left France with only a fraction of the hundred thousand pounds with which he had arrived. Law bet his life on an idea, an adventure of knowledge. From the time he wrote his first treatise in 1705, *Money and Trade considered with a proposal for supplying the nation with money,* his bet was that he alone had understood why people acted as they did and could, on the basis of that knowledge, establish a system guaranteeing universal prosperity. His

97

bet was that he had understood a previously unperceived truth that, even as he exposed it, his fellows remained incapable of recognizing.

Law devoted his life to proving that his doctrine of credit was true and workable. Before winning the support of Philippe d'Orléans, he had been an itinerant *projecteur* wandering through Europe from prince to prince trying to find a royal sponsor who would provide him with the means to prove his hypotheses. The actual period of the System, 1717 to 1720, was for him one of total absorption in every detail of its construction, operation, and defense. During the twelve months of the System's triumph Law was everywhere—opening new offices, advising the regent, drafting new edicts, and fine-tuning every aspect of a national economy now totally under his control. When the System faltered, Law frantically tried every possible tactic to outwit his enemies, shore up the price of the stock, and keep the System afloat. Once it collapsed and he was forced to flee France, Law devoted the rest of his sad life to composing endless justifications of what he had done and hoping for an impossible return to grace with the regent.

Saint-Simon, in his careful final portrait of Law, describes him as "un homme doux, bon, respectueux," who never cheated or profiteered, who remained modest and unassuming even at the center of immense wealth and power, and whose only shortcoming was to have let himself become, in the final days when all was lost, dry, morose, and *mal mesuré* in his answers to others. At the center of his portrait, Saint-Simon describes Law the gambler: "He was a man of systems [un homme de système], of calculation, and of comparison, well and deeply versed, the kind who, without ever cheating, had everywhere won immense sums at gambling because he could predict, as unbelievable as it seems even to me, the sequence of the cards [la combinaison des cartes]."[14] Even for someone of Saint-Simon's imperial phlegm, Law was a man of surprises, a man who possessed a knowledge so startling that describing it risked striking the reader as "unbelievable." Law knew what Saint-Simon calls "la combinaison des cartes." As its first definition of *combinaison* the Littré offers "the assembling of multiples two by two, three by three, or, in general, of any number by any number in a determined order," and explains that the word is most often applied to numbers, letters, colors, and playing cards.[15] What Saint-Simon here struggles to describe is the effect created by Law's ability— somewhat like what we saw in Fontenelle's breathless description of Dangeau's astute cardplaying—to apply to his gambling the lessons of what we now call probability theory. Judging from Saint-Simon's description, either Law had worked out the odds governing the games he played himself or he had used Montmort's *Essai d'analyse sur les jeux de hasard* (1708) to develop that skill. Saint-Simon's concern that the reader might find his claim "unbelievable" suggests that actually applying probability theory to gambling was rare even a half-century after Pascal's work.

Saint-Simon's half-fascinated and half-puzzled attitude toward Law never completely clarified itself. The relation between them was symbolic of how one system of values was replacing another. Saint-Simon was happy to serve as Law's political godfather so long as he saw the Scotsman's rise as a way of humiliating the duc de Villeroy, the rival whom Phillipe d'Orléans had chosen over him to head the Conseil des finances at the beginning of the Regency. Villeroy's early and vocal opposition to Law's plans made it a pleasure for Saint-Simon to defend him behind the scene. Once Villeroy had been dismissed, however, and Law began to assume more and more complete control over crown finances, Saint-Simon grew at best tepid in his support. Saint-Simon was the spokesman for a way of life in which open and public acts of display—bravery on the battlefield, ostentation in ceremony, obliviousness to losses at the gaming table—proved a nobility of character adequate in itself. Law, to the contrary, was the forerunner of a quite different ideal that only a century later would completely displace that of the traditional nobility. Both as gambler and as creator of the System, Law was the scientist: the individual whose value depended, not on acts of public display, but on his knowledge of a hidden truth no one had as yet perceived. Law was Law because he built his System on a new understanding of an unrecognized truth presumed to be at work in the actions of all his fellows. His conviction that a desire for financial gain functioned as the hidden mainspring of all human activity not only allowed him to demonstrate the spectacular powers of credit but also presupposed a vision of human motivation antithetical to the aristocratic ethos of disinterested service carried out in the name of personal honor. Sacrificing everything to his passion for knowledge, Law became the harbinger of the reign of science to come.

While Saint-Simon may have felt a half-repressed affection for Law, Montesquieu saw his System as the principal agent of corruption at work within the Regency. For Montesquieu, Law was a far more dangerous figure than the pathetic would-be commander of the imagination we saw earlier. As the person whose state-sponsored appeal to greed had destroyed what for Montesquieu was the very foundation of social order, Law was the incarnation of evil. For Montesquieu, the rise and fall of the System had reduced society to an immense wheel of fortune destroying the reality of rank: "All who were rich six months ago are now impoverished and those who couldn't buy bread are bursting with wealth. Never have those two extremes touched so closely" (*Les Lettres persanes*, 293). Law is the Foreigner who has violently taken hold of the state and turned it inside out as if it were a piece of old clothing. The System's rapid fortunes created a new and ever-shifting hierarchy built on no firmer basis than the possession of wealth: "What unhoped for fortunes, unbelievable even for those who have made them! Not even God more quickly created men from nothing. How many lackeys are now served by their comrades and perhaps tomorrow by their masters!" (293–94).

Montesquieu's most vigorous condemnation of Law comes in letter 146 of *Les Lettres persanes,* a letter of particular importance as the work's final statement on European society before the scene shifts to the revolt in Usbek's harem. Composed shortly after the System had fallen and while Law was on his way into exile, this letter shrilly condemns Law's celebration of self-enrichment as antithetical to all true virtue and honor: "I saw suddenly born in every heart an insatiable thirst for wealth. I saw come together in a single moment a detestable conspiracy to get rich, not through honest work and generous effort, but through the ruin of the prince, of the state, and of its citizens" (322). This letter stands as Montesquieu's most concerted attempt to designate Law as the universal scapegoat, as the personification of an evil responsible for sins committed by vast numbers of people. The stridency of Montesquieu's anathema comes in great part because the success of Law's System had demonstrated that his hypothesis of universal cupidity was far from invalid. And not even the most naive observer could claim that the System's collapse had resulted from any collective return to virtue on the part of its shareholders.

Law's System was a scandal for Montesquieu because it undercut in the most spectacular way his own conviction that true nobility was distinguished by a devotion to honor incompatible with lucrative self-interest. As *L'Esprit des lois* would make clear, Montesquieu felt that only a nobility indifferent to financial gain could resist the debilitating emoluments offered by the crown and retain the independence necessary for that order to serve as a bulwark against despotism. The System's speculation was scandalous because it provided numerous and daily proofs of the most avid self-interest at even the highest levels of the nobility. The beginning of the System's end came, we saw, when none other that the duc de Bourbon and the prince de

Conti forced their way into Law's offices and demanded millions in gold. The comte de Horn, a grandson of the prince de Ligne, had at roughly the same time lured a wealthy stock speculator into a tavern, where he murdered and robbed him like a common criminal. For Montesquieu, something more than individual weakness had to be responsible for these degradations of the order on which the stability of the realm depended. Since, in other words, the premises of Montesquieu's own ideological position could not tolerate so obviously widespread a corruption of the nobility, the real responsibility for what was happening had to be placed on John Law, on the devil who made them do it: "What crime can be greater than that of the minister who corrupts the morals of an entire nation, who debases its most noble souls, tarnishes the splendor of high office, obscures virtue itself, and subjects the highest station to universal scorn?" (322–23). As always in such anathemas, the innocence of the many depends on a transfer of guilt onto the elected victim, who is then punished as the unique incarnation of an evil to be exorcised through the scapegoat's destruction.

Montesquieu's denunciation of Law as the Foreigner who corrupted an entire nation was symptomatic of a far more extensive, methodic, and costly exercise in collective denial that touched the whole of France. The motivation for this denial was obvious: if the Foreigner alone was responsible, we need only forget the lies with which he has gulled us and return to the truths of the past.

Law and his System had revealed to French society something so traumatizing about itself that it was willing to march resolutely backwards toward a past about which few illusions could be harbored. The System's fall brought with it a massive return to all the worst fiscal and financial practices that had characterized the stagnant twilight of Louis XIV. The vastly corrupt and inefficient system of tax farming was restored. The French economy, which would not see the reestablishment of a public credit institution for over fifty years, had to function without the financial instruments that could have facilitated economic expansion. Every aspect of a bankrupt fiscal policy resurrected from the past became a subject of endless and debilitating debate between crown and parlement.

The price of this return to the past was enormous. Once deprived of the credit mechanisms through which Law had aggressively set out to rebuild the maritime fleet, establish new ports, and invigorate the colonial economies, France divested herself of the means to resist her loss of power in the New World. The naval defeats of Quiberon Bay and Lagos in 1759 may, by giving the English supremacy in the Atlantic, have sealed the fate of New France, but the underlying fragility of a fleet that could be neutralized in two engagements was the direct result of a stagnation in maritime armaments stemming directly from the dismantling of Law's methods and priorities. Domestically, the wholesale return to the grossly inequitable fiscal practices of the past played an important role in consolidating a hostility toward innovation that would stymie all efforts at fiscal reform throughout the century even as, with the approach of 1789, their necessity became more and more obvious to all.

If France was willing to pay so high a price for rejecting the System, it was because its foundation in the free play of credit revealed the fragility of a whole series of institutions and practices sustaining the established vision of the world as stable, fixed, and predictable—as existing beyond the power of chance. Montesquieu denounced Law's System not only because it was an affront to aristocratic honor but because it led to a loss of faith. For the nobility, it had destroyed their belief in an equivalence of land and identity. For the low-born, it had destroyed their belief in the value of regular work and the slow accumulation of savings. The System's innovations had to be evil because they dissolved the construct of mutually sustaining assumptions through which the social order of the *ancien régime* had defined and preserved itself.

Law's System brought with it massive doses of expansion, energy, and gambling. Its transformation of the country on the basis of speculation made it all too clear that it was the child of chance and that its new wealth flowed from none of the traditional formulas defended by church or state. Law's System was a scandal because it made clear for all to see the dynamism unleashed by the gambles of a credit system unrestrained by any allegiance to the limits of some supposed reality.

The story of Law and his System is important because it was through it that the French Enlightenment most spectacularly elected chance and gambling as its scapegoats of choice. Writing seventy years after the System's fall, it is nonetheless to Law and his System that Edmund Burke implicitly alludes when, describing that other great gamble at the end of the Enlightenment, he seeks a scapegoat for everything the Revolution has wrought:

> Your legislators, in everything new, are the very first who have founded a commonwealth upon gaming, and infused this spirit into it as its vital breath. The great object in these politics is to metamorphose France from a great kingdom into one great playtable; to turn its inhabitants into a nation of gamesters; to make speculation as extensive as life; to mix it with all its concerns and to divert the whole of the hopes and fears of the people from their usual channels into the impulses, passions, and superstitions of those who live on chances.[16]

Part Two

Chance and the Novel

4

Toward a Novel of Experience

The year 1678 saw the publication of two works that redefined their respective genres and changed the way we think
of chance. Madame de La Fayette's *La Princesse de Clèves* is
most often cited as the first fully formed example of the
modern French novel. Wilhelm Gottfried Leibniz's *De aes-
timatione* is a seminal study of probability theory that not
only built on the work of Pascal and Huygens but argued
that a deductive, computational ethics was possible within
the context of that new science. The coincidence of their
publication dates symbolizes a fundamental congruence,
perhaps even a monadic harmony, between these two cultural phenomena: the rise of the novel and the elaboration
of a science of probability. Working in the same direction,
both were linchpins in what was to become modernity's
predominant attitude toward chance. Each, when examined in the context of the other, tells us something that
would otherwise go unrecognized.

Addressing the question whether there actually was any
specific period or succession of works that might be referred to as a "probabilistic revolution," Ian Hacking describes the development of probability theory from the
1650s to the 1930s (when Kolmogorov's work effectively
redefined the field)[1] as "the great philosophical success
story" of those centuries: "Other philosophical ideas have
waxed and waned and sometimes grown again, but probability has been monotone. It has waxed and waxed, shone
and shone. It has been a success in metaphysics, epistemol-
ogy, and pragmatics, to mention three of the classic philosophical fields."[2]

Hacking's claim underlines the important role probability theory was to play throughout the eighteenth century in consolidating the consensus within the scientific community that chance was an illusion, that the physical and even the moral world was ruled by strict laws of cause and effect whose workings could be successfully fathomed once we had sufficiently refined our instruments and protocols of observation. While some would see the workings of a divine principle within that order and others would opt for a pure materialism, both groups shared a belief in an ultimately knowable order of causality. The universality of probability theory's triumph brought, however, its own ambiguities. Could so unrelenting a denial of chance have occurred had it not been rooted in an abiding fear that the world of men and of things might in fact remain intractable to the calm domination of knowable and predictable laws?

The novel, more than any other literary genre, reflects this ambiguity of the eighteenth century's attitude toward chance. The novel of that period always tells two stories. On the one hand, it speaks of a deterministic universe in which actions are followed by reactions. On the other, it tells the story of how, within that predictability, the chance event may at any moment redefine the individual's place within the world's apparently ordered sequences of cause and effect. Prévost's *Manon Lescaut* tells the story of three parallel worlds each of which is in itself perfectly predictable: the worlds of the provincial nobility, of the monied bourgeoisie, and of a recently urbanized proletariat. Yet the real story of des Grieux and Manon is that of a chance encounter threatening the predictability of each of those worlds.

Probability theory and the novel worked together to consolidate a bulwark against chance. Grasping what was at stake in that collaboration can best begin by contrasting their shared vision of causality to the earlier understanding of chance and its role in human affairs that it replaced. That earlier view of chance is well illustrated in a woodcut from the early sixteenth century, a woodcut serving as the frontispiece to the 1524 French edition of Petrarch's *Remède de l'un et l'autre fortune prospère et adverse*. This image speaks of an absolute separation between chance and wisdom, between *fortuna* and *sapientia*. At the left of the woodcut, Fortuna sits under the head of the unwise man, the *insipiens*, who proclaims: *Te clamus fortuna dea celoque locamus* ("We proclaim you a Goddess, O Fortune, and place you in the heavens"). To the right, Wisdom sits under the head of the wise man, the *sapiens*, who proclaims: *Fidite virtuti: Fortuna fugatior undis* ("Confide in virtue; Fortune is more fleeting than the waves").

The figure of Fortune is blindfolded. She holds before her an ever-turning wheel over which none of the figures arrayed around it exercises any control. The reigning king, momentarily imperious at its summit, will soon, like the plummeting figure below him, be toppled by the figure rising from the right. Traditionally, these figures were tersely but eloquently designated as Regno, Regnavi, Regnabo, and Sum Sine Regno. Wisdom, to the contrary, calmly contemplates the mirrored image of her own virtue, a wisdom undistracted by the vicissitudes of human endeavor. The figure of Fortune sits on the *sedes fortune rotunda*. Her rounded throne totters precariously on the edge of a triangular base, itself at an angle formed by the wedge upon which it rests. The figure of Wisdom sits on the *sedes virtutis quadrata*, the solid throne of virtue. Rigorously squared, that seat rests firmly on two flat and stable planes.

This woodcut stands as a Renaissance summary of the classical and scholastic understanding of the human situation. Sapientia sits as a metaphor for *scientia*, for a knowledge that, like wisdom, is concerned only with universal, unchanging truths susceptible to logical demonstration and in no way contingent on specific circumstances that change over time. While individuals will come to apprehend such knowledge at a specific time and in a specific

Fig. 2. Fortuna and Sapientia. Frontispiece to Petrarch's *Remède de l'un et l'autre fortune prospère et adverse.* Courtesy of Bibliothèque Nationale, Paris.

place, the truths so perceived lift them out of that specificity to the realm of the atemporal and the unchanging, because they exist independently of the circumstances of their perception. As J. G. A. Pocock has expressed it: "Reality of this order consisted of universals, and the activity of reason consisted of the intellect's ascent to recognition of the timeless rationality of universals."[3] The disciplines through which these truths came to be apprehended were the abstract sciences of philosophy and logic.

To the left, Fortuna sits as a metaphor of *opinio*—the base, uncertain, ever-changing opinions we have of everything situated in and dependent on the specific moment and the particular place. Opinion is circumstantial rather than demonstrable, accidental rather than necessary, temporal rather than eternal. As philosophy and logic were the elected disciplines for the discovery of science's universal truths, so rhetoric, the cunning ability to sway men's minds, was the vehicle of the always partial interpretations leading individuals to form their opinions of events.[4] The eyes of the figure representing wisdom are downcast and nearly closed both as a gesture of stoic humility and because true wisdom refuses any concern with the realm of opinion and what it says of a world given over to change and fortune.

We have, with this woodcut, returned to a world operating on premises totally different from our own. What we today think of as "factual" and therefore true was to be dismissed as meaningless circumstance. What we would instinctively distrust as vague abstraction was seen as bearing therein the hallmark of universal truth. The most important seventeenth-century modification of this paradigm came with Descartes' attempt to redeem a knowledge of the real by proposing its submission to the rigors of mathematical investigation, thus preparing the development of previously oxymoronic "physical sciences." Working in astronomy, optics, and geometry, Descartes argued that only the universality, abstraction, and logical rigor of a mathematized real could allow the newly emerging sciences of the physical world to present themselves as something more than a ludicrous contradiction in terms.

For Descartes, mathematics allowed an attention to the real that respected the classical hierarchy of genres. Philosophy, logic, and now a mathematized analysis of the real world occupied the summit by reason of their shared foundation in universal categories of the unchangingly true. At the other extreme, mired in the limiting specificity of circumstance, history and all forms of narrative offered only moment-to-moment depictions of what may have existed at one moment but would inevitably cease to do so in the future. This devaluation of history and narrative reflects an allegiance to the traditional Aristotelian doctrine of the incommensurability of wisdom and chance, of the universal and the contingent, of knowledge and opinion, of logic and rhetoric, of philosophy and story. All was to be apportioned to one or the other of these contrary realms. Nothing was intermediate. Nothing was shared.

What we refer to as the Enlightenment, the Age of Reason, but also the age of probability theory and the novel was nothing less than a previously unthinkable merging of these categories, a multiplication of knowledge and control of the real flowing from a systematic erasure of the once uncontested boundaries between chance and science. Rather than a world divided between the eternally true and the fortuitously factual, the Enlightenment saw the birth of a mixed, resolutely intermediate world in which even the aleatory would become the object of a science claiming to offer all but certain knowledge.

If Fortune was brought so docilely to heel, if the woodcut accompanying Petrarch's text represents a world-view antithetical to the eighteenth century's, it is because the Enlightenment redefined the status and implications of chance. No longer Rome's blind goddess of Fortune or the Christian figure of providence, chance came to be seen as the reactionary illusion that there exists a point beyond which human knowledge could not extend. Laplacian optimism promised an all-conquering advance in our knowledge of a deterministic world in which chance would have no role to play.

Probability theory and the novel played complementary and mutually sustaining roles in the Enlightenment's evacuation of chance. The events with which the nascent science of probability dealt most effectively were of a specific kind. As we saw, the doctrine of chances grew out of the analysis of gambling, of wagers decided by the turn of a card or the roll of a die. What made cards and dice so precious for gambling was the fact that as randomizers, they have no memory. A given roll of the dice is never, in other words, part of a "well-told story," a story in which what precedes the roll as event can determine what point will appear. Buffon, in the same *Essai d'arithmétique morale* in which he defined his concept of "moral certainty," used the example of a simple dice game called passe-dix—a game in which the player wins by throwing a total of ten or more points with three dice—to explain how the events analyzed by probability theory differ from those of our everyday lives. The chance event for Buffon is characterized by its lack of any causal relation to past or future, by the absence of any relation to what has gone before as cause or to what will come after as effect. The chance event exists outside determinism, outside any concatenation of cause and effect providing the armature of narrative. Describing the situation of the passe-dix player before each throw, Buffon insists that "each such experiment yields results quite unlike those produced by experiments involving natural effects. I would call it a certitude as to the inconstancy rather than the constancy of causes [la certitude de l'inconstance au lieu de celle de la constance des causes]."[5]

The chance event is recalcitrant to narrative. A story exists, is cogent, and achieves meaning only to the extent that it coaxes its reader into discovering some coherence of cause and effect, some rationality of the narrated events.

To read narrative is to participate in a movement of understanding toward which each event beckons the readers as
they participate in its illusions of discovery and compre-
hension. The proudest claim of the new science of probability was that it would eliminate the irrationality of
chance's capricious abruptness. In so doing, probability
theory paralleled the novel's similar ability to elaborate
representations of life's chaos where causal sequence vanquished the threat of chance.

What is less obvious about the relation between narrative and probability theory is the way that new science, as
it set out to analyze chance, itself depended on narrative
frames providing contextualizations of the fortuitous
event. The birth of probability theory is, as we saw, usually
dated to Pascal's 1654 essay on the arithmetic triangle. The
specific problem Pascal addressed in that work was that of
'partitions', of how one might equitably divide the stakes
in a game of chance when the contest is interrupted before
its conclusion.

In his study of pre-Pascalian treatments of such problems, Ernest Coumet stresses the fact that there is no single
self-evident and obviously superior approach to the resolution of such problems.[6] He offers as an example the
straightforward problem of partitions, first treated by the
Italian mathematician Luco Paccioli in his *Summa de arith-
metica* (1494). An elderly landowner visiting his country
estate offers a prize of one hundred ducats to the first of
two young peasants to win six games in a contest in which
both players have an equal chance of winning each round.
When the score stands at five games for A and three for B,
the game is interrupted. How should the stake be divided?

One approach to the problem assumes that only the
games actually played should be considered in dividing the
prize. Eight games were played, with A winning five and
B, three. On that basis Paccioli decides that five-eighths of
the stakes should go to A, and three-eighths to B. As logical
as that approach seems, it in fact ignores the contest's basic
premise: the prize will be awarded only when one of the

players has won six games. A second approach thus insists on considering the games not yet played. Assuming that there could be no more than a total of eleven games (six for the winner and a maximum of five for the loser), this approach suggests that A has moved five-elevenths of the way along this longest possible path toward the prize, whereas B has moved only three-elevenths of the way. A should clearly be awarded five-elevenths of the hundred ducats, and B, three-elevenths. There still remain, however, three-elevenths, more than a quarter of the whole, for which, as it were, no contest has as yet taken place. Given that line of reasoning, one could argue that the remaining three-elevenths should be divided proportionately to the number of games each player has already won, with A receiving roughly twice the share of the remaining three-elevenths as B.

To divide the prize that way would, however, be to assume that chance must continue to act in the future exactly as it has in the past—hardly a self-evident assumption. Coumet cites an argument offered by Lorenzo Forestani in his *Pratica d'aritmetica* (1682) in favor of an equal split of the remaining three-elevenths on the premise that since fortune can reverse itself at any moment, B as the apparent loser might well have gone on to win the next three rounds and thus the entire prize. From that perspective, an equal distribution of the undisputed remainder would most respect the unpredictability of the chance event. The important thing to understand about these analyses is that each depends not so much on the facts of what happened—that A won five games and B, three—as on the way those facts are woven into different narrative contexts. Each version of the narrative, by ordering and emphasizing the facts in a different way, motivates a different outcome.

Pascal's solution to this problem, one all probabilists have adopted after him, involved still another way of telling the story. We must, Pascal insisted, look at the five-to-three score as an unfinished story, as a story that will be complete only when the contest is played through to its conclusion and one player has actually won six games. This can happen with a minimum of one additional game (if A wins it) or with a maximum of three additional games (if B wins them all). For each additional but unplayed game the probability that A or B will win remains one-half. There are, then, three chances for A to win: by winning the first new game, the second, or the third. A's overall probability of winning the contest is thus the sum of the probabilities of his winning each of those three possible rounds $(.5 + .5^2 + .5^3)$, or seven-eighths, and B's probability of winning is the remaining one-eighth. Narrativized in this way, the prize should be divided such that seven-eighths goes to A and one-eighth goes to B.

The crucial innovation in Pascal's approach came in his insistence that to solve the riddle of the unfinished game, the prize must be divided upon any interruption in such a way that were it to become possible for the players to continue the game, the provisional partition of the prize would guarantee that both players saw it as being in their interest to play the game out to its originally defined conclusion. The split at any moment before the original conditions for closure have been met must, in other words, provide odds that motivate both players to complete the game's narrative as it was originally scripted. Pascal's solution is "correct" because it reflects the fact that were the game to be resumed, A would only have to win one additional round in three tries to take the prize, while B would have to win all three. After the interruption, then, A must hold a share sufficient to allow him to offer his considerably disadvantaged opponent the seven-to-one odds B would need for it to be in his self-interest to risk the one-eighth he already holds and finish the game.

Pascal's change of perspective on this classical problem is fraught with implications. In their earlier resolutions, Paccioli and Forestani had confined their analyses to a purely retrospective view of the games already played as a finished process cut off from any possible future. Pascal's innovation came as he enlarged the narrative frame. For him, the moment of the game's interruption had to be approached, not as the end of the story, but as one point in an ongoing narrative—as a present moment to be understood through its relations to future expectation as well as past performance. An adequate resolution of the problem had to involve not only a memory of the past but an anticipation of the future, an assurance that both players would be motivated to complete the scenario as originally written.

In their study of the role of mathematics in contemporary life, Philip J. Davis and Reuben Hersh point out that the field of probability analysis has undergone an enormous extension. Beginning as a theory, it was "mathematical, axiomatic, deductive. [Its] statements [had] the same epistemological status as in any branch of pure mathematics."[7] Its significance grew, however, because of the ease with which that pure theory extended its apparently validating mantle over ever broader sectors of individual and public decision making. As the science of probability assumed extended applicability, its methodology became distinctly different from what had characterized it as a mathematical theory. Probabilistic analyses were "accomplished by art, cunning, experience, persuasion, misrepresentation, common sense, and a whole host of rhetorical, but non-mathematical devices" (24). As probability theory merged with practice, it depended more and more on effects that could be achieved only by an encompassing and motivating narrative fitting the theory's abstract present to a relevant past and projected future.

Like probability theory, the novel imposed itself during the eighteenth century as a form privileging a representation of the present as the movement from a known past to an uncertain future. Like probability theory, the novel depended for its significance on an ability to solicit the reader's identification with its rationalized and causally integrated sequencing of events. Like probability theory, the novel promised a greater understanding and mastery of life's apparently random events.

The novel shares with probability theory the assumption that individuals act within a world of preexisting causal sequences, of multiple determinisms compelling their reactions. Parallel to probability theory's rationalizing of chance, the focus of novelistic representation shifted away from the purely evenemential and giddy unpredictability we find in the picaresque *nouvelles* and *contes* of the early seventeenth century to a didactic analysis of moral character within an ultimately rational world. The novel of experience became for its audience the cornerstone of a new individuality and a new identity. Characters existed not so much in terms of what they did as in terms of their awareness of the reasons why they acted as they did. The novel's narrative of choice became the story of a reflexive self-awareness moving along determined and compelling pathways. Narrative man became cerebral man, the individual marked by and existing through an acute awareness of self. More than any other single work of the period, Diderot's *Paradoxe sur le comédien* stands as a foundational text for the age of the novel. Speaking of the theater, it argues that the most effective actor on the world's stage is the person who, rather than empathizing with and losing himself in the role he plays, stands entirely outside it, watching, analyzing, and adjusting every aspect of his *jeu* to its effect on the audience for which he plays. Diderot's actor incarnates the self-conscious and always self-regarding posture of novelized, narrativized man. The script is written, and its actions decided. Our one prerogative is to analyze and learn from the effects of our individual inflections as we execute that script's commands.

Probability theory and the novel of experience shared a didactic vocation consolidating their popularity as responses to the needs of an audience forced to live within ever larger and more complex social contexts. Daniel Defoe, in the same year that he published *Robinson Crusoe*, wrote a short pamphlet entitled *The Gamester*. A satiric depiction of the widespread gambling in the London of 1719, it ends with Defoe's claim that a firm knowledge of the probabilities governing the various games he discusses has now become as essential a part of the young gentleman's education as was once the study of law: "As several of our gentlemen of great estates bred up their sons to know something of the law, to enable them the better to keep their estates when they came to inherit them, so they should now think it equally necessary that they should study the mathematics, at least so far as to understand the Law of Chance, to make a just computation in all games, to prevent their losing them at play, and being bubbles to sharpers."[8]

On the other side of the channel, the entry "Probabilité" in Diderot and d'Alembert's *Encyclopédie* promised far broader and less satiric benefits from an understanding of this new science. Once adequate records of such events as epidemics, fires, and shipwrecks are kept, once death registers include the facts of the decedent's age, condition, temperament, and cause of death, the calm regularities of laws imperceptible at the scale of the single event but irrefutable at the scale of society as a whole will banish all belief in "what people quite inappropriately call the effect of chance."[9] The didactic value of these laws will be such that once their lessons are perceived, they will close even the gap between youth and experience by their power to "give to attentive young people all the experience of age" (3:105).

The consolidation of the novel's didactic function during the late seventeenth and eighteenth centuries was most apparent in its refusal of the term 'novel'. The word *roman* was unacceptable because it carried with it the liability of evoking the rough comedy of works such as Scarron's *Roman comique* and Furetière's *Roman bourgeois*. Centered on the serial adventures of picaresque heroes exuberantly open to the eruption of the chance event, such novels entertained their readers with the vitality and humor of their socially marginal heroes as they rose to the challenge of any predicament chance might throw at them. As in to-day's James Bond or Kung-fu films, the center of interest lay not in the logic of plot but in the cartoonlike resilience of a central character surviving even the most perilous hazards.

The new novel of experience as it developed alongside probability theory was something entirely different. Insisting on its status as *histoire,* it refused the arbitrary concatenation of events so prevalent in the earlier forms of the genre. Rather than a stringing together of episodes, this new form depended on a coherence of plot and character justifying the genre's claim to inform and mold the reading public by revealing the workings of the world as it actually was. Realism became a paramount value within the novel, because it was only to the extent that its characters and situations were perceived as pertaining to the same world as the reader's that they could become the vehicle of a moral lesson. In his preface to *Manon Lescaut,* Prévost claims for the novel a didactic value equal to, if not surpassing, that of life itself. The story we are about to read will supplement the reader's limited experience through narrations so well drawn that they will teach lessons equally as vivid and equally as valid as those the reader has learned from life itself. Analyzing the importance to the novel of what he calls "the incomparable didactic value of the concrete example," Georges May underlines the abiding importance of this function to the eighteenth-century novel by quoting a text as late as Restif de la Bretonne's preface to *Les Françaises* (1786): "What is a novelist? He is a moralist who, rather than imperiously commanding 'Do this! Do that!,' acts as a skillful Nestor setting forth the actions of other men and other women whose conduct, good or bad, and often both at the same time, he traces out for you. The novelist holds a map in his hand and shows us the way."[10] Unlike its picaresque predecessors, the novel of experience justifies itself, not by the pleasure of its read, but by the value of its lesson.

Probability theory and the novel share the claim to show

the world as it is and to provide their audiences with a more complete understanding of how it works. As probability theory developed through its elaboration of the law of large numbers and its mutation into the science of statistics, it effectively defined itself as the novel of experience par excellence, as the novel of novels, whose central character was none other than that perfect average representing all its potential readers. Adolphe Quételet, the father of statistics, pointed with pride to the necessarily fictive status of the *homme moyen* at the center of his new science: "The person I am considering here is analogous within society to the center of gravity within an object. He incarnates the average around which individual social beings oscillate. He is, if you will, a fictive being for whom everything will happen in accordance with averages valid for society as a whole."[11] The novel of experience shared with probability theory and statistics the intention of revealing society's multiple determinisms and intersecting causalities in such a way that its audience might draw from them a more complete and more effective mastery of its world. Not only would the novel add to the reader's limited experience but, because its representation of events was susceptible to infinite analysis and clarification, it would provide a supplement more reliable, more eloquent, and more valuable than those experiences too often lived as little more than mute chaos.

I have tried to describe here a number of crucial parallels between the emergence of the novel and the probabilistic revolution. Both, I argue, worked toward a domestication of chance, toward the elimination of its threat to the Enlightenment's faith in a rational and knowable world. There is, however, no single or simple relation between the actual practices of the eighteenth-century French novel and the protocols of probability theory. The shape of the novel as it developed throughout this period was far too varied to allow any direct equation of content with form or theme with genre. The rest of this study is therefore devoted to the analysis of specific novels and how they exemplify the divergent forms of the genre's relation to the conquest of chance. While the majority of the works I consider clarify that subversion of chance, others, fewer in number but equally significant, work in the opposite direction—toward a celebration of chance necessarily challenging the conventions of the novel of experience and problematizing the form of the genre.

5

Jean de Préchac and the Noble's Wager

Historians of gambling like to find patterns in the changing fashions of the games people play. Following Philippe Ariès's thesis that the seventeenth century's increasing moralization of everyday activities led to a stigmatizing of games played for money in a family context, Thierry Depaulis argues that the *ancien régime* saw an evolution away from betting and bluffing games of pure chance such as glic, flux, and prime (all mentioned by Rabelais as part of Gargantua's pedagogy and usually recognized as ancestors of modern poker) toward more mathematically complex games based on an accumulation of tricks where skill and calculation played a far larger role than aggressive betting.[1] According to this view, nineteenth-century whist and contemporary bridge represent the highest stages of this evolution. While pure betting games are now rare in the context of family pastimes that interested Ariès, the continuing popularity of blackjack, poker, baccarat, and other casino-style games makes it difficult to agree that there was any general evolution away from one pole of Depaulis's opposition to the other.

It is true, however, that card games come into and pass out of fashion as part of a broader social praxis involving such diverse elements as the game's identification with a particular milieu or class, foreign influences, and police repression. With regard to the period that interests us here, the intertwining of gambling with the larger social fabric is nowhere more evident than in the case of the game called basset, *la bassette*. One of the most popular card games of the seventeenth and eighteenth centuries, basset had the further distinction of figuring in the titles of two of Jean de Préchac's best-known novels, *La Noble Vénitienne ou la bassette* (1679) and *Les Désordres de la bassette* (1682).

First appearing in France in the second half of the seventeenth century, basset had all the social cachet of its Italian origin. Eminently simple to play, it quickly became one of the most popular games of chance. Each player holds a *livre*, a pack of thirteen cards from the ace to the king, and bets against the dealer acting as banker on whichever individual cards from the *livre* he wishes. With suits irrelevant, basset amounted to a kind of roulette with thirteen choices played with cards instead of a wheel. The players would bet by placing on the table whatever card or cards they wished from their *livre* and putting money on top of them. The players, in whatever number, all wagered against the banker, who held a deck of fifty-two cards. Once the players had placed their bets, the dealer shuffled and cut the deck. Turning it over so that the bottom card became visible, the dealer then placed the upturned deck of fifty-two cards in a shoe, allowing only the upper card to be seen. That first upturned card represented a win for the dealer, and he collected as his winnings all bets placed by the players on the card of that value. The next upturned card in the dealer's deck represented a win for the players, and the banker paid a sum equal to the amount on the players' cards to all who had chosen that card. The game continued with cards being revealed two by two, the first winning for the banker and the second for the players, until the full deck of fifty-two cards was exhausted. Players could make additional bets at any time as the dealer moved through the deck. Two qualifications modified this simple structure: players who had bet on the very first of the dealer's upturned cards lost only two-thirds of their initial bet rather than all of it. And what was more important, the dealer did not pay the players for the last card of his deck, the fifty-second, which would otherwise have been a winner for the players.

The game took on added excitement whenever a player won his original bet. Having earned even money on, say, a nine, the player could then, by twisting the corner of his card closest to him, indicate that he was going for the *alpiu* or *paroli*. This parlay bet meant that if a nine came again as a winner for the players, that player would remove his already doubled original stake and receive from the banker three times the amount of the bet. The *sept et le va* and *quinze et le va* were additional parlay bets that the player would win if his card came up a winner for a third and fourth time, with the banker then obliged to pay seven and fifteen times the stake on such bets.

Addictive in its rapidity and simplicity, the game was highly lucrative for the banker. Carefully studied by Sauveur in the *Journal des savants* (1679), by Montmort in his *Essai d'analyse sur les jeux de hasard* (1708), and by Jakob Bernoulli in his *Ars conjectandi* (1713), the game held a banker's advantage of two-fifteenths, meaning that on the average, the banker could expect to win slightly more than one-eighth of all the money wagered. The game's notoriety and the large number of otherwise respectable Parisian families who ran games in their homes led to a series of edicts forbidding it. The entry for basset in Diderot's *Encyclopédie* of 1751 begins with a tongue-in-cheek tip of the hat to the effectiveness of that repression by claiming that the game was "once quite popular in France, but since banned and no longer played."[2] In fact, the game continued, well after the 1750s, to be one of the most popular forms of gambling both in the city and at court.

Jean de Préchac's *Les Désordres de la bassette* is a love story built around basset. Its portrayal of gambling places it at the center of what we saw to be the growing confrontation throughout the seventeenth and eighteenth centuries between two opposed ideologies: that of a traditional aristocracy defining itself through an ethos of disinterested service and that of a less articulate but ever more powerful

bourgeoisie championing the values of self-interest and lucrative exchange. In fact, the groups involved in this conflict were, as we saw, by no means so distinct as the use of
terms such as 'aristocracy' and 'bourgeoisie' would imply.
By the time Préchac wrote *Les Désordres de la bassette,* the
nobility, thanks to Louis XIV's selling of titles, already existed as an amalgam of antagonistic elements ranging from
an "old" nobility totally aligned with the aristocratic ideology of disinterested service to a recently ennobled bourgeoisie whose identities and careers embodied the successful pursuit of financial profit.

Les Désordres is part of and draws its significance from
the intense ideological conflict between these two factions
within the single order of the nobility. Préchac's novel
shows how one element within that amalgam attempted to
influence how the growing reading public for the novel
would perceive the nobility as a class. It is not so much that
Préchac sets out to include within his love story some secret
allegory but rather that his entire portrayal of aristocratic
characters presupposes and confirms one group's negative
view of the other. This novel stands as a case study of
how the eventual victory of one ideological current over
another depended not so much on how each might portray
itself as it did on the effectiveness of the negative and polemic distortions one faction was able to impose on society's
understanding of its adversary.

In his introduction to the 1980 reprint of *Les Désordres
de la bassette,* René Godenne calls attention to Préchac's col-
orful use of specific details to convey the dangers of playing basset. Préchac tells us how doctors discouraged those
with weak hearts from exposing themselves to its often
mortal excitement, how the turning of a card could make
a pale woman blush red as a burning coal and bring out
a sweat in even the most reserved gentleman. This, for
Godenne, is the basis of the work's real interest: "Details
of this kind . . . reveal the face of an aristocracy which
never shows itself in the *nouvelles galantes* of the period. In
that sense, the world of this novel is a true world."[3] The

problem with this claim lies in the way Godenne's notion of "the aristocracy's true face" assumes as fact precisely what was the novel's most polemic hypothesis. To presuppose the veracity of this "hidden face" of the aristocracy is to render invisible the novel's profoundly ideological function as a motivated misrepresentation of the traditional aristocracy. Préchac's entire portrayal of the nobility flows from and consolidates the beliefs and values of the most recent arrivals within that class. To see *Les Désordres de la bassette* as providing us with a more complete picture of the nobility is like claiming that the violently anti-Semitic *Protocols of the Wise Men of Zion* helps us to better understand the aspirations of modern European Jewry. Préchac's novel is important not for any hidden truth it reveals but for how deftly and significantly it distorts the adversary it sets out to portray.

Préchac makes no attempt to hide his allegiances. His sixteen-page *Dédicace* is addressed to Michel Le Tellier, Louis XIV's chancellor since 1677. It praises him for a series of measures each of which was an important part of the crown's bringing to heel a proud and independent aristocracy. When Préchac lauds Le Tellier for having managed to "rétablir la discipline militaire" (v), he is referring to his successful consolidation of royal control over a traditionally independent officers corps composed almost exclusively of the older aristocracy. What Préchac sees as Le Tellier's enlightened prohibition of dueling in fact continued a longstanding royal attempt to stigmatize a practice associated exclusively with the nobility and their concept of personal honor. Finally, looking not at what had been done to check the power of the traditional nobility but at what favored the ascendancy of the ennobled bourgeoisie, Préchac describes Le Tellier's recent reform of legal education: "This judicious decree concerning the study of law will eliminate [the university's past laxity in awarding degrees] and make Roman law as flourishing in France today as it was at the time of Justinian" (ix). What might at first glance seem a minor point on which to flatter one's patron derives its importance from the fact that Le Tellier's reform of legal studies meant that the crown had finally taken a clear (and highly paradoxical) position against the traditional nobility's argument concerning the education necessary for occupying judicial positions and rendering the king's justice. Reacting against the growing number of positions on royal tribunals sold to non-nobles whose ostensible merit lay in their strong education in Latin and Roman law, the nobility had long argued that such training in classical jurisprudence was perfectly useless and that in the golden age of French justice from Charlemagne to Philip the Fair, noblemen had admirably administered the king's justice exclusively on the basis of royal ordinance and local custom. Some voices within the aristocracy had even gone so far as to argue that references to Roman law, or to any law other than the king's, should be explicitly forbidden in French courts as a form of *lèse-majesté*. The King's answer may have come slowly, but Le Tellier's reform could not have been more firmly on the side of the aspiring bourgeoisie.

Préchac himself was a near-perfect example of the new man fashioned by the changing rules of social ascendancy put in place by Louis XIV and his ministers.[4] Born near Pau in 1647, Préchac was not, in spite of his claims, a *noble de race*. He gained his title late in life from a property his maternal grandfather had purchased in 1621 and which Préchac himself inherited, along with the title, only in 1709. His claim to noble status existed, in other words, only on the basis of what in Béarn was called *noblesse réelle*—the "real" here referring to an estate carrying with it a title that passed from owner to owner. As a young man, Préchac studied law and was admitted to the parlement de Navarre at the age of twenty-two. No sooner, however, had he begun his legal career than he set off on what would become twenty years' residence at Paris and frequent travels meant to further his career at court. In 1676 he became a *lecteur* for Monsieur, the king's brother, and four years later he assumed the intriguing position of professor of

Spanish to the queen of Spain, Marie-Louise d'Orléans, the niece of Louis XIV who had married Charles II of Spain in 1679.

During the eleven years between 1677 and 1688 Préchac wrote the more than twenty-five literary works for which he is best known. Two of these, *Les Désordres de la bassette* and *L'Illustre Parisienne* have recently been reprinted.[5] Unjustly neglected, Préchac is mentioned in only the broadest histories of the French novel. Henri Coulet, for instance, cavalierly dismisses Préchac in his *Le Roman jusqu'à la Révolution* as only a particularly prolific example of those many late-seventeenth-century novelists who failed to anticipate the proper future of the mainstream French novel of the eighteenth and nineteenth centuries: "Préchac's abundant production testifies to the state of insignificance [l'état d'indistinction] to which the novel had fallen, the leveling it suffered during the classical period. . . . He was a realist who lacked the tools of realism [un réaliste à qui les instruments du réalisme ont manqué]."[6]

In 1693 Préchac returned to Béarn, where he was named conseiller to the parlement de Navarre and, three years later, garde-scel of the royal chancellery at Pau. For the next fifteen years he functioned as a royalist spy, providing important information about the confidential proceedings of the parlement to the local intendant as well as to his personal protectors at Versailles. As a native son now working for the crown at home, he was vulnerable to both local resentment and to the ever evolving machinations of court cabals. Even playing a careful game, he was not always able to come out a winner. When, in October 1704, the king issued an edict making it illegal to hold simultaneously the offices of conseiller and garde-scel, Préchac not only had trouble being exempted from the new law but found himself caught in the crossfire of the local parlement, which took advantage of the edict to declare that he could no longer be considered a conseiller, and of the king's intendant, who tried to strip him of his crown office as garde-scel. Préchac fought this simultaneous exclusion from parlement and chancellery through repeated and desperate appeals to his friends at court. The closing paragraph from his letter of January 24, 1705, to Pontchartrain, the contrôleur général, nicely captures the tenor of the man: "And that, Sir, is the situation of a poor man who paid ten thousand écus for his position after having spent thirty years pleasing his Prince and paying court to his ministers. Imploring your justice, I remain, dear Sir. . . ."[7] Préchac's problems were only resolved a year and a half later, when, after more letters and carefully distributed financial considerations, he was renamed to his two positions. Things took a definitive turn for the better in 1708, when his maternal uncle died and left him the estate at Poey that brought him his title as well as his admission to the ordre de la noblesse of the Etats de Béarn. Now a "real" noble, Préchac continued until his death in 1720 to provide the crown with secret information about the deliberations of the local nobility as well as whatever else was happening along the always intrigue-laden Spanish border.

"One day at Madame Genrille's basset game, the banker's dealing was making him the happiest man in the world" (1). If things are going so well for the banker in this opening scene from Préchac's *Les Désordres de la bassette,* it is because the players are losing heavily. Madame de Landroze has lost four times in a row on the same card. The marquis de Roziers, ever the solicitous suitor, suggests that she bet on the jack. "You never brought me luck" (3), snaps Madame de Landroze. But she bets on the jack and wins. When the marquis then suggests that she go for the *alpiu* parlay on the jack, she complains, "You weren't born to make me happy" (4), but follows his advice and wins again. When Madame de Landroze then asks the marquis what she should bet on next, he pouts. Repeating her cruel words to him, he refuses to choose a card. Madame de Landroze, after picking the ace and losing everything, shouts, "I would be amazed if anything went right for me with you even once in my life. Believe me, we were born to ruin things for each other" (5–6).

This opening scene weaves together the two passions that will determine everything that happens in this text: gambling and desire as forces continually intersecting with and redefining each other. This brisk dialogue of love declared and love spurned over the turning of a card shows the connection between the two components of Préchac's novel: tableaux from a gambling house and scenes from an unsuccessful seduction. Gambling and courting, money and desire, represent within this novel two parallel devaluations of a single figure: the *chevalier servant* of chivalric tradition as faithful to the code of disinterested service and the ideal of courtly love. For Préchac, the marquis smitten with the shrewish Landroze becomes the only *chevalier servant* possible in the last quarter of the seventeenth century—an anachronistic and ridiculous holdover from another age. The marquis's approach to society and to women is comically out of date precisely because he continues to act according to an aristocratic ideal unrelated to the real world of money and desire, of venality and misogyny. *Les Désordres de la bassette* is the story of a Don Quixote who is laughable and pathetic but never grandiose.

Determined to win Madame de Landroze's love, the marquis asks his worldly-wise friend, the comte de Charlois, what he should do. The comte's suggestion is simple: since Landroze has such a passion for gambling, he should help her find the money to open her own basset game. This, the comte insists, will initiate an intimacy between them that is bound to become sexual as well as financial. The marquis is horrified at everything the comte suggests. The woman he so esteems would never compromise herself by inviting into her home an indiscriminate mass of people with no other merit than the money they can put on the table: "Turn her house into a gambling den, a meeting place for all classes of people, where rabble and thieves are welcomed like honest men!" (30). Not only, the comte corrects him, have many of the most distinguished names in Parisian society set ample precedent but the marquis understands precious little about women and nothing at all about Landroze: "All women are avaricious, and she more than any woman in the world" (32).

Much as the comte predicted, Landroze is ecstatic about opening her own game once she has understood how lucrative it will be. Without the slightest thought to the kind of people she will have to receive, her only concern is with getting together sufficient cash to set up a respectable bank. The marquis volunteers to put up three hundred louis and reports that his friend, the chevalier de Brière, will supply an equal amount as well as provide from among his friends a daily crowd of avid players. Landroze, even though tapped by her recent losses, manages to borrow the final three hundred louis she needs against an additional lien on the revenues her tax collector will extract from the families on her estate during the next year.

Every major character in this novel—the marquis, the comte, Madame de Landroze, the chevalier—is a noble, yet every challenge they face and every action they undertake turns exclusively on money. The marquis may wish only to win Landroze's love, but he quickly learns that love is a function of cash. The reader could not be farther here from the traditional world of the romance dictating that characters of high birth confront a series of martial and amorous adventures outside any vilifying concern with finance. Money determines the actions of everyone present in this novel. Once Landroze has opened her game, players are quick to arrive from all levels of polite society: nobles, merchants, officers, judges, tax collectors, abbots, husbands and wives, sons and daughters. "Sometimes it was a son still in mourning for his father's death who gambled away years of the man's work and savings. Sometimes a clerk with the office till. Abbots brought their benefices, officers their stipends, a new groom his wife's dowry, a tax collector the year's revenue, a judge his bribes, women the money from pawning their bracelets and diamond pins"

(41–42). Préchac's emphasis on the source of each player's money explains the attraction of basset and the source of its intoxication. If the son bets an inheritance accumulated over a parent's lifetime, the groom his bride's dowry, the merchant his cash, the judge his fees, and the abbots their benefices, it is because the lure of an immediate multiplication of their wagers by two, seven, or fifteen renders absurd the slow accumulation of money through the position or work that produced the original stake. Only a coward, someone afraid to lose, could prefer the protracted effort of day-by-day savings to the immediate payoff of the big gamble.

Such an attitude is possible, however, only when it is assumed that self-interest and gain are the exclusive motivations for all who are included in Préchac's long list. The significance of this universal leveling to an obsession with quick profits becomes clearer when we compare Préchac's portrayal of his world with the very different assumptions concerning wealth and nobility offered only thirty-seven years earlier by René de Ceriziers. Describing the true nobleman, Ceriziers's *Le Héros Français* declares that simply amassing wealth can never be the goal of the true noble. On the contrary, wealth is a means to be used for the sole purpose of reaffirming the disinterested service of one's prince: "The passion to own things [La passion d'avoir] is legitimate only when property is used to obligate others. Rather than establishing himself, the noble dedicates his wealth to the service of his prince. We have in our midst a Hero whose merit could lay claim to everything of excellence in France. But after twenty years of faithful service, he has in his home not even half what one would expect to find in the homes of even mediocre men of finance."[8] The "hero" Ceriziers praises here is the chevalier d'Harcourt, a man whose devotion to honor and frugality made him the perfect exemplar of true nobility for his age. If that best and most valiant of nobles never possessed even half the wealth of a mediocre financier, it was because the man of finance can never be more than what the wages of his trade might buy. The true noble, to the contrary, needs no physical accouterments to prove who he is and what he represents.

One of Préchac's favorite devices for introducing secondary characters and enunciating the lessons they represent is to have the chevalier de Brière follow and spy on players as they leave Landroze's game. One day a woman loses heavily but is so taken with the game that she returns home twice for more money, which she promptly loses. When she leaves the game for the last time, it is with a close female friend, her cousin. The chevalier follows them and overhears the cousin's practical advice as to how her friend might recoup her losses: "You certainly understand, cousin, that there is no point in hesitating to give your daughter to that tax farmer. He promised that money would be no problem, and she is the only resource we have left. Afterwards he can marry her off to one of his agents. And even if he doesn't, there are plenty of others in worse straits who had no problem making quite suitable marriages" (44–45). Under the press of money, the mother-daughter relation effortlessly becomes that of procuress-whore. It is not, however, gambling that is the real culprit here. Losses at basset only accelerate a mutation of values already well under way. This scene and its many equivalents throughout the novel do not so much denounce any supposed evil of gambling as they reveal what to the author's eyes was an all but universal venality. Nobles, abbots, soldiers, judges, and bourgeois *mères de famille* are engaged in little more than an elaborate charade when they pretend that their real motivations are anything other than money. The comte and the chevalier know this and act accordingly. Only the marquis is foolish enough to take people's masks at face value.

One evening the comte d'Angluron, a friend of the chevalier's, visits the game. Once an inveterate player, he has now renounced gambling out of love for the beautiful mistress who accompanies him and for whom his passion is so strong that there is no room left in his heart for any other.

Angluron's arrival and the story of his reform sets off among those present what might be described as a revival of the *jeu parti,* the medieval genre of the multivoiced debate about some aspect of courtly love and its proper display. The question before the assembly is, Which is the stronger passion, love or gambling? While only the marquis defends Angluron's position, the chevalier offers the counterargument that most appeals to the crowd: "A mistress may repay her lover for the pain and suffering she causes, but can she ever offer him odds of seven, fifteen, and even thirty to one? No, a mistress's favor has never gone that high" (58–59). The debate's real resolution comes, however, in the narrative itself. Angluron sits at the table with his mistress and, briefly turning his eyes away from hers, decides to place a small bet. One bet becomes two, and the bets become heavier and heavier as he tries to recoup his losses with one large parlay. After losing 150 louis, he calls the chevalier aside and restakes himself by selling his horse and carriage. As his losses continue, he sells his mistress's pearls and then her diamonds and finally asks the chevalier how much he would offer for his mistress herself.

This comic restaging within a gambling house of the medieval *jeu parti* comes as a confirmation of the premise motivating the narrative's entire intertwining of money and desire. It was the story's other count, the comte de Charlois, who first suggested that the surest assault on Madame de Landroze's heart would be to buy it. The supposed wisdom of that position derives from the equally medieval but distinctly anticourtly tradition of those *fabliaux* proposing a profoundly misogynistic view of women, a fear and suspicion of what were assumed to be their always irrational and venal motivations:

> You don't know women. Almost all of them, and Madame de Landroze most of all, are tender only out of weakness. Their emotions move in directions one can never predict. They love and hate without reason and by caprice. They

are faithful only out of self-interest, fear, or lack of an occasion. Coquetry is the foundation of their character, and their virtue is nothing more than skill in hiding their coquetry. Behind all their words and all their actions there are lies. (123–24)

Everything Madame de Landroze does corroborates the comte's position. When the marquis first tries to win her love by making her rich from the profits of her basset, she cannot find a moment to listen to his suit. When the marquis then decides to make it appear she has lost everything so he can prove his love by offering the money to open another game, her response is a masterpiece of manipulation. Playing on her suitor's courtly illusions, she puts him off by claiming that to avow her until now so carefully hidden love while accepting a gift of money would create the intolerable impression of a possible venality on her part: "I love you far too delicately to accept your offer. To do so now would be to pay what I owe you, and you could not accept my action as an overflowing of my love" (88–89).

Madame de Landroze ignores the marquis's love when she is winning and refuses it when she is losing. Instead, however, of reincarnating the inaccessible mistress of courtly tradition, she anticipates the coquette of eighteenth-century *libertinage*. When she finally decides to tell the marquis her true feelings, she explains that she feels no desire for him because she knows he desires her. Her proof of the impossibility of reciprocal desire is the fact that she herself is obsessed with a former lover who lost all interest in her once he realized she had fallen in love with him. Relating to this absent third party exactly as the marquis does to her, she enunciates the law of desire that will become the guiding principle of the next century's long succession of coquettes and *petits maîtres:* "Such is the strange caprice of love: to desire what hurts us and to have no interest in what can make us happy" (152).

If Landroze anticipates the future, the marquis is clearly

a throwback to the past. No matter what happens around him, he remains convinced that his love will prevail because he alone remains faithful to the courtly ideal of disinterested service and sacrifice for the beloved: "I have sacrificed my pleasure for her protection and her interests, proving I love her more than myself, and that alone will bind her to me for the rest of her days" (120).

Madame de Landroze is clearly a woman of her world. Intense, impetuous, always able to find the response or invent the story that will get her exactly what she wants, she is as alluring and elusive as the fortunes promised by basset. The marquis, on the contrary, is an unreal and profoundly ineffectual character drawn with an ambiguity that takes us to the heart of the novel's ideological intent. On the one hand, the marquis is a true aristocrat acting on motivations that parallel the disinterested ideal presumed to be at the heart of the nobility's self-definition. On the other, the marquis is an anomaly within his class, someone utterly unlike all the other aristocrats portrayed in this work. Since the vast majority of the nobility, Préchac is saying, act openly in contradiction to the explicit ideals of their class, any individual respecting that ethos can only be a pathetic anachronism. The marquis is the fool all nobles would be were they not instead the consummate hypocrites they so obviously are.

Les Désordres de la bassette closes with the gamblers gathered together to discuss how they might respond to the decree just issued by the Chambre des vacations forbidding basset and imposing fines of five hundred livres on anyone caught playing and three thousand livres plus the walling up of the premises on anyone hosting a game. After much deliberation, the game's strongest defender suggests a strategy based on the fact that the prohibition has come from the Chambre: "We must go to the king and convince him that basset has hardly had the noxious effects on Paris some are claiming. We have to arrive at an understanding with him that allows us to hold a game. I am ready to do my part and will offer up to eighty thousand livres a year" (184).

The implications of this strategy are as ambiguous as its fate is uncertain. The gambler's proposal is that the king be persuaded to institute, as was the case in numerous other areas, an annual license fee of eighty thousand livres for the right to run a basset game. While 'license fee' may be the preferred term, this offer of eighty thousand livres is also quite clearly a bribe—a payment from subject to sovereign for a privilege promising profits far greater than the sum paid. Mirroring the financial relation between tax farmer and king, such an arrangement is the antithesis of the disinterested service presumed to link noble to king. As the group debates what might be their proposition's fate, some point out that such an offer will surely appeal to the crown's voracious appetite for additional revenue. But how, other voices ask, can the king endorse an arrangement flying in the face of the crown's economic policy of mercantilism, the specific encouragement of the production of consumer goods for profitable resale? "Tradesmen, wig makers, tailors, and shoemakers can't earn a cent from basset players. Their purses are consecrated to the game, and they make no other use of them. Only moneylenders and pawnbrokers make a profit from them" (176). Separated from any production of goods or services, gambling maintains a symbiotic relation with usury, because both deal exclusively with money, with the signs of wealth rather than any real production of wealth. Gamblers and moneylenders grow rich from manipulating and multiplying what was traditionally seen as only a representation of true value. If Paris has become a city of gamblers and moneylenders, it is because the king, as he sought to finance his endless wars, made such manipulation an essential part of the realm's finances.

Whether fee or bribe, whether successful or not, the premise behind the players' strategy is clear: monarch and gambler are as one in their cynical acceptance of the fact that the world is governed by venality, that everyone, including the king, can be bought. *Les Désordres de la bassette* ends with the irony of a group of ostensible aristocrats making plans on the basis of assumptions about themselves and their king that invalidate any claim they might have to a specific identity and necessary function within the political community of the *ancien régime*.

Préchac's portrayal of gambling satirically dismantles the code of aristocratic honor as a viable alternative to self-interest. Traditionally, the noble was noble because he was willing to die for his king. As Ceriziers succinctly puts it, "When a man risks his life, he justifies it" (176). The real intent of Préchac's satire becomes clear when we remember that this positive view of a *noblesse désintéressée* was by no means a lost ideal at the time he wrote. How the noble was seen, à la Ceriziers or à la Préchac, was precisely what was at stake in the vast transformation of roles and orders initiated by Louis XIV's fiscal practices and ending only with the cataclysm of the Revolution. Préchac may well, writing in 1682, reduce the French nobility to either avaricious hypocrites or laughable anachronisms, but as we saw earlier, even as late as the mid-eighteenth century writers such as Montesquieu in *L'Esprit des lois* (1748) and the chevalier d'Arcq in *La Noblesse militaire* (1756) continued to define and justify the nobility in the same terms as those proposed by Ceriziers a century earlier.

Préchac's closing description of the gamblers' colloquy presents it as a formal assembly convoked to deliberate on important matters of state. The group elects a president. They decide the times and places for subsequent sessions. If they are sanguine about their future, it is because the ever resourceful chevalier de Brière has applied to their problem what is always the best of political solutions. If basset has been forbidden, he suggests, we need only change some of its rules, give it a new name, and continue our profession while scrupulously respecting the law: "Let's transform basset into a different game . . . making it unrecognizable and protecting ourselves from arrest and penalties. We need only to keep a banker with the same advantages but change the game's name" (188–89). That, the history of gambling tells us, is exactly what happened. Basset was replaced by a new game called pharaon, and the real beauty of it was that both were the same game. The one difference was that while in basset each player used his own *livre* of thirteen cards to indicate his bets, pharaon used a *tapis* spread out on a table and divided into thirteen sections labeled ace through king. Soon, of course, new decrees would prohibit pharaon. And just as quickly, new variations and new names would replace pharaon.

Les Désordres de la bassette announces within its satire a new age where power, as surely for king as for gambler and usurer, will depend on the manipulation of signs. The gambler-politicians of this closing scene operate on the premise that language, like gambling and money, is a sign system open to endless manipulation. Language and law have become, for Préchac and the bourgeoisie he represents, purely symbolic systems gloriously abstracted from any reality they claim to represent.

Préchac's other novel centered on basset, *La Noble Vénitienne ou la bassette* (1679), uses the game's structure as the basis for an extended allegory confirming the parallel between gambling as a manipulation of signs and what will become the two principal themes of the modern novel: the love story and the epic of social ascension.

The noble Venetian, that most beautiful, most alluring, yet most dangerous of women, is none other than the game of basset. Throughout this novel, Préchac plays on the ambiguities of a passion oscillating between the literal and figurative meanings of her suitors' ever rekindled desire to "risk everything for the love of the noble Venetian."[9] "La Bassette" is the pseudonym adopted by a young woman of noble birth who left home when her father "tried in vain to make her recognize her duty. But with her hot temper she mocked his warnings and continued to follow only her whims. In spite of all her father's counsel, she did exactly as she pleased" (8). Free to do as she wished, she scandalously spent entire nights in any number of different houses lavishing her favors on the delighted host, who served as dealer and banker. If she came to be known as "La Bassette," it was both because of her short stature—she was "ordinarily seated in an armchair" (11)—and because in paying their court, "her faithful always lowered their eyes when looking toward her" (11).

Préchac's allegory plays on every aspect of the game's structure. La Bassette travels with an entourage of fifty-two servants as well as a certain comte Dalpiu, a *dangereux compère* always ready to put things right when she has too long granted her favors to any one suitor: "As soon as his mistress is in debt, he takes care of it and the interest by promising to triple the sum if one just trusts him" (22). She is also accompanied by the even more imposing Capitan Sept et le Va, who handles those few who can outwit the comte. A steady succession of princely suitors from France, Germany, and Spain are momentarily favored by this seductress, but each inevitably goes on to ruin in his vain attempts to extend the period of his favor. A Florentine *gentilhomme* and a Greek merchant go so far as to kill themselves when La Bassette grows weary of their suit.

Halfway through the novel, Préchac shifts the focus of his allegory away from the dynamics of sexual desire to the protocols of social ascension. Bored with her facile conquests, La Bassette decides that she would like to hold public office in her native Venice. That, she is told, is impossible. Such honors go only to those who have served as ambassadors of the republic and know firsthand the workings of the various courts of Europe. La Bassette wastes no time solving that problem: she will go to France and study "the court that sets the tone [qui donne le branle] for the whole of Europe" (64). Her debut in Paris is inauspicious, as she makes the mistake of accepting the offer made by Iustiniani, the Venetian ambassador, of lodgings at the embassy on the condition that he assume the highly profitable position of dealer. Many are drawn by her charm, but confined to the Venetian embassy, she cannot compete with the president Piquet, the marquis de Berlan, the Catalan chevalier d'Hoca, the German baron de Lansquenet, or the Spanish comte d'Ombres (all names of other popular card games), who seem to be everywhere at once. La Bassette's stock finally begins to rise when she leaves the ambassador and takes up residence with a number of French hosts. Her social ascension becomes truly dizzying when she chooses women as her favorites and has them act as her dealers. Soon her victory is complete not only in Paris but even at Versailles, where she is given what were once the private apartments allocated not only to "le grave Espagnol," the comte d'Ombres, but to the marquis de Berlan, who takes refuge with the cooks, and the baron de Lansquenet, who is reduced to living with lackeys and servants in common taverns.

Court and city are so taken with her charms that "people have stopped gossiping about love affairs since basset came into fashion. If two people are whispering to each other, it is about basset" (184). La Bassette's one remaining desire is to enthrall the king to her charms. And here she experiences her unique defeat. While Louis certainly enjoys her company, he maintains a "noble indifference" (138) to those favors other men find so irresistible. If the king remains unmoved, it is because, as Préchac would have it, "the king never acts out of self-interest" (142). Rather than adding the king to her long list of conquests, she provides the proof of his royal singularity: "She was never able to distract that wise prince from any of his duties" (143). The king, however, is not the only person who has escaped the wiles of La Bassette. Préchac himself has, as the author of the novel we are reading, all but entirely recuperated from it the losses he suffered in learning firsthand how alluring yet demanding a mistress she could be: "The author, having lost at basset, managed to recoup by writing a book on the game that earned back for him most of what he had lost" (186).

Préchac and the king stand apart from the endless succession of princes, dukes, and noble courtiers readily sacrificing everything for the favors of La Bassette. The king is unlike the nobles surrounding him by reason of a singular (and entirely fictive) indifference to financial gain. Préchac is unlike the other players because he alone has had the practical good sense to turn a profit as author from an activity that cost him dearly as player. Préchac's allegory of gambling thus inscribes the desired ideological solidarity of monarch and bourgeoisie within a shared ability to recognize and exploit the hypocrisy of a nobility only pretending to any motivation beyond self-interest.

6

Chance, Reading, and The Tragedy of Experience: Prévost's *Manon Lescaut*

*Venus et la Fortune n'avaient point d'esclaves
plus heureux et plus tendres.*
—PRÉVOST, *Manon Lescaut*

L'abbé Prévost's two best-known characters, Manon Lescaut and the chevalier des Grieux, certainly number among the most famous "happy and tender slaves of Venus and Fortune" in the eighteenth-century French novel. Far more than for such characters as Usbek, Meilcour, Candide, or Saint-Preux, literally everything happens to them as a stroke of luck—alternately good and bad but always beyond their control. 'Fortune' in this novel, rather than a vague synonym for whatever joys and sorrows life might bring, carries all the weight of the succinct definition Prévost offered for the word in his *Manuel lexique:* "un mot tiré du latin qui signifie *hasard.*"[1]

Chance and games of chance play an important role throughout this novel. For Manon, life without gambling would be so dreary that even when des Grieux frugally calculates how they might stretch a meager sixty thousand livres out over ten years, he allows Manon to gamble as often as she wishes—but hoping that she will limit each loss to no more than two pistoles. It is during a game of piquet (a two-handed belote with no trump suit but with many more initial point declarations) that Manon and Monsieur de G—— M—— *fils* decide to dispatch one of

his former mistresses to the rue Saint-André as a consolation prize for the abandoned des Grieux. The single point
of even temporary equilibrium in their topsy-turvy love
story, the one period when des Grieux's income equals and
even surpasses Manon's expenses, comes when he supports
himself as a pharaon dealer at the Hotel de Transylvanie.
Des Grieux wins there, not because he is particularly lucky
or skillful, but because he cheats. Introduced by Manon's
brother into the underworld of cardsharps known by such
deliciously conspiratorial names as la Ligue, l'Ordre, l'Association, and la Confédération, des Grieux quickly learns
the sleights of hand allowing him to become a master me-
chanic renowned among the initiated for his ability to force
or hold back any card of his choice. Des Grieux enters the
arena of chance, the world of the upturned card bringing
riches or ruin, but he does so by trying to eliminate chance
as the force determining who wins and who loses.

Chance, however, allows no such mastery and tolerates
no such equilibrium. Des Grieux may control the cards
that fall on the tables at the Hotel de Transylvanie, but he
is powerless to prevent their servants from disappearing
with his accumulated winnings. What seemed to be his victory over the raw power of money that he first encountered when Manon left him for the rich financier, Monsieur de B——, is shattered not because he could not have
continued his trade at the Hotel de Transylvanie and won
just as much as before but because Manon, petrified at
how quickly their fortune has turned, follows her brother's
practical advice and takes refuge with Monsieur de G——
M——, the *vieux voluptueux*. No matter how stable any situation in this novel may appear, there is always a fire, a
theft, an arrest, or a powerful rival to upset it. Des Grieux
may vanquish chance as he presides over the cards, but
that same chance takes exquisite revenge on his passion
for Manon.

Manon Lescaut portrays a world at the mercy of chance.
Chance erupts in this novel, however, not in the metaphysical and moral forms of earthquakes, shipwrecks, and hu-

man perversities. It is instead the banal, far more realistic variant of the random encounter and the costly error. If such everyday chance is so much at work in this novel, it is in large part because *Manon Lescaut* is one of the first novels in which a constant search for money by impoverished characters plays a crucial role. No other work of the period offers the reader so acute a sense of how society had been transformed by the dizzying inflation and deflation of Law's System and the way, within only a few years, wealth was sundered from its identification with the stability of land and distilled into the volatile ether of banknotes and shares successively making the fortune and assuring the ruin of those who held them.

Manon Lescaut stages the confrontation of two antithetical worlds: that of a doomed stability anchored in the old order of the nobility and clergy with the hyper-dynamic, chance-driven instability of money and its circulation. Des Grieux comes from the first of those worlds. As the younger son of a provincial noble, he is expected to safeguard the family's stability by leaving intact for his older brother both title and estate. As the novel opens, his choice is between the quasi-religious Order of Malta (whence his title of chevalier), to which his family has destined him, and the priesthood, which the bishop of Amiens, impressed by his philosophy studies, has strongly urged. Later, after he has been forcibly separated from Manon by his family, des Grieux will return to Paris as a seminarist at Saint-Sulpice, as someone destined to assume a position of importance in the hierarchy of the first estate. Arrayed against that stability of sword and altar is the ever-shifting world of money. It is present in the form of Parisian financiers, for the most part wealthy *fermiers généraux,* whose well-paid pleasures everyone is anxious to provide. Money is also at the center of a nascent urban proletariat straddling the boundary between the legal and the criminal as well as in the police-soldier-guard caste paid by the old order to preserve the illusion that control might be maintained over those whose motives are openly and exclusively mercenary.

At its most obvious level, the story of *Manon Lescaut*, a story in fact told entirely by des Grieux, is that of how one woman, thanks to des Grieux's fascination, initiated a threatening and ultimately impossible conjunction of those two worlds. Manon, at least as far as the reader confined to des Grieux's version of the tale will ever know, is herself a bewitching synthesis of love and venality, devotion and exploitation.

Manon Lescaut tells a story of circulation—the circulation of money and people, with the first always motivating the second. The novel's narrator is the elderly marquis de Renoncourt, whose normally sedentary life well represents the stasis of the landed nobility. If he meets des Grieux at all, it is because he has taken what he describes as the unusual step of journeying to Rouen to help his daughter establish her claim to an inheritance being adjudicated by the parlement de Normandie. It is as he is returning home that he happens to arrive at the village of Pacy just as there arrives a group of *maréchaux* escorting a dozen prostitutes on their way to Le Havre.

As prostitutes, these women incarnate the synthesized circulations of money and persons. Among them is Manon Lescaut. While not a prostitute, her being caught up in this forced circulation of persons has everything to do with a parallel and motivating circulation of money. Manon is on the road to exile because des Grieux's father and the wealthy Monsieur de G—— M—— have enlisted the power of the state to punish her theft of money and jewels.

If this convoy of impressed women is at Pacy, it is because their journey is part of what was the eighteenth century's most important circulation of people and wealth. The economic development of France's New World colonies, as well as the protection of her claims to the huge land areas joining them, depended on the presence there of a visible and growing French population. A sufficient number of single men might be drawn to the rigorous life of the colonies by true or false promises of fortunes to be made, but any long-term political establishment demanded the presence not only of wandering trappers and traders but of settled couples founding families and populating the colonies. *Manon Lescaut*'s opening scene of the forced exile of urban prostitutes destined to become wives and mothers in the wilderness of New France was part of an attempt to safeguard the all-important flow of wealth from colony to metropolis by a reciprocal flow of reproducing bodies from metropolis to colony. Des Grieux loyally follows Manon into exile, but the convoy guards impose their own regulations on this circulation: des Grieux may talk with Manon only so long as he pays the guards one écu per hour—a sum corresponding to the going rate in Paris for a prostitute.

This first chance encounter at an intersection of roads built to facilitate the circulation of people and goods is followed two years later by a second meeting, which is no less extraordinary and no less a product of chance. Arriving at Calais from England, Renoncourt finds his stay there unexpectedly prolonged by the indeterminacy of what he qualifies as "quelques raisons" (16). It is during an aimless afternoon walk meant only to pass the time that he again happens upon a paler and more careworn des Grieux, who, invited by Renoncourt to dine with him at the *Lion d'Or*, tells the tale of woe we read under the title of *Manon Lescaut*.

Des Grieux's story, like the narrative frame enclosing it, is born of chance. In explaining to Renoncourt how he first met Manon, des Grieux begins: "The very evening before my departure, as I was walking with my friend Tiberge, we saw the Arras coach arrive" (19). As for Renoncourt, it is during a moment outside regimented time—the time of killing time before the next day's departure—and at a place outside regimented space—the pure randomness of an itinerary covered "as I was walking with my friend"—that there occurs the decisive event in des Grieux's life.

In his *Exposition de la théorie des chances et des probabilités* (1843), the mathematician and scientist Antoine Cournot formulated what would be the nineteenth century's sole demurral to Laplace's contemptuous and by that time all but universally accepted dismissal of chance. For Laplace, as for the entire Enlightenment tradition he represents, the idea of chance was a vulgar folk belief, a precipitate of human ignorance only hindering the advance of true science. Cournot, uneasy with this exclusion of what he saw as a very real dimension of human experience by so imperious a position, argued for a different understanding of chance and its role in human life. In expressing his view, Cournot chose as the key image for his model a situation that is in fact inscribed at the inception of Prévost's novel. For Cournot, the chance event might best be defined as one occurring at the intersection of two distinct and independent causal series. Because they are distinct, their conjunction produces an effect that could never have been predicted by looking at either of the series in isolation. The story of *Manon Lescaut* begins at the moment when two independent causal series, des Grieux's desire for a last walk with his friend Tiberge and Manon's resigned presence in a coach taking her from Arras to the convent at Amiens, produce an event—their encounter—whose effects could never have been predicted from the examination of either of those sequences in isolation from the other.

Cournot's rehabilitation of chance, his insistence that it is grounded in something more real than superstition, introduced within the scientific community an understanding of chance's role in the life of the individual that had in fact long been a staple of novelistic convention. My point here is not that Prévost should be seen as a precursor of

Cournot but that Prévost's attempt to represent the unpredictability of life led him to adopt a narrative form that implicitly challenges the presuppositions of the various scientific discourses contemporary to his work. The explicit elaboration of Prévost's narrative model would come only a century later in the work of Cournot.

The chance encounter at Amiens not only produces a present undeducible from the past but initiates for des Grieux the discovery of a sense of self unrelated to any earlier conviction as to who he was: "She seemed so beautiful to me—to me who had never before thought of the difference between the sexes or paid even the slightest attention to a girl; to me whose wisdom and reserve everyone admired. I found myself immediately inflamed to the point of fainting. . . . Thinking back on it, I am still amazed that I showed such boldness and facility of expression" (19–20). The astonished des Grieux not only discovers that he is an inspired lover but also learns that he is perfectly capable of lying without compunction to his most trusted and trusting friend.

As a narrative, *Manon Lescaut* repeatedly emphasizes how the unexpected intersection of distinct causal sequences produces a chance event: the money meant to support the couple for ten years is lost in a fire; the winnings from the Hôtel de Transylvanie are stolen by servants; Manon's brother is killed in the street just when des Grieux most needs his help. It is not surprising that when des Grieux tries to summarize what he has learned from loving Manon, he should speak of a joy made all the more intense by the uncertainty of its future: "Why call the world a place of suffering when it can provide a life of such charming delights? But, alas, they are too soon over [leur faible est de passer trop vite]" (66). This traditional theme of fleeting earthly joys is, however, less important in itself than for the way it sustains a narrative technique centered on the portrayal of chance as the agency of the unsuspected but inevitable reversal. Before beginning his story of what was to happen in Paris, des Grieux offers a generalized, extradiegetic statement emphasizing how all is subject to change, how everything that most surely should have been never was, and how from all that was best came only what was worst: "Her mind, her heart, her sweetness, and her beauty formed a chain so strong and so charming that I would have staked all my happiness on never casting it off. Terrifying change! What is now the source of my despair could have assured my happiness. I am the most unhappy of men thanks to the same constancy from which I might have expected the sweetest of fates and the most perfect return of love" (25).

Manon Lescaut is one of the best-known love stories of the eighteenth century. Yet it is a love story that never dwells on the depiction of whatever joy or happiness the couple may have known. Each mention of joy is instead prefaced and inflected by the immediate recognition of its inevitable abolition. At those points in the story where the couple enjoys a relatively extended period of happiness the narrative focus shifts away from any portrayal of that joy to a description of its exterior circumstances: while they live happily on des Grieux's winnings, the narrative describes his initiation into the League and his disquisitions on how a beneficent providence sees to it that the poor are smart and the rich, stupid. At no point does the narration linger over or attempt to convey to the reader any sense of the sexual, social, or psychological *entente* actually holding the couple together. In terms of the way des Grieux tells his story, *Manon Lescaut* is not so much a love story as it is a story of reversals and changes, of chance and its unexpected detours always and everywhere at work.

Prévost's clear predilection goes to the moment when everything changes: the impending doom behind a knock at the door during supper or the way a declaration of love in a seminary parlor sweeps aside all previous plans. The emphasis is on things as they turn upside down, on the moment values are reversed, on the moment joy becomes despair and despair, joy. The direction events take is less important than the fact of change and the rapidity of the shift. To the opening door of the interrupted supper there corresponds the similar abruptness of love refound at the opening of Manon's cell: "'When?' she asked. 'This very day,' he replied. 'That happy moment is not far off. It will come this very instant if you so wish.' She understood at once that I was at the door. I entered just as she was rushing toward it. We embraced with an outpouring of tenderness that an absence of three months makes so delicious for those who truly love" (103).

Early in the novel's second part Manon offers the most eloquent declaration of her love for des Grieux. Courted by a wealthy Italian prince, she humiliates her suitor by holding up a mirror to his face and asking him to compare himself with the handsome young des Grieux. At this very instant when, as des Grieux puts it, "the intoxication of triumphant love made me applaud everything" (124), he nonetheless warns the reader that "I have noticed throughout my life that heaven has always chosen to strike me with its harshest punishments at those moments when my fortune seemed established on the firmest basis" (124).

One effect of this work's emphasis on unforeseen chance events is the fact that des Grieux, as he tells his story, finds himself obliged to narrate situations whose uniqueness and unexpectedness rendered them incomprehensible at the moment of their occurrence: "This was one of those situations so unique that no one has ever known anything comparable. It is impossible to explain them to others, because they have no conception of them. It is difficult to explain them even to oneself [à se les bien démêler à soi-même], since they are the only ones of their kind, are related to nothing in our memories, and can be compared to no known feeling" (69). *Manon Lescaut* tells a story of events for which des Grieux was so little prepared that whether it be the joy of love discovered or the despair of love lost, he lives them as an incomprehensible mystery. Whatever wisdom might be distilled from these experiences comes not at the moment of their befuddling occurrence but at those later moments of their narration at the *Lion d'Or* and of their reading by Prévost's audience. Only when integrated into the retrospectively ordered world of the story told and the novel read does what was experienced as a series of fragmentary bafflements provide a basis of understanding and judgment.

Prévost uses his preface to the stories Renoncourt and des Grieux will tell, his "Avis de l'auteur," to alert the reader to the singular value of a narration capturing the chaos of life's surprises and reversals as they are lived. The novel, Prévost argues, is a literary form particularly well suited to addressing and resolving the most puzzling paradox of the human condition. How can it be, he asks, that what he calls "moral precepts" are universally esteemed yet universally ignored? How is it that at the level of the abstract idea, all can readily agree on what is morally correct, yet such unanimity vanishes once it is a question of practical action, of what should actually be done in a specific situation? Analyzing virtue, friendship, and happiness provides, alone or in conversation with others, the most exhilarating stimulation possible for the life of the mind. Yet, in our everyday lives none of us lives up to what we so readily concede in the abstract.

The explanation of this paradox, Prévost insists, lies not at the level of our intentions but at the level of our knowledge—of our ability to see clearly how abstract moral principles can be applied to the ambiguity of real life situations: "Since all moral precepts exist as vague and abstract principles, it is difficult to apply them to the specifics of our attitudes and actions [au détail des moeurs et des actions]" (6). How, the question becomes, can this inability to act morally within the thick of life be addressed? How can we be helped to see more clearly the relevance of the abstract rule to the specific situation? The most obvious answer is experience, the slowly accumulated wisdom that accrues from living through and reflecting on the events we actually encounter. Experience has, however, two disadvantages: it enlightens us only after the fact, and it is available only to the person having that experience. To rely on experience as an ethical guide is, for those reasons, to surrender moral responsibility to the rule of chance: "Experience is an advantage not all have been blessed with. It is a function of the different situations in which our fortune has placed us" (6). There is, however, a second strategy for closing this gap between principle and action. Open to all independently of the specific situations in which fate has placed them, stories of someone else's experience allow the reader to understand through them what might be the intersection of abstract principle and concrete situation.

The argument Prévost offers here is central to the development of the novel. At one level, he directly challenges the traditional view of the novel at the beginning of the eighteenth century as a genre limited to the frivolous, the fantastical, and the licentious. Prévost suggests that the novel, like the case studies used in the training of confessors, can tell stories whose value lies, not in the entertainment they offer, but in the lessons they teach, in the wisdom these distillates of experience communicate to their readers: "Each narrated event is a ray of light, a lesson that complements experience [une instruction qui supplée à l'expérience]. Each adventure provides a model for fashioning ourselves [un modèle d'après lequel on peut se former]" (6). This new function of the novel depends, however, on an additional step that must be taken by the reader if the genre is to achieve its moral purpose: "The only thing missing is its application to our specific circumstances [d'être ajusté aux circonstances où l'on se trouve]" (6). The novel may be, as Prévost puts it, "a moral treatise pleasingly fleshed out in applications [un traité de morale, réduit agréablement en exercice]" (6); but the real value of that treatise finally depends on the readers' ability to apply the story's lesson to the specifics of their own lives. The case Prévost makes here for the novel as a means of adequating represented experience to life lived adopts exactly the same strategy, and has the same weakness, as the arguments offered by the major figures of probability theory for the practical relevance of their science. The real person, like the gambler wondering which card will fall next, is inevitably frustrated with the theory's inability to speak of *this* event within *this* situation at *this* moment.

Prévost, enunciating what will become a dominant tradition within the eighteenth-century novel, asks his readers to approach the tale he tells as two distinct stories, with each demanding a different understanding. Because the novel speaks of individual experiences, its most immediate story will, as we saw, be that of a series of unexpected, apparently chance-driven events that are as often as not misunderstood by the characters at the moment they experience them. Yet this evenemential surface of chance, specificity, and circumstance is also intended to initiate an act of interpretation moving from the random signifiers of that first story to a second level of signified meaning where the fragmented pieces coalesce into a unified whole. The novel's real unity and utility lie not at the level of the story told but at the level of the reader's personalizing appropriation of that story through interpretation. The perception of this second level depends on the readers' understanding that the apparent chance of the first story leads to a moral lesson that, once grasped, will allow the readers to profit from the narrated experience as though it were their own.

The invitation Prévost offers his readers is twofold. In one direction, the readers are asked to approach the circumstance of story as the prolegomenon to an act of interpretation referring the story's random shards to a greater unity establishing them as the illustration of a moral truth. In the other, that first voyage from the specific to the abstract through interpretation prepares the way for a second voyage allowing the readers to apply the intent of the properly interpreted story to the specifics of their own situations and, in so doing, reorganize the perception of their own circumstantiality within an equally meaning-laden interpretation. The novel, Prévost suggests, initiates an alchemy of interpretation moving back and forth be-

tween the specific and the general, between the situation
of the story and the situation of the reader.

How, the question becomes, must the novel be written
and read if these interpretations are to take place? How
can the story told be both of specific persons and of universal moral significance? How, in other words, can the novel
achieve a discourse of the generalizable specific? *Manon
Lescaut* is particularly fascinating for its lack of any obvious
answer to the questions raised by its preface. Its story
hardly reads as a moral fable, and generations of critics
have, for the most diverse reasons, condemned it as
amoral. It is, it would seem, not so much the story told that
is important but how we as readers become aware of and
go on to interpret the story. *Manon Lescaut* is, we saw, a
misleading title. First published as an addendum to the six
volumes of *Mémoires* Prévost attributed to the marquis de
Renoncourt, *L'Histoire de Manon Lescaut* was, according to
that fiction, a story told to the marquis. It becomes the
story we read thanks to his apparently verbatim transcrip-
tion of the tale told by des Grieux at the *Lion d'Or*. Rather
than the story of Manon Lescaut, it is, at the most literal
level, the story of des Grieux. His telling his story to Renoncourt thus represents in a very real sense an aggressive
taking control of all that remains of Manon's life.[2] Storyteller and reader share a knowledge of Manon everywhere
mediated by her story as des Grieux chooses to tell it. Yet
the reader cannot help but be aware of a startling gap
between des Grieux's active role as storyteller and the passivity he displays throughout the story he tells as a character at the mercy of chance. The moment of his most spectacular turnabout, his reaction to Manon's arrival at
Saint-Sulpice, subtly illustrates how this passivity is transformed by his telling of the tale: "It has never surprised
me that human resolutions are subject to change. They are
born of one passion, and another can destroy them. But
when I think of the sacredness of those that led me to
Saint-Sulpice and of the heartfelt joy I discovered in obey-
ing them, I shudder at the facility with which I abandoned

them [je suis effrayé de la facilité avec laquelle j'ai pu les rompre]" (42). Presenting himself as a victim of passions beyond human control, des Grieux can only fear where they will lead him ("je suis effrayé de la facilité avec laquelle . . ."). Yet, because it is he who actually tells the story, he himself remains the spectacle beheld by that frightened gaze ("j'ai pu les rompre").

Des Grieux's story is simultaneously the chronicle and the denial of his passivity. Speaking to Tiberge after he has left Saint-Sulpice, des Grieux again presents himself as fate's hapless victim: "I presented it [my passion] to him as one of those strange strokes of destiny which draw the poor soul to his ruin, and which it is as impossible for virtue to resist as it is for wisdom to foresee" (59). Not only does this luxuriance in passivity allow des Grieux to cloak himself in the becoming guise of fate's victim but it is part of his ploy to extract still more money from the ever-trusting Tiberge. The lamented passivity becomes, in context, an actively executed ruse.

Manon Lescaut is, at two distinct levels, the story of a story. On the one hand, the marquis de Renoncourt is telling us the story of the story he heard from des Grieux. On the other, des Grieux tells the story of his story, the story of how his abiding passivity has come to be transformed within the active gesture of narration. If, as Prévost would have it in his preface, this novel is of moral significance to its readers, it is by reason of this reconciliation of active and passive carried out at the intersection of the story told and the act of its telling. At the level of the story told, *Manon Lescaut* stages a literal pageant of individuals either crushed by or amorally submitting to the dictates of random configurations of money and power demanding compliance and collaboration. Des Grieux's one escape from that passivity lies in the control of reader and listener he achieves as the teller of his tale. If the readers accept the pact offered in the preface, if they identify with the story sufficiently to find in it a moral significance pertinent to their own situations, it is because this transformation of passive into active through storytelling evokes a universal human dilemma.

Des Grieux invites the reader's sympathetic identification not because Renoncourt is careful to insist on his natural nobility and dignity but because his passivity stems, not from any fault of his own, but from his finding himself in a world ruled by chance—a world of implacable and conflicting causal sequences whose random intersections occur as a result of the most outrageous coincidence. Des Grieux's immersion in the aleatory ends only when, at Renoncourt's invitation, he abandons the dark night of experience within the present and turns instead to a narration of his past. The story I tell, des Grieux invites his reader to agree, may be tragic, but it is mine and it is me.

This interplay of active and passive solicits the reader's identification because its pardoning ambiguity corresponds to a need anchored in what must be the reader's own experience of the world. To acknowledge chance is, as des Grieux does, to become actively aware of our passivity, of a limit to our control of the real dictating that it is only within the story of the self that each might one day tell that there resides all we might become beyond the ineffable facticity of the random present.

Prévost was one of the first novelists to portray a modern awareness of chance. What is so often referred to as his "realism" results in great part from his attention to a new dimension of the way chance inflected life in society. *Manon Lescaut* continually underlines the fact that within the array of unrelated causal sequences intersecting in the production of the chance event, money and its concomitant power have come to constitute a vector of new and unsuspected force. Within Prévost's novels no distinction is made between the chance event understood according to Aristotle's classical model of the individual's being struck by a falling roof tile and that same individual's being robbed by a trusted servant or evinced in the affections of his lover by a wealthy rival. While the classical paradigm for chance minimized the presence of any human agency within that event, the press of money makes that specifically human and social dimension of chance explicit. By casting the chance event in this new mold, by insisting on chance's role in deciding the individual's position in a societywide circulation of money and power, Prévost offered a novelistic representation corresponding to the experience of a growing number of readers from all quadrants of society.

·Prévost recognizes the power of chance and uses the victimization it imposes to solicit and ensure the reader's identification with the suffering character. At another level, however, this reign of chance, like the passivity that accompanies it, is abolished by the act of narration. "It is necessary [Il faut]," says des Grieux during his first encounter with Renoncourt, "that I accept my fate in all its rigor [que je me soumette à toute la rigeur de mon sort]" (14). This sentence, with its sequencing of the impersonal and the reflexive, captures the way a confrontation with the inevitable—"Il faut"—serves to justify a reflexive self-creativity paradoxically springing from the very act of submission—"que je me soumette." With his entire story continuing the interplay of these two verbal forms, des Grieux's life is an epic of passivity, chance, and fate. At the same time, however, his telling of his story transcends that subjection by situating events in a narrated past, no longer open to the random disruptions of chance. The temporality of the story told, unlike that of the lived event, is one always rooted in a past and determined by a future.

The moral significance of the novel, Prévost argued, depends on an identification of reader with story such that the narrated events become for the reader an equivalent of actual experience. The novel's didactic function and the identification on which it is based imply a parallel between the chance-free present of the story told and the similarly transmuted present of the reader engaged in the act of reading. Reading is a refusal of chance both because it abstracts us from the contingency of our own real present and because it initiates an identification with a story inviting us to discover within its narration an ideal past and an imaginary future, both of which give ballast and meaning to an otherwise free-floating present.

The story des Grieux tells in *Manon Lescaut* says little of any future beyond his sad experiences in Paris and the New World. Des Grieux does, however, speak early in his tale of one future project, a project placing the acts of reading and writing at the center of the story he tells. Remembering the time he spent as a prisoner in his father's house after his first stay in Paris with Manon, he describes a project that relates not only to that period from the past but to the future, to a time after the telling of his tale to Renoncourt: "I composed a loving commentary on the fourth book of the *Aeneid*. I intend to publish it and flatter myself that it will find its public" (38). Des Grieux's promised commentary on Dido's love for Aeneas and her suicide upon losing him is at one and the same time the resurrection of an earlier past of reading ("I reread all my favorite authors" [38], he says of the same period), the idealization through writing of the more recently lost past of his time with Manon in Paris, and a distorted anticipation of Manon's death in the wastes of New France. Des Grieux reads the fourth book of the *Aeneid* in precisely the way Prévost invites his readers to read *Manon Lescaut*. The story to be told may begin with the chance event of a storm at sea or an unexpected encounter at Amiens. Through its representation in story, however, that present becomes, no matter how unexpected its adventures, that of a tamed chance caught between predetermined past and anticipated future.

As a novel, *Manon Lescaut* offers much more than a supplement to experience. Rather than simply adding something not previously there, the novel refashions the very status of the present. As des Grieux's rereading, reliving, and rewriting of the fourth book of the *Aeneid* make clear, to accept the identification of self with text implicit to every successful act of reading is to infuse the chance-driven contingency of the present with a direction, a determination, and a necessity rooted in a relationship of mutual appropriation joining reader and story. To read the text and live its story is to substitute a domesticated simulacrum of chance for what without it can only be the tragedy of experience.

7

The Ironies of Chance:
Voltaire's *Candide* and *Zadig*

No French novel of the eighteenth century confronts the
question of chance more directly than Voltaire's *Candide*.
Its hero wanders through a world governed by chance and
evil. Yet Candide struggles to keep faith with Pangloss's
proclamation that everything is for the best in the best of
all possible worlds. Juxtaposing that belief with a reality
everywhere contradicting it, Voltaire's novel becomes a reflection on what it means to tell a story in and of a world
of circumstance, accident, and coincidence. Writing a
chronicle of chance, Voltaire discovered the impossibility
of being both philosopher and novelist, of recognizing
and, with the same voice, representing the reality of
chance. In accommodating the novel to his epic of the aleatory, Voltaire initiated a practice of narrative ironies crucial to the genre's survival of its confrontation with chance.

Candide stands as a question mark appended to the Enlightenment's proud proclamations of order, reason, and
justice. Born of Voltaire's horror at the Lisbon earthquake,
which on the morning of All Souls' Day 1755 killed fifteen
thousand people during its initial six-minute tremor and
then caused another fifteen thousand deaths over the next
few days, the novel was bitterly subtitled "Optimism." Vol-

taire's decision to satirize the Leibnizian claim that ours is
the best of all possible worlds was not in itself particularly
iconoclastic. The short entry in Diderot's more or less contemporary *Encyclopédie* under the heading "Optimisme"
concluded with the dismissive statement, "It must be said
that this metaphysics of optimism is perfectly hollow."[1]
Leibniz's insistence on the best immediately made his position ludicrously suspect for those unable to accept the con-
voluted metaphysics of its defense in his *Theodicy* (1710).
The parallel but less extreme doctrine of providence—a
concept based on the same premises as Optimism but lacking its insistence on the best within the possible—remained
a central point of Christian dogma, Reformed as well as
Roman. The *Encyclopédie* entry "Providence" is circumspect
not only because it was an article sure to be examined by
the royal censor but also because there was in fact no fundamental incompatibility between a providential view of
the world and the convictions of even the most secular
philosophes. So long as the agent of providence was sufficiently blurred into the vague presence of a disinterested
watchmaker, that view of the universe meshed easily with
their Newtonian, scientistic belief in the order and rationality of the physical world. The *Encyclopédie*'s "Providence"
in fact takes on a decidedly "optimistic" and even parodic
hue as it explains how a lack of knowledge can jeopardize
our understanding of a given phenomenon: "We see many
things as disorders because we are ignorant of their causes
and effects. Once we understand them, we see a marvelous
order. . . . Thus, for instance, of rain falling into the sea:
perhaps it decreases the water's salinity, which would otherwise be harmful to fish; and it provides a much needed
refreshment for sailors" (3:135). The one real anathema
within the *Encyclopédie*'s treatment of providence is hurled
not at Leibnitz but at the idea of chance, *le hasard:* "Chance
[Le hasard] is nothing. It is a fiction, a chimera bereft of
possibility and existence. People attribute to chance effects
whose causes they do not understand. But for God, know-

ing all causes and all effects, actual as well as potential, in the clearest detail, nothing can be an effect of chance" (3:135).

This argument is one we have encountered frequently. The perception of chance is a function of our ignorance, a projection onto the objective world of our own lack of knowledge. According to the tenets of deism, God is by definition all-knowing, and it logically follows that for Him, chance has no meaning. For the more agnostic mainstream of the Enlightenment, the argument remained much the same. Only the identity of the knowing and therefore chance-banishing subject changed. Rather than to an omniscient God, it fell to humankind and its ever more comprehensive inquiries to extend the limits of knowledge and, in so doing, to unmask chance as a figment of our ignorance. If there was one point on which the otherwise warring factions of church and Enlightenment agreed, it was on the absurdity of chance as an equal affront to the glory of God and the glory of man. There was an order and coherence to the universe. Our duty is to study that universe as closely as possible, to penetrate the levels of causality at work within it, to understand their integration within a unified whole, and to accept the lessons of the system as it existed. The adoption of this posture excluding even the possibility of chance was common to all the major figures of the French Enlightenment, whether they were deist, rationalist, or materialist.

Candide, written in anger and frustration, flies in the face of this consensus. The physical world portrayed in this novel is one of storms, shipwrecks, plagues, earthquakes, and other forms of senseless destruction. The storm heralding the Lisbon earthquake comes, at the level of Voltaire's prose, as nature's response to Pangloss's reaffirmation of his optimism when Candide points out that it is difficult to see the inventions of the bayonet and cannon as the necessary building blocks of the best of all possible worlds: " 'All that was indispensable,' replied the one-eyed doctor, 'and private misfortunes add up to the general good, and the more private misfortunes there are, the more all is well.' While he thus reasoned, the sky grew dark, the winds blew from all four corners of the globe, and the vessel was besieged by a horrible storm as it drew in sight of the port of Lisbon."[2]

The innocent Candide provides Voltaire's reader with a resolutely singular perspective on the world. All his actions spring from his commitment to a single goal: to find and marry Cunégonde. Once expelled from the baron's castle, Candide becomes a man with no short-range strategy, a man prompted by no proximate or intermediate goals determining his moment-to-moment activities. His ultimate goal is defined, but it remains for the most part irrelevant to all options within the possible. He is indifferent to everything unrelated to his reunion with Cunégonde. With no immediate agenda of his own, Candide becomes the unperturbed and ideally empty mirror reflecting whatever coherence and rationality might be at work in the world around him.

The people he meets, where he goes, and everything that happens to him occur by chance. Candide is like a pinball in the machine of life. Jean Starobinski has pointed out that Voltaire achieved this effect in part by restricting his field of narrative vision to the "causalité courte."[3] Limiting his description of events to their proximate causes and immediate effects, Voltaire effectively isolates them from any larger ideological justification. The Bulgare and Abare armies mercilessly slaughter each other and any number of innocent civilians, but there is never the slightest hint as to what might be the larger political motivations behind their conflict. Voltaire achieves a similarly absurd effect by juxtaposing the personal, most immediate motivations of a given action with larger consequences never suspected by the acting subject. One day Candide takes a walk "believing it was a privilege of the human species to use one's legs as one pleased" (140) and finds himself arrested for desertion and offered a choice of execution by firing squad or regimental beating.

The sway of chance within the novel is further consolidated by Voltaire's continual emphasis of two action patterns eminently subject to the aleatory: the hero's journeying through unknown lands and his encountering
people who act on the most rapacious desires. *Candide* is
an epic of traveling and taking. Its hero's journey takes
him from Westphalia to Holland, to Lisbon, to South
America, to Europe, and to Asia. But no matter how much
the locale changes, the people he meets are pockets of
solipsistic desire grabbing for whatever they can get. With
the exception of his few more philosophical friends, everyone Candide meets or hears about wants either money or
sex. His and their chaotic routes are the products of a
random series of robberies and rapes. This conjugation of
the indeterminacy of travel with the randomness of desire
is nowhere better illustrated than in Pangloss's "genealogy"
of his syphilis: "Paquette had received this present from a
very learned Franciscan who had gone back to the source.
He had received it from an elderly countess, who had received it from a cavalry captain, who owed it to a marquise,
who had it from a page, who had received it from a Jesuit,
who as a novice had received it directly from one of the
companions of Christopher Columbus" (144–45).

The majority of the characters in this novel—Cunégonde, her brother, Pangloss, Paquette, Cacambo, Martin,
the deposed kings in Venice—are no less buffeted by
chance than Candide. The old woman with one buttock,
now Cunégonde's maid, takes over the narration during
the voyage from Cadiz to Paraguay. In response to Cunégonde's claim that no one could have suffered more unjustly than she, the old woman tells the story of her lifelong
wanderings from Rome, where she was born the daughter
of Pope Urbain X; to North Africa, where she was captured by pirates; to Asia, where she was sold as a slave; to
Azof, where her lost buttock nourished the starving janis-
saries; to Moscow and across northern Europe, where she
worked as a servant once her youth and beauty had given
out. If the old woman tells her story in such detail—it

accounts for two of the novel's thirty chapters—it is because it illustrates how, at the level of those personal narratives through which the characters define themselves, all would claim the status of chance's most exquisite victim. The old woman ends her story with a heavy bet as to the other travelers on their ship: "Have some fun, ask each passenger to tell you his story, and if it turns out there is a single one who has not often cursed his life, who has not often said to himself that he is the unhappiest of men, throw me headfirst into the sea" (164).

After a hundred days wandering in the jungle, Candide and Cacambo come upon the Dutch possession of Surinam. "We have reached the end of our troubles and the beginning of our happiness" (182), thinks Cacambo. But the first person they meet there is a black slave. Prostrate in his one earthly possession, a loincloth replaced by his master every six months, he explains in a few sentences how his right hand was cut off for losing a finger in the sugar mill and how his left leg was amputated for trying to escape from the plantation. As though addicted to such tales of woe, Candide ends his stay in Surinam by organizing a contest whose prize of return passage to Europe will go to the person whose life story proves him to be the most unhappy resident of that city.

All those stories, like the novel itself, are tales of evil—of human and metaphysical evil, of individual and social evil. Their constant reiteration has, however, the effect of undercutting everything the term 'evil' implies. How can so many people, in so many places, be either evil themselves or the victims of evil? The cumulative effect of these tales is to call into question the very concept of evil, to reveal it as a misnomer, an inadequate shorthand presupposing a coherent agency where in fact there is none. 'Evil', like 'good', becomes a word without a referent, a testimonial to the abiding human desire to moralize chance, to see some principle of causality as responsible for the random events that befall us. 'Evil' designates the chance event for which someone can be blamed. 'Evil' is the scapegoat of chance.

The terms 'good' and 'evil' were at the core of the Enlightenment's evacuation of chance. We saw how chance in a neutral sense—the chance event qualified as neither good nor evil—was dismissed as a by-product of ignorance, a meaningless term masking our temporary inability to identify correctly the cause of a given event. When, as is constantly the case in *Candide*, chance took on a less benign form, *le mal* was the term used to designate any situation against which one was obliged to struggle. Ignorance and evil, like knowledge and good, form the mutually sustaining poles of the Enlightenment's struggle against chance, its parallel strategies for controlling and evacuating it. Any instance of chance that could not be consigned to either ignorance or evil had to be denied. To do otherwise would have been to jeopardize knowledge and responsibility as the parallel imperatives of Enlightenment ideology.

Candide extends its portrayal of evil so far and in so many directions that even though the proper code words *mal* and *malheur* are used, it becomes impossible for the reader to preserve any faith in an ultimately unified and coherent principle demarcating the separate domains of good and evil, knowledge and ignorance. The one-buttocked old woman's tale of woe begins when she and her mother are captured by Moorish pirates off the coast of Italy. The situation they discover as they arrive in Morocco is the prototype of *Candide*'s world: "Morocco was swimming in blood when we arrived. The fifty sons of the emperor Mulei-Ismaël each had their faction, and there were fifty civil wars of blacks against blacks, blacks against tans, tans against tans, mulattoes against mulattoes. There was a continual carnage throughout the entire empire" (159–60). This description of fragmented and uncontrollable civil strife directly anticipates the novel's closing scene in the garden outside Constantinople. The fifty factions locked in civil war carry out within a single moment what Constantinople experiences sequentially as the world-weary pilgrims watch the endless succession of boats carrying deposed rulers to exile in one direction as their temporary replacements arrive from the other. *Candide*'s is a world where everyone's fate corresponds to that of the old woman's mother and the other Italian women as they arrived in Morocco: with each faction claiming the booty, "I saw all our Italian women and my mother torn, cut, and massacred by the monsters who fought over them" (160).

This ripping apart of the innocent victim by forces locked in murderous envy becomes an emblem of the human condition. It lays bare a fundamental chaos of desire and violence that appears again and again in almost every setting where Candide and his tellers of tales happen to set foot. It is Martin, the winner of Candide's sad tale–telling contest in Surinam, who best enunciates the general principle:

> I have rarely seen a town that did not desire the ruin of the neighboring town, nor a family that did not wish to exterminate some other family. Everywhere the weak loathe the powerful before whom they crawl, and the powerful treat them like flocks whose wool and flesh they are ready to sell. A million regimented assassins, wandering from one end of Europe to the other, murder and pillage with discipline to earn their bread because they have no more honest occupation. (187)

Martin's indictment not only covers the obvious dangers posed by soldiers and thieves but includes within its inventory even those apparently peaceful communities that are in fact racked by more suffering than a besieged city: "In towns that seem to enjoy peace and where the arts flourish, men are devoured with more envy, cares, and worries than all the scourges suffered by a town under siege" (187).

Civilization, law, the humanly created dimensions of language and community, rather than offering an escape from envy and violence, only exacerbate them. Quite unlike the Mandevillean voice of *Le Mondain,* which could, twenty-three years earlier, describe the humanly fabricated reality of the city as infinitely preferable to any pristine nature, Voltaire now presents language and society as a hopeless logomachy, as wars of words cut off from reality and turning futilely on their own contradictions. An agent of the Inquisition hears Pangloss declare ours to be the best of all possible worlds after a day spent extracting corpses from the ruins of Lisbon. His attention is caught not by the absurdity of the statement in its context but by the way Pangloss's "All is for the best" contradicts the doctrines of original sin and divine punishment. Unfazed by the inquisitor's suspicion, Pangloss, in his ready reply, only consolidates language's exile from any contact with reality and meaning: " 'Man's fall and condemnation necessarily entered into the best of all possible worlds.'—'Then the gentleman does not believe in free will?,' asked the familiar.—'Your Excellency will excuse me,' replied Pangloss, 'free will can coexist with absolute necessity: for it was necessary that we should be free' " (148). Pangloss's defense of a liberty compatible with necessity enunciates the ultimate cacophony of language, the bankruptcy of man's attempts to represent reality, to offer anything more eloquent than silence as a way of making sense of what happens in the world. All attempts at understanding, like Pangloss's braying atop the ruins of Lisbon, form little more than a fragile crust of language proclaiming its categories of good and evil, knowledge and ignorance, causality and rationality, over a volcano of chance poised to contradict and abolish them.

Voltaire, reacting to the enormity of the Lisbon earthquake, offers in *Candide* a representation of the world that goes beyond his vocabulary. Writing against the doctrine of Optimism, Voltaire moves beyond any recourse to its cozy twin of pessimism. Pangloss may be a fool, but Martin's visions of universal evil provide no real answers. Best and worst, like good and evil, work together as mutually sustaining opposites whose real function is to exclude the reality of chance. *Le hasard,* simply and irrationally there, makes a mockery of all attempts to domesticate it within the anthropocentric categories of good and evil.

Candide's world writhes in the throes of chance. It savagely undercuts all its characters' pitiable attempts to understand, rationalize, and control what happens around them. Yet Voltaire never explicitly addresses the question of chance in this novel. In part, this was because any recognition of chance was antithetical to the enterprise of the didactic novel as Voltaire conceived it. Narrated events had somehow to hold together in terms of a logic relating part to part and subordinating part to whole. The problem was clear: On the one hand, the novel offered the advantage of reaching an audience far greater than that willing to read any directly philosophical disquisition on the human condition. On the other, the very form of the novel necessitated an order and coherence of events antithetical to a vision of the world as ruled by chance. How, the question became, could chance be tamed? How could it be included within the novel as theme yet not destroy the genre as form? In addressing this question, and in understanding the importance of the solution proposed by *Candide,* it is important to remember that Voltaire had addressed this problem before. He had, in fact, already told Candide's story—only differently.

First published in 1747, *Zadig* predates *Candide* by twelve years. Yet their stories are the same. Both tell of a hero, forced into exile because of a forbidden love, who wanders through a world of violence, envy, and injustice. Zadig and Candide have been made and broken by chance. One day Zadig tears in half a sheet of paper on which he has written a poem. His jealous neighbor, Arimaze, happens to find the torn sheets and realizes that one part, separated from the other, reads like a seditious threat to the king. Zadig is imprisoned and awaiting execution when it happens that the king's parrot flies into Zadig's garden and returns with the other half of the sheet, revealing that Zadig's poem was written in praise of the king's martial valor. Zadig's reaction to the world as he finds it would be in no way inappropriate for Candide: "All the good I have done has only been a curse for me, and I have been raised to the pinnacle of greatness only to fall into the most horrible abyss of misfortune. If I had been wicked like so many others, I would also be happy like them" (23). Again, as in *Candide*, the loosely knitted episodes of Zadig's adventures are held together by his unflagging desire to rejoin the woman he loves. In his case, it is the beautiful Astarté, the wife of King Moabdar, who fell in love with him but with whom he never acted in any way that would justify the blind jealousy that led Astarté's husband to force him into exile.

Zadig, too, carries a subtitle: "La Destinée." And, again like *Candide*, *Zadig* is a meditation on how, within a world of unrewarded good and unpunished evil, one might continue to believe in any destiny or providence turning life into something other than pure chance. In many ways *Zadig* is a less extreme, less somber consideration of the same questions at the core of *Candide*. While Zadig's destiny is decided by a series of chance events every bit as unjust as those that befall Candide, Zadig, unlike Candide, always manages to scramble out from under. Falsely accused of murder when he arrives in Egypt, Zadig is made a slave and sold to Sétoc. In no time, however, Zadig's sage counsel has established him far more as Sétoc's senior partner than as his slave. *Zadig* ends more happily than *Candide*. Rather than in the ambiguity of a self-enclosed garden all must cultivate, Zadig's adventures establish him as the new king of Babylon and as husband to his beloved and beautiful Astarté.

My point in making these comparisons is to underline how *Zadig* and *Candide* reveal on Voltaire's part a continuing obsession with the role of chance in the individual's life and how that subject might be addressed within the tradition of the novel, in this case the particular variant of the *roman philosophique* or *conte philosophique*. Both works portray a universe at the mercy of chance, yet in both cases that chance is ultimately denied in order to preserve the narrative and semiotic form of the didactic novel. Voltaire did, however, carry out his dismissal of chance in two quite different ways, and our appreciating how this is done in the more extreme case of *Candide* depends on understanding the earlier resolution of the problem in *Zadig*.

As a character, the learned, brilliant, and brave Zadig is clearly different from Candide. Whereas Candide wanders the world scratching his head and wondering how Pangloss would justify the latest horror he has encountered, Zadig becomes educated, rich, beyond vanity, open to the lessons of nature, and a fine student of human character. Like a Babylonian Sherlock Holmes, Zadig is able to provide exact descriptions of the king's lost dog and horse with nothing more to go on than the tracks they have left in the forest. He is an astute, Solomon-like judge whose "principal talent was to uncover the truth all men seek to hide" (16). When a contest of jousting and solving riddles is opened to determine who will be the new king of Babylon, Zadig proves himself the best and brightest.

Zadig is the story of a dialectic between a world whose events are ruled by chance and one eminently rational individual who is able to win no matter how bad a hand he is dealt. *Zadig* opens with a long description, entirely in the imperfect tense, of the story's hero: "In the time of King Moabdar there was [il y avait] in Babylon a young man named Zadig, whose fine native disposition had been fortified by his upbringing. Although rich and young, he knew how to moderate [savait modérer] his passions, he had no affectations [n'affectait rien], he did not insist on [ne voulait point] always being right, and he was able to respect [savait respecter] human frailty. . . . He was [était] as wise as a man can be, for he sought to [cherchait à] live with the wise" (2–3). This portrait of Zadig's virtues continues until it is interrupted by a single verb in the simple past. The appearance of this abrupt, momentary tense signals an event situated, not in the slowly accumulated and abiding temporality of the imperfect, but in the specific then and there of a single moment causing the future to veer in an unexpected direction: "They [Zadig and his fiancée, Sémire] saw [virent] two men coming toward them armed with sabres and arrows" (3). These armed men are in the pay of Orcan, who, envious of Zadig, has dispatched them to steal the beautiful Sémire. Zadig manages to fight off his attackers but is wounded near his left eye. His surgeon predicts that he will certainly lose it, and Sémire, who detests one-eyed men, decides to marry Orcan. This opening episode establishes a pattern that will repeat itself throughout the novel. From his first appearance Zadig is endowed with an identity sufficiently firm that no matter how threatening the events within the register of the simple past, he retains a ballast, a contact with talents situated in the abiding continuity of the imperfect.

Zadig adopts what was the most traditional form of the novel, a narration alternating between imperfect and simple past. Plot, the events that occur, may appear to be nothing more than the aleatory dictates of chance. It is at the level of character, of a continuing individual identity surviving the chance events of the simple past, that the story will achieve its real coherence. Character, the traditional formula goes, is generated through and revealed by events. The momentary, chance-driven temporality of the simple past takes on meaning only as it inflects a continuing temporality of character expressed by the imperfect. Zadig suffers any number of trials and tribulations, but he always emerges as a better and stronger version of what he was from the start. A sense of self situated within the imperfect has been tried and tempered by the random blows of the simple past. Chance may be everywhere, but it only confirms a continuity at the level of character that stands ready to learn and profit from whatever surprises it might deliver. The imperfect absorbs the simple past, character absorbs plot, and individual virtue triumphs over chance.

In terms of both its narrative form and the story told, *Zadig* is a perfect illustration of the Enlightenment ideal of the rational and self-sufficient individual. Zadig's identity depends not on birth or rank but on the same careful exercise of observation, analysis, and reason we saw to be the guiding ideals of the mathematicians who developed the theory of probability. Each time Zadig stops and looks back only at what has happened to him, only at events within the simple past, only at plot, he despairs at the workings of what seems the most absurd chance. The day after defeating all the other contestants for Astarté's hand, he oversleeps and his white armor, the only proof that he was the winner, is stolen: " 'That's what comes,' he said, 'of waking too late. If I had slept less, I would be king of Babylon, Astarté would be mine. Knowledge, morality, and courage have only led to my misfortune' " (51). Yet each such moment of despair is followed by Zadig's choosing to rely on himself, his wit, and the exercise of his abiding talents in such a way that he is sure to succeed: Zadig's reputation for honesty leads to his being allowed, even though he does not wear the winner's armor, to participate in the riddle contest, in which he easily triumphs over the thieving Itobad. Chance, this constantly repeated pattern shows, ultimately serves to reveal a stable truth of the self.

Toward the end of *Zadig*, during the moment of despair between the episode of the stolen armor and its recuperation through the solved riddles, the question of chance is raised explicitly. For three days Zadig has traveled with the wise hermit able to decipher the *livre des destinées*. Zadig is appalled when the old man first drowns the fourteen-year-old nephew of an impoverished widow and then burns down the house of a man who has just extended them the most generous hospitality. Responding to Zadig's amazement, the hermit explains that the boy would have killed the widow if he had lived another year and that their gracious host will discover an immense hidden treasure under the ruins of his house. After revealing himself to be the angel Jesrad, the hermit enunciates the truth all must recognize about the status of chance: "People will think that this child who has just perished fell into the water by chance and that it was also by chance that that house burned. But there is no chance. Everything is a test, a punishment, a reward, or a forethought" (56).

Chance, the story tells us once again, is only a product of human ignorance. The angel Jesrad, a literal deus ex machina, insists that all events serve to accomplish a moral end when once they are understood as parts of a whole, which more often than not remains hidden from human eyes. Jesrad's lesson comes as the final fruit of Zadig's travels. His reaffirmation of a coherent universe beyond chance is accepted as wisdom grasped and a mystery revealed. Jesrad's dictum is perfectly consonant with the form of *Zadig's* narration: although life as it is lived may appear to be a concatenation of chance events, those events finally contribute to the forging of an identity whose coherence can be appreciated only retrospectively and, in Zadig's case, while basking in the pleasures of a happy ending giving him both queen and kingdom.

Twelve years later everything has changed. While Zadig might display physical prowess, a fine flair for human motivations, and real wisdom, Candide is a naive adolescent stumbling through a world he rarely understands and never masters. Events may lead him to question his allegiance to Pangloss, but his is hardly the epic of an independent character shaped and confirmed by the trials of experience. Rather than *Zadig's* dialectic of imperfect and simple past, *Candide* offers only the inaugural abruptness of a simple past excluding the continuities of the imperfect. While Pangloss may remain Candide's interlocutor of choice at the end of the story, his status as the parodic equivalent of Jesrad shows how, during the twelve years separating these two works, Voltaire's attitude toward chance and the form of the novel had changed. What could still in 1747 be presented as the beginnings of wisdom is in 1759 mercilessly pilloried. A world everywhere given over to envy and violence now makes a mockery of Pangloss's serene assurance.

There are, however, two moments in *Candide* when the reign of evil and the sway of chance are suspended. Candide's visit to El Dorado and the closing scene in the garden outside Constantinople are crucial to understanding how Voltaire was able to write this work as an epic of chance yet safeguard the narrative form of the novel. El Dorado is the reverse image of the destructive passions reigning everywhere else in the world Candide discovers. With gold and jewels everywhere, no one accumulates them or envies another's. The people of El Dorado are naturally and fervently religious. Their religion, rather than protecting them from any threat or guaranteeing them any favor, serves exclusively to express their gratitude for everything they already are: "'We do not pray to him,' said the good and respectable wise man. 'We have nothing to request because he has given us everything we need. We thank him ceaselessly'" (178). El Dorado has no law courts, no police, and no government buildings—facts whose explanation lies less in what El Dorado is than in what it most emphatically is not: "We have until now always been sheltered from the rapacity of the nations of Europe" (178). El Dorado is the anti-Europe. Outside envy and violence, it is outside time. The only sense of history, of change over time, at work in El Dorado is that of a single event referring its people back to the original sin of a distant other. Their history began and ended in that one past moment when a part of the tribe left its inaccessible sanctuary and, as Incas, set about conquering other peoples until they themselves were enslaved by the arriving Spaniards. Much like the virtuous Troglodytes of Montesquieu's *Lettres persanes,* the inhabitants of El Dorado draw their most essential lesson from the story of how a past egotism destroyed the society of their ancestors. El Dorado preserves its perfection through a ritualized commemoration of how horribly wrong everything went for another version of

177

themselves situated in another time and another place. This history of the Incas, of the self as an anticipation of the European other, is the only story ever told in El Dorado. Outside desire, envy, and violence, these people have no other story to tell. Their lives have reached a stasis of perfection excluding all change and chance.

The description of El Dorado occupies two chapters toward the end of the second third of *Candide*. While these chapters offer the rough summary of a possible utopia, the description of that ideal seems quickly to bore Voltaire. Rather than articulating any real coherence within its traits, he offers what amounts to a catalog of its edifying features. Candide then abruptly remembers that he can never be truly happy without Cunégonde and decides to leave. The one other motivation for his departure comes as he discovers the boredom of a life lived in such serenity, of a life lived outside comparison, envy, and story: "If we remain here," he insists to Cacambo, "we will only be like the others; but if we return to our own world with only twelve sheep laden with the pebbles of El Dorado, we will be richer than all kings put together" (180).

By the time Candide arrives at the garden outside Constantinople he has lost all the treasures he carried out of El Dorado, he has been reunited with his beloved but now hideously ugly Cunégonde, and he even demurs at Pangloss's unfailing proclamations that all is always for the best. This final moment in the garden is far from the timeless contentment of El Dorado, yet its delineation of a possible ideal depends on a similar separation from the world at large, from the world of envy, violence, and chance. Unlike the sensual euphoria of El Dorado, this enclave of the tired travelers is far from perfect. When they are not arguing with each other, they quickly grow bored. The old woman wonders whether, after all, it was not better to have suffered all the horrors each of them has known than to live out deadly dull lives in a safely circumscribed world like the one where they now find themselves. Martin goes so far as to conclude that man's only real choice is between "les convulsions de l'inquiétude" and "la léthargie de l'ennui" (219).

Candide's closing response to this dilemma is the famous "il faut travailler notre jardin," suggesting that practical work for the common good can create a third alternative to the tortures of the world and the boredom of separation. Many critics have condemned *Candide*'s ending as a justification for what they see as the eminently bourgeois ethic of an isolation from political strife devoted entirely to personal enrichment. Jean Starobinski nicely corrects these critics when he points out that "the age that is beginning here is insufficiently defined through the familiar concept of the 'bourgeois.' In fact, the moment here forming and affirming itself is that when man, no longer the admiring spectator of a totality including him, refashions himself as the producer of his own world: a partial, momentary, and provisional world."[4] For Starobinski, in other words, the critics of Voltaire's supposedly bourgeois ideology disfigure his position when they equate it with the triumphalism associated with ideologies of science and progress, which are themselves rooted far more in the nineteenth and twentieth centuries than in the eighteenth. The world this ethic of personal labor for the common good might create is, to use Starobinski's terms, partial, momentary, and provisional. Unlike the mastered determinisms of the universe imagined by scientism, the world Voltaire recognizes is a world of chance and change, a world where men may be the collaborators but never the victors of chance.

Zadig tells the story of how one man vanquished the illusion of chance and became king of his country. *Candide* tells the story of how the shards of one man's world came to be washed up with him on the perilous shores of a distant country. This change signals Voltaire's recognition of chance as a force savaging the world and rendering impossible the calm centrality of any single, unified character within a well-told story. Candide, unlike Zadig, is one character among many. Hardly the wisest and hardly the bravest, he reflects on his experience, shares his thoughts with others, and listens carefully to their responses. The novel closes with a version of its opening: the now discredited mentor and the now incredulous pupil halfheartedly discuss yet again the enigma of chance and necessity.

Five years later Voltaire reopened the question of chance in a context evoking both *Candide* and *Zadig*. In his *Dictionnaire philosophique* (1764), in an entry whose title "Destin" clearly evokes *Zadig*'s subtitle "La Destinée," Voltaire chose to address the problem of chance by contrasting two mutually exclusive attitudes toward it: "The peasant believes it has hailed on his field by chance [par hasard]; but the philosopher knows that there is no chance and that it would have been impossible, by reason of the world's very constitution, for it not to have hailed on this day in this place."[5] The simple peasant is convinced that it was by chance that hail destroyed his field. The wise philosopher, on the contrary, knows two things: first, and most definitely, that chance does not exist; second, and most abstractly, that the entire history of the world has predetermined, from the first second of creation, that hail was to fall in that place on that day.

The peasant sees his world as a fragmented locus of constant danger where the labor of an entire season can be wiped away in a few short moments. But not always. Sometimes. By chance. Were he to describe his world, it would necessarily be through a story, a series of simple pasts abruptly stating what happened first, and then next, and then after that. His part in the story would limit itself to his resolve to accept whatever comes, good or bad, and move on to the next cycle of planting and harvesting with a minimum of wasted effort. The philosopher, however, accepts no such fragmentation, but sees the world as the unified expression of a single principle. Whatever has happened had to happen. There is, for the philosopher, no story to tell, no circumstantial sequence of events worth recounting. There is only a system to analyze, a theory to elaborate, and a unity to admire.

In this text of 1764, Voltaire approaches the riddle of chance, not by presenting what might be called his position on the question, but by accepting it as irresolvable, as the subject of an endless debate within every human consciousness between two attitudes here identified with the peasant and the philosopher. To be fully lucid on this subject is to continue within one's consciousness the debate between these two opposing voices. Were either to fall silent, the individual would be left with the uncomfortable alternative of becoming either a Manichean like Martin and renouncing all attempts to understand the world or a systematic philosopher like Pangloss and assuming all the dogmatic pomposity of his refusal to recognize the real. Voltaire sees balance, sanity, and truth as lying neither with the peasant nor with the philosopher, neither with Martin nor with Pangloss. The truth of the human condition is an oscillation between these two poles, an internalized dialogue between these two voices with each ironically relativizing the proclamations of the other. In the paragraph following his evocation of this eternal debate, Voltaire ironizes even the title of his entry by describing those who would refuse that dialogue as "people destined to reason badly" (166). Developing his thoughts on chance and destiny, Voltaire abandons more and more completely the univocal position of any single voice claiming to master the subject and composes his entry in the *Dictionnaire philosophique* as a dialogue between two voices locked in a forever irresolvable argument: "I necessarily have a passion to write this, as you have a passion to condemn me. Both of us are equally fools, equally toys of fate" (167).

To tell the story of chance was for Voltaire in 1747 to tell the story of a philosopher-king whose last lesson is the absurdity of any such notion. Twelve years later that same story has become for him a tale of ruined dreams and distant exile. In a world devastated by forces beyond human control, certainty has become impossible. His ironizing of any single position one might take—Martin's as well as Pangloss's—left only the option of an oscillation between the positions of the peasant and the philosopher, of the tale teller and the system builder, but only so long as the voice of the one continually qualified that of the other. *Candide* is rife with tale tellers, but they are interrupted by those who would philosophize. *Candide* is rife with philosophers, but they are interrupted by those who would tell their stories. On the last page of the novel even Pangloss, the arch-systematizer, evokes not just one tale but a potential infinity of tales—those of Eglon, Absalon, Nadab, Ela, and all the way up to Henri IV—telling of kings, perhaps even Zadig, who took power only to be dethroned and killed. But before he can begin any of them, he is interrupted by Candide's "I know too that we have to cultivate our garden" (221).

Voltaire's response to the problem of chance through a dialogue of oppositions mutually relativizing each other is at the core of his contribution to the development of the novel. Even the preferred labels for his narrative works, *roman philosophique* and *conte philosophique*, testify to how closely he is identified with a combining of discursive forms usually seen as mutually exclusive: narrative and philosophical exposition. Voltaire's importance to the history of the novel lies in his development of a continually self-ironizing discourse. His growing concern with the question of chance, no longer as laughable superstition but as insoluble problem, led him to reject what had been *Zadig*'s centering of the narrative on the triumph of a single character. The ferocity of chance's sway in *Candide* is such that no single character can assume responsibility for the work's meaning. The insolubility of chance's enigma meant that what this novel "says" can no longer be identified with the voice of any single character. Whatever perception of truth *Candide* generates comes as the result of its narrative isometrics, its ironic balancing of voice against voice.

Yet no story can content itself with simply mirroring the world's chaos. To tell only the story of chance would be to sacrifice narrative's status as a vehicle of meaning, as a communication between author and reader. Any representation of unalloyed chance strikes at the very raison d'être of the novel as a form. Voltaire's taming of chance, his subordinating it to the needs of novelistic representation, was accomplished through a constant ironizing of his own narrative discourse. On the one hand, all the horrors of war, rape, slavery, and earthquakes, as well as religious and political tyranny, are portrayed in the fullness of their chaotic violence. On the other, that representation is enclosed within a second level of authorial discourse continually winking at its readers, beckoning them to understand what is never directly stated and thus consolidating a hidden and all the more seductive communication between author and reader. The predatory recruiters convince Candide to accept his enlistment stipend with the words, "We would never allow someone like you to be without money. Men are created to help one another" (140). One moment in the carnage of battle is described as follows: "The musketry removed from the best of worlds approximately nine or ten thousand scoundrels who infected its surface. Bayonets then provided the sufficient reason for the death of a few thousand more" (141). As they try to ward off a second earthquake, the Lisbon authorities decide that "the spectacle of a few persons burned over a slow fire in great ceremony is an infallible secret for keeping the earth from quaking" (149). A palace revolution in Constantinople has the result that "this news of this catastrophe was on everyone's lips for a few hours" (220). These are only a few of the more obvious examples of Voltaire's constant inscription within his narrative of a second level of ironic comment assuring his readers that no matter how chaotic and absurd the events recounted, the story they are reading is firmly under the control of an authorial consciousness separate from and superior to the chaos of character and story.

Candide is important to the history of the novel for its unparalleled recognition of chance in all its forms. Yet this vision of the world's irrationality, of the absence within its workings of any unified causality, could only be narrated by domesticating the very savagery of chance it represents. Voltaire's all-encompassing irony allowed him to preserve *Candide*'s didacticism while, as the myriad interpretations of "Il faut travailler notre jardin" attest, never stating precisely what lesson he would teach. Voltaire was able to express the full force of events, their domination of all who experience them, and at the same time reassure his readers by offering them refuge in their complicity with an ironic but never directly stated perception of the narrated events.

Voltaire's irony opens the way to that form of the novel we associate more frequently with the nineteenth century than with the eighteenth. It is with authors such as Stendhal and Flaubert that we find the most complete exploitation of the twin implications of Voltairian irony. On the one hand, the invitation to the reader to participate in a hidden complicity sustained by the ironies of the authorial voice will become the cornerstone of a practice of reading as connoisseurship that anticipates Stendhal's definition of his audience as the elite of the Happy Few. On the other, the qualifying parentheses of authorial irony make possible the intense identification between narrative voice and character that will one day allow Flaubert to claim, "Madame Bovary, c'est moi."

Candide tells the story of a world given over to chance, of a world beyond malefic as well as beneficent human control. What escapes this reign of chance, however, and at the same time makes possible its narrative portrayal is Voltaire's practice of irony, his hollowing out of a space within the rush of events for the affirmation of a consciousness able, if not to eliminate, at least to recognize, denounce, and struggle against the moral insignificance of chance. It is in this that Voltaire is most eminently a man of the Enlightenment.

8

Writing of No Consequence:
Vivant Denon's *Point de lendemain*

*Vous me feriez croire que je suis un homme
sans conséquence.*
—VIVANT DENON, *Point de lendemain*

Few literary works capture more succinctly or with more
panache what was at stake in the Enlightenment's refusal
of chance than does Vivant Denon's *Point de lendemain*.
First published in 1777, hardly twenty pages long, it tells
the story of one night as a moment in time severed from
history, of a moment with no tomorrow and no yesterday.
One evening, as the young narrator waits for his mistress
to join him in her box at the Opera, he is swept up by the
beautiful Madame de T—— in an adventure that will take
them to a mysterious château outside Paris, where, to their
mutual surprise, they make love deliciously and repeatedly. At every turn of this unexpected excursion, convention and chance, *société* and *hasard,* mutually redefine each
other. When the story ends the following morning, everything appears to remain the same, but nothing is as it was.

Point de lendemain centers on what it means for a person
or an event to be *sans conséquence*. It asks whether being of
no consequence is in fact a narrative possibility. Rooted
in the past participle of the Latin *cum-sequi,* 'consequence'
designates that which follows closely from something else.
The word's history is that of a progressive strengthening
of the link between the events to the point where the conse-

quence is now seen as following from its cause with absolute necessity.

Point de lendemain speaks of how an awareness of consequences, the agreement as to what must follow what, constitutes the definition of any society. To be a person of no consequence, *une personne sans conséquence,* is not only to be of no importance but to act in such a way as to stand scandalously outside the social contract holding the community together through its implicit designations of causes and effects, actions and consequences. As the story of a moment defined as inconsequential, this text describes a utopia—the impossible dream of a moment cut off from past and future, of a now with no tomorrow to extend its implications beyond the present of the event's occurrence. In tracing the undoing of that utopia, this story speaks not only of how society enforces its vision of the consequential but of how chance, as a momentary, unexpected, and inconsequential surprise, opens up new temporalities of experience, memory, and writing.

This short text presents itself as the first-person memoir of a man who is never given a name. Its opening is a tour de force of disabused self-analysis whose staccato alternation of imperfect and simple past summarizes all the illusions and self-deceptions that were so much a part of the eighteenth century's conventional *libertinage:* "J'aimais éperdument la Comtesse de ——; j'avais vingt ans, et j'étais ingénu; elle me trompa, je me fâchai, elle me quitta. J'étais ingénu, je la regrettai; j'avais vingt ans, elle me pardonna: et comme j'avais vingt ans, que j'étais ingénu, toujours trompé, mais plus quitté, je me croyais l'amant le mieux aimé, partant le plus heureux des hommes. (I was madly in love with the Countess de ——; I was twenty years old and I was naive; she betrayed me, I became angry, she left me. I was naive, I missed her; I was twenty years old, she forgave me. And as I was twenty years old, and naive, still betrayed, but no longer alone, I esteemed myself the most beloved suitor and even the happiest of men.)"[1] One evening, while patiently waiting for his mistress at the Opera, the narrator is summoned by the woman in the next box, the comtesse's good friend, Madame de T——. With no explanation, Madame de T—— issues an order lifting him out of the Opera's social ritual and plunging him into the uncharted space of chance. To Madame de T——'s leading question, "Do you by chance [par hasard] have plans for this evening?" the narrator, suspecting he has been stood up by his mistress, is well advised to answer in the negative. They leave the Opera together on a late-night ride taking them to a château on the banks of the Seine that belongs to Madame de T——'s estranged husband. The narrator, who knows Madame de T—— only vaguely as an acquaintance of the comtesse and as the faithful mistress of a certain marquis, discovers that he has been chosen by this woman to serve as her "companion" during the first evening she will spend with the husband from whom she has been separated for over eight years. The trip to the château is part of an official reconciliation that has been planned for over six months.

For the narrator, this evening and everything it brings are products of chance. For Madame de T——, it would seem, the opposite is true: her choice of the narrator at the Opera was the single as yet undetermined element within a carefully laid plan. Once she had chosen him, she dispatched two servants with messages, one to the narrator's home with word that he would not be returning, the second, instructed in whispers the narrator could not hear, to a destination unknown to him. It is only the next morning, at the end of the story, and to the narrator's great surprise, that he discovers to whom that second message was sent: to the marquis, Madame de T——'s lover, telling him that he should arrive, as if by chance, at her husband's château early the next morning. The whole scenario, from Madame de T——'s perspective, is a carefully constructed ruse to mislead her husband, to have him assume that the narrator is her current lover and, when the narrator returns to Paris the morning after their arrival, that his wife has properly deferred to the spirit of their reconciliation.

The happily reunited couple can then receive the undoubtedly longer visit of the marquis—who just happened to be passing their way.

Madame de T—— enters the story as the careful planner, as someone who pays close attention to and deftly manipulates all the appearances demanded by society. What her plan does not anticipate, however, is chance's power to upset all plans, to confront her with an experience that will redefine her relation to the lover whose arrival she has so carefully prepared. This mutual yet unsynchronized experience of chance begins for the hastily thrown-together couple soon after the second change of horses in their hurried journey away from Paris. Drawn by the beauty of the moonlit countryside, the narrator and Madame de T—— lean toward the open window of their speeding coach, when a chance movement upsets their balance: "As we leaned toward the same door, the lurching of the coach led to Madame de T——'s face and my own touching. In that unexpected movement she grasped my hand, and I, by the purest chance [par le plus grand hasard du monde], held her in my arms" (386–87).

What is planned and what happens by chance? Whose plan is in fact being executed? To make a plan like Madame de T——'s is to declare oneself the master of chance, and it is to that power that she now accuses the narrator of making a claim: "Is it your plan [votre projet] to convince me of the imprudence of what I have decided on [ma démarche]?" (387). To her accusation that his *projet* is threatening her *démarche*, the narrator unconvincingly protests that he is innocent of any consequential intention, that his movement was not part of a plan but an involuntary response to the unforeseeable shock of chance: "Plans . . . with you . . . how foolish that would be! You would see them coming far too much in advance. But a chance movement, a surprise [un hasard, une surprise] . . . that can be forgiven" (387).

Chance can destroy the most carefully laid plans. But chance can also itself become the basis of a plan extending and consolidating whatever temporary advantages it might offer. After a predictably cold reception and huffy good-night from the surprised husband, the narrator and Madame de T—— take an evening walk together in the château's gardens. Madame de T—— concedes as they sit together on the lawn that perhaps she should not have presumed an ulterior motive on the part of a man she knows to be devoted to his mistress, the comtesse. Sensing his opening, the narrator hazards a quibble sure to push Madame de T—— in precisely that direction first opened up by the chance moment in the moving coach:

> "I gathered nonetheless," I said to her, "that the surprise of a moment ago did not terribly upset you."
> "I am not so easily alarmed."
> "But I still fear it has left you some misgivings."
> "What would it take to reassure you?"
> "Can't you guess?"
> "I'd like to be enlightened."
> "I need to be sure you forgive me."
> "And for that I should . . . ?"
> "Grant me the kiss that chance [le baiser que le hasard] . . ."
>
> (388–89)

With geography mirroring desire, the narrator's story is that of a movement from a public to a private space, from an open to a hidden and protected space. Madame de T—— and the narrator move from the public arena of the Paris Opera to a coach leaving the city, to a country château, to its garden, and to the grassy bank on which they kiss until Madame de T—— abruptly decides they must return to their separate rooms in the château.

But they do not. Just as they are about to reenter the château, Madame de T—— changes her mind and instead leads the narrator down another darkened path toward a small pavilion for which Madame de T—— does not have the key—but which turns out to have been left open. This pavilion, by chance unlocked, becomes a space beyond *projets* and *démarches*, beyond any plan establishing one as mas-

ter and the other as instrument. Their entering the pavilion is their entry into a realm where there reigns only the
power of desire as a force born of chance to which both
are equally subject: "We shuddered as we entered. This
was love's sanctuary. It possessed us; our knees buckled;
our weakening arms wrapped around each other, and, unable to hold each other up, we fell onto a canapé off to
one corner of the temple" (392). Outside the consequentiality of any plan, their lovemaking defies linguistic representation. As an act taking them beyond the categories of
planner and manipulated, of active and passive, of taking
and giving, of victory and defeat, it provokes a linguistic
representation pointing to the inadequacy for its expression of language's conventional oppositions: "If, on the
one hand, we wished to give what had been taken [donner
ce qu'on a laissé prendre], on the other we wished to receive what had been stolen [recevoir ce qui fut dérobé];
and both of us hastened to obtain a second victory confirming our having been conquered [une seconde victoire
pour s'assurer de sa conquête]" (392).

The final stage of the couple's journey into the unantici-
pated takes them from the pavilion on the bank of a mean-
dering river to the château's most secret space: the *cabinet
secret* Monsieur de T—— built for his wife when they were
first married. To enter this room is not so much to move
from one point in space to another as to step outside space,
to lose one's basic sense of a continuity between the here
and the there, of any link between where I was and where
I am, between past and present: "The door closed and I
could no longer make out how I had entered. I saw only
an ethereal grove which, with no exit, seemed neither to
give on nor lead anywhere [ne tenir et ne porter sur rien]"
(397). A masterpiece of indirect lighting and trompe l'oeil,
this *cabinet secret* is, with its portico and temple consecrated
to the goddess of love, the perfect replica of a classical
grove, complete with altar, chalice, garlands, grass under-
foot, and the beckoning mouth of a dark grotto. If the

room succeeds so completely in imposing its effect, it is because rather than imitating any physical materiality beyond its self-enclosed confines, it is constructed according to a technique of complete illusion: the room's four walls are mirrors onto which images of the objects represented have been carefully painted. Eye and mind are completely fooled.

The story's journey away from the socialized visibility of the Opera toward the removed, the hidden, and the secret becomes complete as the couple arrive in this *cabinet secret* at the château's center. The room achieves its effect through a self-sustaining multiplication of perspectives making the visitor simultaneously aware of how real everything appears and how false everything is. A lesson in the chemistry of illusion, the parallel mirrors multiply and consolidate every image they project until "they create the illusion of everything they represent" (397).

This world of the mirrored room is preeminently a world of no consequence. Once embarked on the illusion of its infinity, time and space are annulled. Lifting its occupants outside temporality and change, the secret room becomes the symbol of confinement within a pure present of chance, desire, and *jouissance* bringing with them the couple's abstraction from all obligations of socialized reciprocity: "Neither of us had any right to demand anything, to ask for anything" (389). The trip from the Opera to the secret room abolishes society's insistence on the consequential, the responsible, and the determined. To live within society is to live within the realm of consequence, of a remembered past heavy with implications for the future. The seduction of the mirrored room lies in the way its walls offer no breach through which society's anonymous and objectifying gaze might discover and record the events occurring there. The real sweetness of this stolen evening comes from its leaving the narrator and Madame de T—— free of consequences and obligation. At liberty to continue or abolish this pure present of chance, they discover a pleasure uncontaminated by the rules and reciprocities of the social, "pleasure without the slowness, bother, or tyranny of its rituals" (394).

Vivant Denon's life stands as a symbol of the always ambiguous border between the consequential and the inconsequential, between society's insistence that there *is* some overarching coherence within its preferences and advancements and the individual's inability to experience his social position as anything other than the chance-driven product of the most obvious and overwhelming incoherence. Better known as a diplomat and art historian than as a writer, Denon was in one sense most emphatically a "man of consequence," a man of importance and power in his world. Director of the Cabinet royal des médailles and finally the director general of all French museums, his professional career from the 1770s to his retirement in 1815 covered a half-century whose convulsive political changes were such that to have remained throughout them a man of consequence, he was most certainly and in the most profound sense of the word a man of no consequence—a man unhampered by what more pedestrian minds would see as the necessary consequences of earlier actions and commitments.

Vivant de Non, as he was known before the Revolution, was a member of the minor provincial nobility. He first made his way at the court of Louis XV by placing himself each day at some point along the king's route where he was likely to stop until, finally, he was acknowledged and eventually given his first position—this with no small help from Madame de Pompadour and other ladies of the court who had nicknamed him "le faune." At the outbreak of the Revolution he quickly returned to Paris from his diplomatic post in Italy so as to dissociate himself from the antirevolutionary émigrés. His connections with the painter David secured him a commission to design a uniform to be worn by all civil servants in France, and that austere project in turn gave him the occasion to meet and win the esteem of Robespierre—whose friendship protected the now Monsieur Denon throughout even the most turbulent days of the Terror. Legend has it that it was while attending a ball at the home of another eminent survivor, Talleyrand, that Denon happened to make the acquaintance of a young and then unknown general. Hearing the officer ask for a glass of *limonade,* Denon offered the man the glass he had just poured for himself. Their ensuing conversation, thanks to Denon's charm, led to his lasting friendship with Napoleon. In 1798 he asked Denon to accompany him on his expedition to Egypt, and four years later Denon published his famous *Voyage dans la Basse et Haute Egypte,* the much-translated first revelation to the European audience of the richness and diversity of Egyptian art. In 1803 Napoleon named Denon director general of the museums of France. Eleven years later, after Waterloo, his luck still held when Louis XVIII continued him in that position. Living in times that favored the most profound meditations on the necessity or chance with which one event followed another, Denon was well placed to speak of chance's power to redefine all that was once thought to be the necessary consequence of a given state or action.

Point de lendemain's severed interlude with Madame de T—— is not one of unalloyed pleasures for the young narrator. The lesson of chance speaks also of society's struggle against it and how its consequentialities have already affected what the narrator thought to be the freest and most personal dimension of his life. As the narrator begins his story, he presents himself as a man sure of his mistress's devotion and his own happiness. His description of that happiness is, however, infused with a retrospective irony born of everything the evening will teach him. What the narrator has taken to be the fetching impetuosity behind his mistress's minor and supposedly past indiscretions was,

Madame de T—— reveals as they speak in the château gardens, a carefully calculated ruse carried out precisely for its social consequences. The comtesse, as Madame de T—— describes her, is the perfect dissembler: "She is happiest in that little game when she can feign everything while remaining completely uninvolved" (391). Her entire relation with the narrator, Madame de T—— makes clear, was born not of any desire the narrator may have inspired but of a carefully calculated role she chose to play for an audience extending far beyond their couple: "When she became involved with you, it was to distract two particularly imprudent rivals who were on the brink of creating a scandal. She had been too accommodating with both of them, and they had noticed it. They would have ended up unmasking her. But then she brought you onto the scene, distracted them with her interest in you, set them off on new investigations, drove you to despair, pitied you, consoled you, and all four of you were happy!" (391).

Madame de T——'s revelation is all the more unsettling because, it would seem, she too has chosen the narrator not for himself but as a function of two other men: the estranged husband she must meet that evening and the lover scheduled to arrive the next morning. The parallelism between these two situations breaks down, however, as Madame de T——'s chance choice of the narrator has the unexpected effect of creating for them a freedom of speech and action, as well as a potential for understanding and pleasure, otherwise excluded by the duplicity of the charade the comtesse is playing out for society.

If the narrator is able to write this story as someone no longer the dupe of the illusions he describes, it is because his apprenticeship of chance has brought with it a crisis of knowledge, a pervasive doubt as to his ability to distinguish between truth and illusion. Each turn of the story brings with it an experience that fractures the preexisting categories of his understanding. During his walk in the garden the morning after his night with Madame de T——, the narrator's hope is that the fresh air and early daylight will dissipate his confusion and allow him to return to the truth, order, and sense of consequentiality he believed in before his encounter with chance: "I could feel my soul touching truth once again, my thoughts untroubled and *following each other in order* [se suivre avec ordre]. I could breath at last" (398, emphasis mine). No sooner, however, does he begin to feel this return of security than he is again put off balance by a simple but unanswerable question: Is he now Madame de T——'s lover? And what would that status imply? Unable to respond, he discovers that he is no longer sure of anything—not of Madame de T—— and her relation to the marquis, not of his own relation to the comtesse, not even of whether he is awake or dreaming. "What an adventure! What a night! I could not tell if I was still dreaming or not. I doubted, then I was persuaded, certain. And then I didn't believe any of it" (399). Everything he has discovered about life and chance leads him to suspect that what he imagines to be his more penetrating vision may be nothing more than a change of blindfolds: "I felt as though someone had removed a blindfold from my eyes but that I had not noticed the one replacing it" (391).

Chance takes its fiercest revenge against those who would define themselves as beyond its power, those who claim to manipulate it as one more instrument in their arsenal of deception. It was by design that Madame de T—— chose a companion for the evening. But it was by chance that her specific choice of the narrator led to a movement of desire and pleasure initiating another story, unwriteable by the narrator, of how that chance event will go on to affect her relation to her lover, the marquis.

The marquis, too, presents himself as a master of chance, as someone using it as a camouflage for his careful strategy when he meets the narrator in the château garden the next morning: "Everything has been planned. Pure chance seems to have brought me here, as I am supposed to be returning from a visit to the nearby countryside" (399). The marquis, delighted that the coach trip has given the narrator an occasion to know and admire Madame de T——, insists on what their liaison says about him: "Can you imagine that any man could make that woman settle down? It wasn't easy, but I have molded her character to the point where she may well be the one woman in Paris on whose fidelity one can count absolutely" (400). No one, of course, is better placed to appreciate the dubious implications of that claim than the narrator. Swept up by his self-congratulation, the marquis magisterially concedes that Madame de T—— does have one defect: "Between us, I have discovered only one failing in her. Nature, in granting her everything, refused her that divine flame which would crown all her blessings. She inspires everything, makes you feel everything, yet she feels nothing. She is a statue" (400). The narrator, quite unaware of any such flaw—but hardly for the reasons the marquis assumes—fights his laughter by replying, "But . . . you know her as though you were her husband" (400). The marquis's fatuous lament, given what narrator and reader know, becomes an involuntary joke unleashing a laughter that the narrator must control but the reader can freely enjoy.

Embarked on an adventure of chance, the narrator of *Point de lendemain* tells the story of how he lost the innocence of believing in his mistress's love yet simultaneously discovered the intense pleasure he has momentarily shared with Madame de T——. The narrator's ultimate response to this experience is to write the story we are reading. Dictated by chance, it is, as its brevity testifies, a narrative outside narrative. Its story is that of how for one evening the laws, continuities, and consequences of society's intermeshing narratives were suspended. At the story's end, every character occupies a position different from what he or she had originally expected or connived at. Monsieur de T—— has begun a reconciliation with his wife on terms decidedly different from those he had sought. Madame de T—— has found herself far more enchanted by her choice of an evening's companion than she had ever intended. The marquis as secret lover finds himself the unwitting double of the cuckolded husband.

If *Point de lendemain* holds a lesson for the reader, it is one implicit in Madame de T——'s parting words to the perplexed narrator. Addressing his earlier concern regarding what the consequences for him of their night together might be, she whispers: "Goodby, Sir. I owe you many pleasures, but I have repaid you with a beautiful dream" (402). Unexpected pleasure for her; a dream come true for him. But, she makes clear, true pleasure and fulfilled dreams exist only within the exquisite brevity and self-contained temporality of a chance moment cut off from the social. The story's real lesson comes in the narrator's realization that he must stop asking questions and refrain from trying to prolong chance's momentary and inconsequential joys by making them part of a space and time extending beyond the here and now. To prolong chance is to integrate it within the social and, in so doing, sacrifice it to a collective and consequential judgment resurrecting all the deadening charades and impostures of the Paris they have momentarily left behind.

The narrator learns from Madame de T—— that chance's intensity can be prolonged only within the utterly personal idioms of memory and writing. To write the story we read is, as the narrator discovered in Madame de T——'s mirrored room, to renounce whatever reality it might represent and, on the basis of that renunciation, discover a far greater power to preserve and express it as a textualized challenge to the solidity and consequence of the socialized self. *Point de lendemain* confirms the wisdom of how the narrator first overcame his discomfort at finding himself leaving the Opera with a beautiful but unknown woman: "I began to laugh at the role I was playing, and we became quite gay [et nous devînmes très gais]" (386).

9

The Moment's Notice:
Crébillon's Game of Libertinage

*Si vous saviez de plus à quel point je raconte mal
dans un lit, vous ne voudriez sûrement pas
m'y transformer en historien.*
—CRÉBILLON *fils, La Nuit et le moment*

There is little the characters in Crébillon *fils*'s novels would
rather do than gamble. Most of their bets turn, of course,
on the feminine virtue and masculine honor staked or
bluffed as they maneuver each other toward an alcove, a
sofa, or "one of those large armchairs as favorable to te-
merity as they are suited to indulgence [aussi favorables à
la témérité que propres à la complaisance]."[1] With surprising regularity, however, key events in Crébillon's novels
play themselves out around the less lubricious but equally
risky perimeter of the card table—an emblem of the socialized yet threatening *hasard* at the core of Crébillon's esthetic.

Crébillon's dialogue-novel *Le Hasard du coin du feu* takes
place entirely in Célie's bedroom, where, on a cold winter
day, she and the duc de Clerval spend a long afternoon
trying to seduce each other. Célie will yield only if Clerval
first tells her he loves her. Clerval, however, insists that at
least at the level of *le coeur,* his fidelity to his current mistress precludes any such statement. Early on in their conversation Clerval asks Célie if she herself was ever young
and naive enough to have actually believed that the "love"
she so insists on hearing about could ever deliver the eter-

nities it promises. His question prompts Célie to tell the story of her first lover. Norsan, Célie is forced to admit, had carefully calculated every stage of her seduction. And it was the social ritual of the card game that allowed him to force from her, at the level of gesture, the same declaration she would now withhold from Clerval: "We decided to play a game of brelan, and he all too easily forced me to accord to each of his actions that anxious and concerned attention which I have never known to be without danger for us, and which is itself perhaps the first symptom of love" (199–200).

Berland, or more commonly brelan, was an immensely popular card game of the period. Usually played by three or five players, it is deceptively simple. The players, after receiving a three-card hand, are free to bet, fold, or raise according to how strong they feel their hands to be. The best hand is the *brelan,* in the other sense of the word, which French retains today: triplets, or three cards of the same value—three aces, three kings, and so forth. If, as was usually the case, no player holds a brelan, the winner is the person holding the highest aggregate point count in a single suit, with aces counting as eleven, all picture cards as ten, and the other cards at their face value. This count is made, however, only after all the players remaining in the game after the betting and raising have placed their cards face up on the table so that those holding the highest card in each suit can take from their opponents' hands all the cards in that same suit. Played with unlimited raises, brelan was described in Diderot and d'Alembert's *Encyclopédie* in terms that made it the perfect symbol of the kind of seduction Norsan was carrying out: "a cruel game in that one is rarely able to bet only what one wishes."[2]

The *Encyclopédie*'s entry on brelan is surprisingly long, taking up almost two full columns. The entry alternates between an enthusiastic description of the game's simple but fascinating structure and a warning of just how dangerous the game can be: "There is perhaps no game of chance more terrifying yet more attractive. It is hard to play it without becoming obsessed with it; and once possessed, one has no taste for other games."

Brelan is a game, but it is "the most terrifying" game. And it is so terrifying precisely because it is "the most attractive." To play brelan once is to risk becoming obsessed with the fast-moving, constantly changing, high-stakes world it creates around itself. The game's danger lies in its power to transform what began as a moment's diversion into a "fury," a "possession" rendering everything else dull and insipid. There is something monstrous about brelan's simple beauty, because it subverts the very concept of the game. As an entertaining diversion, it is meant to turn the players' minds away from the worries of real life and restore them through play within the fictive universe of the game. The world of the game is momentary; the real world is continuous. Brelan is dangerous and monstrous because the intensely thrilling perils of the moments it creates tempt us to forget their transience and seek instead to extend them as far as possible toward the continuous.

Crébillon's best-known work, the memoir-novel *Les Egarements du coeur et de l'esprit*, likewise tells a story punctuated by card games where everything is staked and won, staked and lost. It is during a card game in her home that Madame de Lursay, secretly worshiped by the young Meilcour, overcomes her scruples at taking the first step with a younger man and reveals the affection Meilcour feels he must be certain of before he can overcome his timidity. "We sat down to cards. During the entire game Madame de Lursay, doubtless more susceptible than she believed and carried away by her love, gave all the strongest signs of it [her love]. It seemed prudence had abandoned her, that nothing now existed for her other than the pleasure of loving me and telling me so, and that she foresaw how much, if she were to beguile me, I needed to be reassured."[3]

Later in the novel, after a chance meeting at the Opera has led Meilcour to fall in love with the young Hortense de Théville and abandon his suit of Madame de Lursay, it is around the same card table that, in no more time than it takes to turn a card, the whole of Meilcour's stake on the *belle inconnue* is swept away by her rival: "Our eyes met. The languor I saw in hers fixed in my heart the effect her charms had initiated and whose force seemed to grow with each instant. The few sighs she seemed to only half utter completed my overthrow, and at that dangerous moment, she benefited from all the love I felt for that unknown woman" (108).

The novel's final scene is also built around a game of cards, a game recapitulating in miniature the back and forth, beckoning and repelling, understanding and mistrusting movement of the entire novel. Now completely smitten with Hortense and duped by the jaded Versac's lies about Madame de Lursay's past, Meilcour returns to her home only because he hopes to find Hortense there. While many guests are present, Hortense is not, and Madame de Lursay is engaged in a card game. Seeing Meilcour, she plays her cards in such a way that the new arrival receives exactly the message she wishes to communicate: "I was seated next to her, and from time to time she commented on the strange hands she was being dealt, but in a detached way. There was so much gaiety in her eyes, and her wit seemed so free, that I had no doubt she had forgotten me" (261–62).

The finesse with which Madame de Lursay masks her true feelings generates for Meilcour a moment of self-discovery within chance that captures the very essence of the Crébillonesque scenario. Suspecting that Lursay may be feigning her lack of interest in him, Meilcour decides to study her closely as she plays. It is precisely as he is taken in and becomes certain he is not being fooled by any feigned indifference on Madame de Lursay's part that he becomes the dupe of his own unsuspected feelings: "To get to the bottom of the matter I studied her carefully. The more surely my scrutiny convinced me her change was real, the more I felt diminish the joy that thought had first brought me" (263). Madame de Lursay invites Meilcour to join the game, to take a hand alongside the marquis de ———, to whom she has been paying particular attention. Once the game resumes, she leaves little doubt who is the desired partner and who the dummy: "Each time I glanced at her I found her eyes fixed on the marquis, and she no sooner noticed my attention in observing her than she quickly brought them back to her cards, as though I were the person from whom she most wanted to hide her feelings [comme si c'eût été à moi surtout qu'elle eût voulu cacher ses sentiments]" (264). As the stakes rise, Meilcour's own play becomes an index of the success of Madame de Lursay's stratagem: "I could not help showing signs of an impatience she knew very well was not my usual reaction to gambling and which I could thus hardly blame on it" (265). Thanks to Lursay's consummate feints, all the pieces are now in place for the game's and the novel's final confrontation, one that will be played out alone by Meilcour and Madame de Lursay after the other guests have left.

Gambling is a privileged activity in Crébillon's novels not only because as social ritual it allows for the communication of nonverbal messages but also because as a conflict of the momentary and the continuous, of what diverts and what obsesses, it is a literal twin to sexual desire as Crébillon's thematics of choice. As a dialectic of the momentary and the continuous, desire provides the organizing polarities of his most popular dialogue-novel, *La Nuit et le moment*. Late one evening, after all her guests have retired, Cidalise is surprised by the arrival in her bedroom of Clitandre. The entire novel consists of the conversation and other activities carried on by these two characters until first light the next morning. At every stage they demonstrate, in the direct present of speech and action, how desire is born, declares itself, and is consummated only to the extent that it disguises itself as what it is not.

Cidalise has chosen her guests carefully: all four of the other women visiting the chateau are former mistresses of Clitandre's. When she expresses her surprise that Clitandre should choose her bedroom as the object of his nocturnal stroll, he replies that those other women are only dim memories from a forgotten past: "Why should anyone imagine that in the midst of everything social life imposes on us, those whom chance, caprice, and circumstance once brought together for a few moments [des gens que le hasard, le caprice, des circonstances ont unis quelques moments] should recall what in fact interested them so little [se souviennent de ce qui les a intéressés si peu]?"[4] Using an *on* that simultaneously depersonalizes his statement and establishes it as a general rule governing society, Clitandre enunciates a philosophy of desire and chance summarizing all the world-weary wisdom of the legions of dissolute ducs, marquis, and chevaliers populating so many novels and plays of early eighteenth-century France:

> We are happy together, we sleep together [On se plaît, on se prend]. And if we grow bored with each other [S'ennuie-t-on l'un avec l'autre]? We separate with no more ceremony than we took each other. Are we happy with each other again? We sleep together again with just as much pleasure as the first time we met. We separate again and never get upset about it. It is true that love has nothing to do with all this; but love—what is it other than a desire we were pleased to exaggerate, a movement of the senses our vanity enjoyed taking as a virtue? (18)

Life and desire are presented as a succession of disjointed moments following one another with no more coherence or continuity than one might expect between cards dealt from a well-shuffled deck.

Speaking in a more personal voice, Clitandre goes on to

insist that his own experience eminently confirms this law. As concerns Julie, for instance, "After all, I only had her one time after a dinner. Can you really call that having a woman?" (102). Had it not been for the heat wave that summer, Julie's state of undress when he arrived, and most of all her blind devotion to the revered physicist Pagny, whose latest lecture she repeated to the effect that—in obvious contradiction to Clitandre's visibly rising excitement— such heat inevitably produces "an annihilation [un anéantissement] . . . caused by an excessive dissipation of the mind and a relaxing of the vital fibers" (104), nothing would have happened between them. If Clitandre provided Julie with "the most furious refutation imaginable of her opinion" (104), it was purely the result of *le hasard* governing this series of chance events over which he exercised no control and for which he bears no responsibility. Speaking of his affair with another of the guests, Araminte, the woman for whom Eraste, Cidalise's former lover, left her, Clitandre repeats that important term: "In returning from our walk, chance [le hasard] led us to pass by a small and dark grove. Equally by chance [Par le même hasard], we had unknowingly separated ourselves from the others" (27).

Clitandre underlines everything that was accidental and ephemeral about his relations with these other women not so much because he would align himself with the promiscuity preached by the societal *on* of the libertine voice but to underline how different is his present with Cidalise from all those past moments. Clitandre's whole seduction of Cidalise turns on his careful manipulation of the period's distinction between desire and love. Characterized by distinct temporalities, desire exists only in the present, lasts only for the moment, and implies nothing about a future it leaves entirely free. Love, on the other hand, redefines the present as the promise of a future assured by the continuity of the lover's passion. Desire celebrates and limits itself to the present moment. Love may begin within the present, but only because that present is the single point of access to an unlimited future giving the present its real meaning.

Within the scenarios of libertinage, love is associated with virtuous women and naive young men; desire with jaded libertines of either sex. The entire plot of *La Nuit et le moment* turns on Cidalise's self-deceiving attempts to convince herself that in yielding to Clitandre, she is responding not to his desire but to his love. Clitandre's stories of his former affairs are reassuring, not because he seems forever ready to blunder into any arms that open before him, but because he insists that none of those moments of past desire imply any interest continuing into the present he now shares with Cidalise. Clitandre's strategy is to raise the payoff on the clear longshot that he is actually in love to such a level that Cidalise's narcissism can no longer resist betting on the possibility that he is not lying. His portrayal of his sexual past as a random concatenation of meaningless desires generates for Cidalise the flattering image of herself as the one woman who, unlike all those who came before, has been able to inspire true love and true passion. These maneuvers constitute Clitandre's response to Cidalise's insistence that she will surrender herself in the present only if she is convinced that their present is the beginning of a shared future.

Love and desire differ not only in their relation to the future but in the way they relate to the past. Listening to Clitandre's declaration of love, Cidalise raises what, since they have known each other for many years, is a logical objection: "Either you do not love me today or, and I have strong reasons not to believe it, you have loved me for a long time" (58–59). Since Clitandre has already consigned his earlier adventures to the insignificance of random desire, he can reply, "Yes, Madame, I have been in love with you since that happy moment I first saw you" (59). If he did not act on his love earlier, it was because Cidalise was herself involved first with Damis and later with Eraste. Women, especially the woman to whom one is declaring one's love, are assumed to love, and as a supposedly virtuous woman, Cidalise cannot, like Clitandre, blithely dismiss her own past with those other men as nothing more than a series of passing desires. Love requires a reshaping of the past, its renunciation as a lie at last recognized as such thanks to the new light of passion's truth. Cidalise declares to Clitandre: "You cannot know how much I love you! How much I abhor having belonged to anyone else! How I hate you for waiting so long to love me [Combien même je vous hais de m'avoir aimée si tard]!" (87). To portray herself as hating the now beloved Clitandre for not having loved her sooner is symbolic of the heavy paradox and self-deception within which Crébillon's characters continually navigate.

Clitandre may seduce Cidalise, but he must do so on her terms. Those terms, however, never remain entirely her own. Clitandre's final words to Cidalise, spoken as he leaves her bedroom the next morning, capture all the ambiguity of their enterprise: "Adieu, may you, if it is possible, love me as much as you yourself are loved!" (150).

Crébillon's novels all tell different versions of a single story: that of how desire, born of a chance moment, transforms itself into, attempts to transform itself into, or disguises itself as something else—as a love capable of redefining both past and future. In telling this story, in underlining the contrasting temporalities of desire and love, Crébillon's characters ultimately speak not only of the sexual mores of the Regency but of the novel itself and its role within the society it addressed. Understanding what Crébillon's thematics of seduction tells us about the novel as a form might best begin by juxtaposing his treatment of the contrastive temporalities of desire and love with the surprisingly similar version of that opposition offered two centuries later by Jean-Paul Sartre in La Nausée and its critique of the illusions of storytelling. Sartre's Roquentin explains his growing disgust with what he calls "the sublime" through an analysis of how storytelling perverts and misrepresents the most fundamental reality of everything it claims to represent. His critique is developed through an extended contrast between living life and telling a story, between the event and the adventure, between a vision of the self as simply a person and the mythologizing of the self as hero.

In the same way that Clitandre presents his past seductions of Cidalise's houseguests as disconnected chance moments bearing no relation to what came before or after, Roquentin comes to accept the arid truth that life is a series of moments during which "the scenery changes, people come in and go out, that's all. There are never any beginnings. Days are tacked onto days without rhyme or reason in an interminable and monotonous addition."[5] In the same way that Crébillon's illusion of love depends on an imaginary future inflecting every moment of the present, the bad faith Sartre denounces at the core of every "story" implies that "we forget that the future was not there yet, that the guy was walking in a night without signs which offered him its monotonous riches in a jumble and that he made no choices" (62). Life becomes story, its events our adventures, and ourselves its hero only when, as with love's promised future, "it all began with the end. It's there, invisible and present, giving these words all the pomp and value of a beginning" (62). Abstracted from existence as a concatenation of chance-driven moments, life-as-story begins from what it is destined to become rather than from what it happens to be: "The story goes on in reverse, its moments no longer pile up haphazardly [s'empiler au petit bonheur les uns sur les autres], they are drawn along by the end of the story [happés par la fin de l'histoire] as it conjures up each of them as well as the ones preceding it" (62).

Crébillon's novels center on seduction, on how those who see life as a series of chance desires are able to manipulate others whose belief in a (love) story promising continuity, purpose, and meaning marks them as the perfect prey. Crébillon's demystification of love through the oppo-

sition of a self-enclosed present to an illusory future parallels Sartre's indictment of narrative through the oppositions of life to story, event to adventure, and person to
hero. To be seduced is, quite literally, to listen to and believe a story. Crébillon's reflections on seduction through
story thus speak of a danger that extends far beyond the
tragicomic, self-deceptive scenarios of sexual conquest
wherein would-be seducers are always on the prowl for
victims sufficiently naive to accept the pledge of a fictitious
future in return for their present surrender.

Les Egarements du coeur et de l'esprit is perhaps the best
illustration of this danger. Often described as a novel of
initiation, a *Bildungsroman* like Flaubert's *L'Education senti-
mentale* or Joyce's *A Portrait of the Artist*, *Les Egarements* tells
the story of its principal character's worldly education.
And the lesson Meilcour ultimately learns is that of the
failure of all stories. The novel opens with its main character in full possession of a firm and unquestioned sense of
self: "I made my entry into society at the age of seventeen,
with all the advantages that can make a man be noticed
there" (47). If Meilcour knows exactly who and where he
is, it is because his identity is defined by a series of mutually
sustaining stories. Since like all the characters in Crébillon's
novels, he is a noble, his story is in one sense another chapter continuing the already illustrious story of his ancestors.
In Meilcour's case, his dead father has bequeathed him not
only a name but—because he was killed fighting in the
king's service—"a noble name whose renown he himself
had increased" (47). The dead father functions as the biological foundation of two complementary stories: the long-
term, generational history of the family dynasty Meilcour
continues and the short-term but more glorious story of
the feats through which the father distinguished himself
as hero. On the other side of the family, Meilcour's mother
is a source of both material security—"I had expectations
of considerable wealth from my mother" (47)—and the
ongoing story of an unswerving devotion compensating
for what has been lost through the death of the father:

"Beautiful, young, and rich, her tenderness for me led her to imagine no other pleasure than that of educating me and making up for all I had lost in losing my father" (47).

The ensuing 250 pages of this novel, describing a period of roughly two weeks, chip away the certainty and sense of identity with which the work begins. The novel may end with Meilcour and Madame de Lursay understanding each other, but the encounter with Hortense as well as Versac's lies about Lursay deprive that ending of the sense of closure and completed quest so ardently desired by Meilcour in the work's opening pages.

Les Egarements is a memoir-novel, a novel written in the first person by the main character long after the events he narrates. This first-person form allows Meilcour to offer a double perspective on everything he relates. At every point in his narration he retains the option of describing events either as he experienced them at the time of their actual occurrence or, using a retrospective past conditional, as he has since come to understand them from the vantage point of age and wisdom. *Les Egarements* ends with a veritable crescendo of this second perspective, and in order for the readers to understand what actually happened during its final evening, they must deduce it, not from what is actually narrated, but from the abstracted lesson Meilcour draws from his experience. The novel ends with the bankruptcy of what Meilcour had until then accepted as the sum of worldly wisdom: Versac's secret doctrine of society as a locus of universal hypocrisy demanding absolute self-control. As Meilcour first listened to Versac's revelations, he was awed by their unveiling of a previously unsuspected intellectual dimension within this older and worldly-wise man he had so long admired. Versac's extended exposition of how the world really works represents the one "true" story that, along with the earlier stories of paternal distinction and maternal devotion, might be seen as defining Meilcour's future. But the experiences of the two-week period narrated in the novel teach Meilcour something quite different. Looking back on the evening with Madame de

Lursay and how her "extreme connaissance du coeur" (293) allowed her, to his astonishment, to render him "enchanted" with the very woman he had hated only a few moments earlier, Meilcour realizes that a continued adherence to Versac's doctrine, "l'usage du monde," would only have rendered him more corrupt and more vulnerable to manipulation: "The conclusion I draw today is that had I been more experienced, she would only have seduced me more quickly, since what we call knowledge of the world only makes us wiser by making us more corrupt" (293).

With Versac's lesson dismissed as "cette commode métaphysique" (293), Meilcour finds himself cut off from the assurance that would have allowed him to control himself and others. Having lost faith in Versac, he has lost the ability to live life as a story whose assumed ending will provide the significance of each of its episodes. Instead, Meilcour's experiences leave him caught up in an immobilizing oscillation of antithetical feelings: "Exiled from pleasure by remorse, and from remorse by pleasure, I could not for a moment be sure of myself" (294).

The key word in Crébillon's title, *égarement,* is all but impossible to translate into English. 'Distraction' is the term to which most dictionaries resign themselves, usually following it with examples demonstrating the English word's inability to capture the more diverse and serious connotations of the French term. Barbara Bray tried, none too felicitously, to finesse the problem by choosing as the title for her 1967 translation of Crébillon's novel *The Wayward Head and Heart.*[6] Jean Sgard makes the point in speaking of Crébillon's text that "the concept of *égarement* is doubly interesting: it expresses an ambiguous and disconcerting state, a 'trouble,' a 'delirium' defying analysis; and it implies at the same time a norm, as an *égarement* can only exist in relation to a straight path."[7] While Sgard claims that *égarement* implies the existence of an abandoned norm, it is significant that Crébillon modifies his own usage of the word with two adjectival phrases—*du coeur* and *de l'esprit*—which themselves, because they represent opposing principles of human conduct, substantially compromise the possibility of any such single "correct path." *Egarement* is, according to *Le Robert*, derived from the Frankish *warôn*, meaning 'to care for, to safeguard, to secure in a sure place.'[8] *E-garer* thus implies a lost security, a setting off into an uncertainty compromising any defined rectitude.

Les Egarements ends with Meilcour unable to continue as the admiring acolyte of a supposedly all-knowing Versac. He finds himself instead in a state where "I could not *for a moment* be sure of myself" (294, emphasis mine). The concept of *le moment* here alluded to functions throughout Crébillon's work as an emblem of life lived as a sequence of fortuitous events determined only by chance. Earlier, in Clitandre's explanation of his past to Cidalise, we saw its role in the libertine's ever-playful dismissal of personal responsibility. At the close of *Les Egarements,* the term appears again, but now as providing the temporality of the character's far more somber inability to know or master his fate once he is deprived of the security of stories and forced instead onto the uncertain seas of experience and contradiction.

In considering the development of probability theory we saw how, from Pascal to Borel, the most important figures within that science emphasized its power to dismiss chance as an illusion. Presenting their finite permutations of the possible, of what *might* happen next, as perfectly adequate responses to the quite different question of what *will* happen next, the probabilists substituted their mathematical models for the reality they claimed to explain. I rehearse this basic strategy of probability theory because it parallels in important ways what are the distinctive characteristics of Crébillon's novelistic style. His plots usually limit themselves to the simplest situations: in *La Nuit et le moment,* Clitandre has arrived in Cidalise's room and sets out to seduce her; in *Le Hasard du coin du feu,* Célie would insist that Clerval declare he loves her before she yields; in *Les*

Egarements, Madame de Lursay wants the timid Meilcour to take the first step before she reveals her own feelings. The actual texture of Crébillon's novels could be described as an infinitely extensible dialectic between two conflicting views as to what should happen next. One character argues the case for one course of action, while the other parries with a contrasting array of reasons for the alternate course.

Crébillon's narrative technique and the protocols of probability theory share a tendency to postpone indefinitely the actual occurrence of the event by opening up what becomes a potentially infinite space devoted to the analysis of its possible implications. It is precisely for this "overly analytical" or "overly psychological" style that Crébillon has been most consistently criticized. It is his style, far more than his undeserved reputation as a pornographer, that explains why, even today, his importance to the history of the novel remains unacknowledged.

There can be little doubt that Crébillon's style frustrated the reader of his time. Accustomed to the more or less realistic or more or less romanesque representation of a rapidly moving sequence of events, the eighteenth-century reader could only be perplexed by Crébillon's insistence on structuring his novels around the analysis of a static situation whose potential implications were then considered in seemingly infinite detail. This deferral of the novel's forward progress, of any easy movement from event to event, has a number of important effects. At one level, it forces the reader to realize that the standard novelistic diction of an untroubled and expeditious representation of events is an *option* rather than a rule of the genre. At another level, Crébillon's concentration on the interval between events, on the intricacies of his characters' feelings as to whether and why something should or should not be done, emphasizes the potential infinity of interpretation each character brings to a given situation. Crébillon's characters are masters of argument capable of initiating an endless dialectic around almost any question. The pleasure of reading Crébillon lies in admiring how his characters find new ways to surprise, parry, and elude the rhetorical traps they continually set for one another. By forcing his reader to recognize the difference between the event and its analysis, Crébillon emphasizes a disjunction between the two. We may speak, reason, cajole, threaten, and plead all we wish; those acts can never of themselves determine what actually happens next. The event occurs in a realm set off from the endless words spoken by its protagonists. And it is chance and the moment, far more than the characters' words, that determine what actually happens.

In writing his novels as he did, in emphasizing a diction all but antithetical to their form, Crébillon undercut what we saw to be the period's justification of the genre through a claim to didactic realism. The most frequent defense of the novel in the prefaces of the eighteenth century grounded the genre's utility in its power to represent people and events as they actually were within the real world. The novel, as Prévost argued, was a less dangerous and more accessible supplement to experience. Furthermore, the novel's ability to portray evil as punished and virtue as rewarded qualified it as teacher and reformer. Novels set in the real world of their readers could teach men and women how they should act not only morally but in accordance with the secular norms of polite society.

Crébillon subverts any such justification of the novel not so much because his characters are hardly paragons of conventional virtue as because his entire portrayal of how things happen between individuals subverts the effortless and purposeful progression from event to event at the core of the didactic novel. Crébillon's style is particularly intriguing because while it borrows probability theory's analytical bent, it works against the implicit belief in determinism that science shared with the emerging ideology of the novel. In *Les Egarements du coeur et de l'esprit,* all the truly decisive events in those two weeks of Meilcour's life occur by chance: one evening he is smitten with an unknown woman who happens to be seated in the box next to his at the Opera; a few days later he happens to hear that same woman's voice through the labyrinth of the Tuileries. Hurrying along its twisting paths, he positions himself so as to cross her path. Hoping to manipulate that chance encounter to his own ends, he learns instead the sad lesson of the novel's inefficacy as a Prévostian supplement to experience: "I then recalled all the episodes from novels I had read that treated of speaking to one's mistress and was surprised that there was not a single one that was of any use to me" (105). Like probability theory, novels may teach us many things—but their lessons are never quite appropriate to the specific situation at hand.

Even Crébillon's seducers, those characters who are masters at concocting the mini-novels of love's promised future, can be stymied by the specificity of the moment. In *La Nuit et le moment*, Clitandre tells how his affair with Luscinde began the evening he took her home from a dinner at which her lover, Oronte, had not only insulted her but left early and taken her carriage. Clitandre's strategy is based on an excellent analysis of where, given the evening's events, Luscinde is sure to be most vulnerable. What better way to avenge herself on Oronte than a brief affair with Clitandre? The abstract appropriateness of his approach, Clitandre knows, is beyond question. The problem, as always with what is only probable, comes in applying that abstract principle to the specific here and now of the actual situation: "I had no problem convincing her she should avenge herself. But as angry as she was, I could not persuade her so easily as I liked to think I could that she should avenge herself at that very moment [dans le moment même]" (116–17).

All the lessons the novel of experience might teach, like those of probability theory, are circumscribed by an inability to address the *hic et nunc* of this situation at this moment. Toward the end of *Le Hasard du coin du feu*, Clerval reacts to Célie's pouting remorse over her surrender with an explicit and brutal parody of all the supposed reassurance to be found in novelistic and probabilistic representations of reality. Anticipating by a century what would become the dominant discourse of statistics, Clerval cavalierly suggests that the best way for Célie to soothe her conscience would be to situate her indiscretion within the context of the large number: "Do you really find your conduct with me so extraordinary? Alas, what has just happened between us is happening in front of more than a hundred Paris fireplaces at this very moment, and between people who, I assure you, have not nearly as good reasons for it as we" (265). It would be difficult to imagine a strategy more alien to Crébillon's esthetics of the moment's singularity than this offhand dismissal of the couple's specificity in favor of the quantifiable aggregate. What is lost in any such referral to the average is the essence of Crébillon's limitless attention to the delicately comic yet ultimately pathetic interaction of individual desires declaring themselves within a universe ruled by chance.

Anchored in the complexities of the present, Clerval—like Clitandre, Versac, and so many of Crébillon's characters—enacts a scenario of libertinage. It is, however, a *libertinage du moment* whose focus on the fleeting opportunities of the passing instant is distinctly different from that portrayed a half century later by Laclos in *Les Liaisons dangereuses*. While Laclos was certainly influenced by Crébillon—*Le Sopha* was part of Merteuil's warmup reading as she prepared herself to be the hundred women in one for her lover, and many critics have chosen to read Merteuil as a feminine version of Versac—his scenarios of libertinage are always part of projects far larger and more ambitious than those found in Crébillon. When Merteuil and Valmont set out to seduce, sexuality is never an end in itself. A means for achieving something else, sexual conquest in *Les Liaisons* is only one among a number of ploys for controlling another person. And that control of the seduced other is itself more often than not an instrument whose real purpose is a more effective aggression against a third party. One tactic within a larger strategy of domination preceding and completing it, Laclos's libertinage is, in every sense of the word, *un libertinage conséquent*. Crébillon's *libertins*, on the contrary, do not act in terms of a long-range plan but are confined to an acute awareness of everything happening around them as they stand ready to seize every unexpected opportunity. Crébillon's seducers rely, not on a carefully planned strategy, but on the unpredictable luck of the hunter. His Clitandres, Clervals, and Versacs move through their world like stalkers in search of game. Never knowing when or where their quarry will appear, they are always at the ready. The success of their hunt depends on chance, on whether stalker and quarry happen to intersect at the same place at the same moment. Versac goes to Madame de Lursay's only so he can bring with him Monsieur de Pranzi, Lursay's former lover, and thus consolidate her humiliation in Meilcour's eyes. Once there, however, he comes upon a woman he has never seen before: the young and beautiful Hortense de Théville. After only a moment's surprise, he begins a stalk of which no one is more perfectly the master than he: "Surprised that so rare a beauty had so long remained hidden from him, he stared at her in astonishment and admiration. . . . He displayed his charms: he had a good leg and showed it off. He laughed as often as he could so as to show his teeth and assumed the most imposing postures to set his figure off to best advantage and demonstrate its graces" (155–59). In this case his almost comic stalk is unsuccessful, but like the veteran hunter, he is always ready to try.

Crébillon often uses the term *le moment* in its more restricted sense of a specifically feminine susceptibility, often unsuspected by the woman herself, to the maneuvers of seduction.[9] "No one is answerable for the moment; it is a realm where nature acts unhampered [il en est où la nature agit seule]," we read in *L'Ecumoire ou Tanzaï et Néardarné*.[10] Answering Célie's query as to what he means by *le moment*, Clerval responds: "A certain movement of the senses as unexpected as it is involuntary. A woman may hide it, but if it is noticed or sensed by someone interested in taking advantage of it, it puts her in the gravest danger of being more compliant than she believed she should or could be [un peu plus complaisante qu'elle ne croyait ni devoir ni pouvoir l'être]" (209). The element of chance inherent in *le moment* concerns, in other words, not only the objective coordinates of time and space inflecting a given *rencontre* but an aspect of our own psyches as repositories of intentions that, whatever our resolve, remain open to the possibility that we will surprise ourselves, that an unexpected event will lead us to act in ways we could never have anticipated. If Crébillon sees this aspect of *le moment* as particularly characteristic of women, it is because most of his male characters, the *libertins,* have constructed their entire persona through obsessive protocols of self-control and deception adopted as frantic attempts to extirpate all susceptibility to the tug of *le moment.*

Le moment as a force disrupting the continuity of the present with past and future inflects not only Crébillon's thematics of seduction but the very form of his novels. Listening to Clitandre's story of his brief affair with Julie, Cidalise exclaims: "That certainly worked out well for both of you, and the episode could not have ended more nobly." "Ended!" Clitandre immediately corrects her. "Ah, but we are not there yet" (141). In fact, finishing the story is always a problem in Crébillon's novels. None of them ends on a note of real closure leaving the reader with the sense that earlier expectations have been satisfied and all remaining questions answered. *La Nuit et le moment* ends, as we saw, with Clitandre's ambiguous wish that Cidalise love him "as much as you yourself are loved" (150). *Le Hasard du coin du feu* ends only because Clerval must leave and not because any question has been resolved. In his preface to *Les Egarements,* Crébillon promises at least six parts to a novel that in fact has only three: the first and second, showing Meilcour's innocence and first loves; *les suivantes,* of which we have only one, showing the sad influence of others on his life; and the never written *dernières,* promising his salvation by an unspecified *femme estimable.*

Crébillon's desire to preserve the openness of the present moment likewise manifests itself in his abiding preference for the epistolary form. Three of his novels are collections of letters—the *Lettres de la Marquise de M—— au Comte de R——* (1732), the *Lettres de la Duchesse de —— au Duc de ——* (1768), and the *Lettres athéniennes* (1771)—while another—*Les Heureux Orphelins* (1754)—although it begins as a translation of Haywood's *Fortunate Foundlings*, ends as an original series of letters written by the character Lord Chester to a friend in France. Crébillon's tendency toward the epistolary is a sign of his reluctance to adopt toward the events his novels recount anything like the distance and control implied by the alternative of a third-person narration. The epistolary form privileges each sentence as a statement open to whatever disruptions the present may bring.

As though even the writing present of the epistolary implied a form too determined by the remembered past of a time before pen touches paper, Crébillon's most profound stylistic tendency is toward reproduced speech, toward dialogues representing the characters' voices as they speak within a shared present. Even in a memoir-novel like *Les Egarements*, Meilcour's properly narrative voice does little more than stitch together confrontations between characters that consist for the most part of directly quoted conversations. Like an unsettlingly gallicized Ivy Compton-Burnett, Crébillon seems most himself when his writing retains the openness of actual speech to whatever might happen within an unpredictable present. His characters speak, not in complete, fully articulated sentences summarizing themselves and their positions, but in broken, interrupted fragments generated by the continual clash of all who would have their say. Speech in Crébillon's novels is speech as dialogue. Just as his narrative interest centers not on the sequence of events but on the intervals between those events, his dialogues portray not the substance of the isolated character in monologue but the interaction between characters, their repartee, the way they respond to and are redefined by what the other happens to say. Crébillon's characters continually interrupt, clash with, and rebound off one another in directions none could ever have anticipated before the actual exchange.

Novels such as *La Nuit et le moment* and *Le Hasard du coin du feu* read far more like plays or film scripts than novels. In each there is an unnamed narrative voice telling us (or winkingly hinting at) the movements and amorous activities not explicitly referred to in the dialogue. Rather, however, than consolidating any illusion of the carefully structured tale, these anonymous narrative voices satirize the conventions of the genre by alluding to the work's existence in yet another dimension of the present: that of the reader reading and imagining. In response to Cidalise's "Is it really true that you still love me?" the narrator breaks in with "Clitandre tries to banish Cidalise's fears by smothering her with the most ardent caresses. But as everyone may not prefer his method of responding to doubts, those of our readers to whom it seems appropriate may adopt another method, such as having Clitandre recite the most touching words or whatever they feel is most effective for reassuring a woman in such a case." Then, as though no break in the dialogue had occurred, Clitandre replies: "So! ungrateful one [ingrate]! are you reassured?" (86).

Crébillon's refusal of narrative closure, his preference for dialogue, and his delight in interruptions of all kinds contribute to the strong sense throughout his work of an always changing and unpredictable present, of life lived *sur le moment.* These choices are, of course, directly contrary to the canons of the novel of experience. Writing in 1754, Fréron excoriated Crébillon's recently published *Les Heureux Orphelins* as, to his eyes, an endless and disorganized conglomeration of dialogues, enclosed stories, moralizing, epigrams, and digressions. However highly some might rate Crébillon's prose style, Fréron insisted, his works clearly lack the indispensable hallmark of the true novel: "facts which are new, necessary, and believable [des faits neufs, nécessaires et vraisemblables]."[11] For Fréron, the true novel was one whose narrative achieved believability because its events followed each other with absolute necessity. Once the initial situation has been established, the novel's episodes should appear to take place as though they could not have happened otherwise. Fréron's rejection of Crébillon is important because it brings into focus the extent to which his novelistic practices differed from the period's mainstream expectations of the genre. It shows how his refusal of sequential determination stamped his work with the marks of the haphazard and the scandalous.

Why did Crébillon write as he did? And why, in terms of the novel's history, did his choices have so little future? The answer to these questions lies neither in hypothesizing on the psychological motivations for Crébillon's esthetic preferences nor in assuming the existence of some archetype of the novel in relation to which his choices were simply aberrant. The answers depend on understanding the audience for which he wrote: the troubled second estate, a nobility very much in transition.

The signs of his choice of audience are everywhere in evidence. Crébillon's characters are always duchesses, marquis, chevaliers, or their parodic equivalents drawn from the repertoire of the exotic and oriental novel. They often lack any further specification and are designated only by a title: *le duc* or *la marquise*. There is an absence within his novels of any description of physical traits attaching these characters to a particular body, a particular place, or a particular family. Crébillon's characters are abstract, interchangeable exempla of a single social class. Some may be younger and more naive, others older and more jaded, but such differentiation never compromises the fact that all are part of a single social world sharing the same set of conventions. Crébillon's characters never challenge the rules of their caste but are nonetheless delighted when the occasion presents itself to cheat in tacitly accepted ways. The conflict within his novels is never that of individuals struggling against the society of which they are a part. No lone voice calls the established social order into question. His novels turn instead on the conflict of private, individual desires where the only real stake is the risk of appearing *ridicule*, of it becoming public knowledge that one has not lived up to the demands of society's shared conventions and hypocrisies.

The less obvious implications of Crébillon's choice of audience are rooted in the historical situation of what we saw to be the changing and conflicted French aristocracy of the eighteenth century. Its troubles were both a heritage from the past and an anticipation of the future—the past of the seemingly unlimited swelling of its ranks through the king's sale of offices and the future of an impending cataclysm which by the end of the century would all but eliminate the nobility as a class. Whether sword or robe, old or new nobility, all segments of the eighteenth-century French aristocracy defined themselves by their ability to appear as the true cognoscenti of their order, as numbering among those who belonged, understood, were at ease within, and had mastered the complex world centered on king and court. Crébillon's readers, true nobles as well as aspiring bourgeois, came to his works because once the question of a socialized savoir-faire at the center of all his novels was posed, no reader could be certain of knowing enough. If *Les Egarements* was the most successful of his novels, it was because so many readers could identify with the situation of the young Meilcour as he entered a society about which he understood very little. Expected to know everything, such readers were acutely conscious of the limits of their knowledge. With regard to a certain way of acting and a verbal agility in polite conversation, Crébillon's novels functioned as a kind of conduct book, a guide for an aristocracy whose knowledge of how things were done was the touchstone of their identity. If the figure of

Versac stands out so clearly in Crébillon's work—he is the only one of his characters alive outside the world of Crébillon criticism—it is because his lengthy treatise on the ways of the courtier lies ambiguously between the revelation of a mystery and the parody of an absurdity. His voice is perfectly modulated to the needs of a readership that might not believe in all the things it must do but certainly wanted to do them correctly.

Few novelists assume a greater complicity on the part of their readers than does Crébillon. Spurning the careful plot development and suspense of the realistic novel, his highly coded and wittingly understated dialogues leave the reader with no choice other than to follow with complicitous fascination or to close the book. When the aristocracy to which Crébillon addressed himself looked not for an instructive vignette but for a story or history, it was to a very different genre that it turned. Whether old or new, the one story all nobles had to tell was that of their lineage. The importance of this self-definition through ancestry had led, well before Crébillon, to the development of a distinct and little-studied narrative genre lying between genealogy and literature: that of the family history.[12] First developed in the sixteenth century, the production of aristocratic family histories grew dramatically throughout the seventeenth and eighteenth centuries. While only 38 were produced in the half-century between 1550 and 1599, the following fifty-year period saw 170, and the period from 1650 to 1699 produced 258. Interestingly enough, it was during the two decades directly preceding the Revolution, 1770 to 1789, that there appeared the near-record total for a twenty-year period of 105.[13] At one level, these family histories were a practical response to the *recherches* carried out by the monarchy to verify the credentials of those claiming noble status, and with it an exemption from certain taxes. Once the legal documents authenticating one's ancestry had been gathered, it seemed a logical next step in the age of the novel to give that disparate cast of characters the continuity and purposefulness of an often quite freely elaborated narrative history and then to endow the whole—documents and story—with the greater authority of the printed text.

The existence and function of these family histories tell us something important about the noble as reader and about the aristocracy as a component of the general reading public. There is a fascinating complementarity between, on the one hand, these family histories establishing a continuity of blood that speaks for both the past and future of the aristocratic reader and, on the other, Crébillon's highly restricted narrative focus on momentary questions opening onto only the most immediate future: Will this character understand the subtlety of what is being said? Will that character yield or resist? Crébillon's novels, most often a loose sequencing of independent stories, are never constructed as a progressive, cumulative movement toward some single point of closure located in the future. For Crébillon's designated readers, the whole question of a future beyond that of the next moment and its thwarted or fulfilled desire was in effect already answered by the long-term continuities of the family history. Defined by blood, that larger future existed not as an opening to real change but as the inevitability of repetition. The future of blood and family would reenact and retell a single story with only minor variations in the names of its characters.

Crébillon addressed himself to and was avidly read by an audience that, at least claiming to be certain of its past and future, could turn its attention entirely to the affairs of the passing moment. This posture of long-term self-certainty allowed the aristocratic audience to acknowledge the moment as the realm of chance. What was to happen next might be affected by their effort, skill, and planning; but such individual qualities could never determine it entirely. Always at work in the present was the unpredictable tug of a *hasard* utterly indifferent to the individual. To recognize the present as moment and chance as inevitable was not, however, to cower before some dark, incomprehensible fate but rather to achieve the freedom that came with accepting a limit to one's own responsibility. To acknowledge chance as a force beyond the individual's control was to escape the potentially unlimited tyranny of responsibility. Crébillon, his characters, and his reader are, in a very real sense, utterly irresponsible. With their focus limited to the present, Crébillon's novels portray a world of liberty and libertinage to which all values beyond the tautology of blood, be they religious or secular, are irrelevant. The very form of Crébillon's storytelling precludes the possibility that the value of a given action should depend on its role in some greater narrative extending beyond the present.

Placing Crébillon's works in the context of his aristocratic readership allows a better understanding of why the subsequent development of the novel relegated him to the status of a minor, secondary figure. Crébillon wrote for an audience whose most important life narrative was defined by a family history. Secure as to who they were, for them the question of their individual identity held little interest as a subject of novelistic speculation. Crébillon's works never dramatize a crisis of social identity. His cast of characters includes no real representative of any Other challenging the fundamental values these novels share with their audience. If critics have so regularly condemned his works as superficial and frivolous, it is because they show no trace of what was to become the central problematic of the modern novel: a crisis of identity born from the recognition of some truly threatening Other. Be it in terms of gender, class, race, or the internal fissure of madness, the narratives most central to the modern novel of plot and character are always those of the Other confronted and the self questioned.

If Crébillon is perceived as a figure eccentric to the development of the novel, it is because the genre's mainstream evolved in response to a very different readership with very different demands. Beyond and eventually engulfing the aristocratic readership for which Crébillon wrote, there existed another quite different audience that came to the novel with no preexisting answer to the question of their individual identities. The eighteenth century saw an important mutation in the composition of the reading public. While the aristocratic audience of old, new, and aspiring nobility made up, at the beginning of the period, a majority of readers, a combination of forces was already at work changing that situation. By mid-century both a general increase in the level of literacy touching all classes and the consolidation of a specifically bourgeois and anti-aristocratic ideology of merit had combined to render any sense of identity through birth a more and more problematic element within the psyche of the reading public. Obsessed with the question of who they were as individuals, this new audience looked more and more to the novel, to narrative as a mirror of self-definition, for the beginnings of an answer. The novel of experience and realism became the dominant literary genre of the eighteenth and nineteenth centuries because its narratives, quite unlike Crébillon's, contained within them an authentic representation of the Other. Be it through the outsider's perspective of Montesquieu's Usbek, the ultimately self-sufficient female figure of Grafigny's Zilia, or the cold manipulation of Laclos's Merteuil, the novel came more and more to tell stories centering on a confrontation with some Other calling into question both individual identity and the social order. It was, however, equally characteristic of novels written for this new readership that such confrontations with the Other should serve ultimately to consolidate an identity redefined and renewed by the trials of the story told. The novel of realism tells a story of change and danger, of the protagonist's identity put at risk. Ultimately, however, that identity is only refashioned and tempered in the fires of adversity and alterity. The novel of realism allegorizes a *felix culpa,* a crisis of identity assuring its consolidation.

With infinitely higher stakes riding on the story it had

to tell, this new form of the novel refused even the suspicion that there might exist within its workings any element of chance. It insisted instead that its entire narrative was a sequence of, to use Fréron's earlier phrase, "facts that are new, necessary, and believable." This illusion of necessity could, as Sartre showed us, be achieved only when the story's telling simultaneously assumed yet held hidden the closure of an ending, an already determined future moment transforming all that might appear as chance and chaos into purpose and necessity. It was this teleology of plot that so admirably suited the emerging novel of experience to the epics of identity that have always been its principal subject matter.

The novel of plot and character, the mainstream novel of the eighteenth and nineteenth centuries, reflects and consolidates a change in where the reading public looked for the foundation of its identity. No longer secure in any aristocratic given of blood, the increasingly important non-noble component of this audience turned instead to the potency of story. To follow the hero's quest was, for its readers, an invitation to live their lives as versions of the stories they read. Such readers, like characters in novels of their own creation, appeared free to write their stories as they wished. With that apparent freedom from any preordained familial or social script came, however, a heavy responsibility. Once the reader/writer had accepted this bargain, any sense that chance played a predominant role in one's personal epic became scandalous. Chance, as the parallel development of probability theory set out to demonstrate, could only be a figment of our ignorance, a diminishing unknown within those territories not yet conquered by our proud march toward a complete knowledge of ourselves and our world. To greet chance with anything other than a dismissive sneer was to subvert the representational foundation on which the modern sense of individual identity had been founded.

With nothing left to chance, this new freedom of the

storied self brought with it an intensified sense of individual responsibility for every moment within the life narrative and within life as narrative. No event was so insignificant that it need not be lived and evaluated in terms of its role in advancing the story toward its determined end. The individual's story and Hegelian History became different versions of a single order of necessity to which every specific moment had to be subordinated. The freedom of life as story brought with it the need for all to pretend to a more and more complete control, a more and more complete domination of a world for which they accepted complete responsibility. Hubris and paranoia were, it would seem, the inevitable conclusions to the story of our stories.

I have rapidly sketched out some of the more ambiguous implications of that other route taken by the history of the novel in order to underline how very different were the world Crébillon described and the audience for which he wrote. We limit our understanding of his works when we dismiss them as frivolous and superficial, as little more than a pandering to the depraved tastes of a social order that was to disappear from the face of the earth not a moment too soon. The problem with such a judgment is not so much that it is false as that it says so little about Crébillon and so much about us. Facile and moralistic, that position is possible only so long as we judge one vision of society and the individual's place within it according to criteria generated by and supporting an entirely alien vision of those same realities.

Crébillon is eccentric to the development of the novel. His is a voice that has disappeared. This is so because he both expressed and addressed himself to an audience that did not yet feel responsible for every moment of a life-narrative making it everything it was to be. Crébillon's characters are gloriously and joyfully irresponsible. They neither feel a need nor claim any power to control totally either themselves or the world in which they live. Less free, but at the same time less responsible, they accept life as a series of moments never completely controlled by the individual and only accidentally providing the closure of the well-told story. Crébillon's novels acknowledge a limit to human power as it confronts the reality of chance. Clerval speaks in *Le Hasard du coin du feu* not only for Crébillon's entire cast of characters but for a world now gone and a truth now scandalous when he describes himself as "reduced as we almost always are . . . to living by chance and awaiting whatever it brings [à marcher au hasard, et à en attendre tout]" (206).

10

Chance's Untellable Tale:
Diderot's *Jacques le fataliste*

Diderot was a man fascinated by chance. His philosophical writings on cosmology and ontology were deeply influenced by the Lucretian notion of the *clinamen* and its aleatory swerve as the physical foundation of chance's role in the universe.[1] Even while working on the *Encyclopédie,* he found time to translate and freely adapt Edward Moore's *The Gamester* into his own *Le Joueur* as a melodramatic caution against the dangers of gambling. He once, half-seriously and in great detail, wrote a twenty-five-page proposal for a universal lottery, compulsory for all estates and ages, structured in such a way that the ticket-buying obligations and system of payoffs would allow it to replace the *ancien régime*'s entire tax system.[2] In 1774, looking back on his life after sixty years of relentless work, he expressed his sense of how the world turned and of his own place in it through a striking image: "The world belongs to the strongest. It is only at the end that I will know what I have finally lost or won in this huge casino [ce vaste tripot], where I have spent sixty years, cup in hand [le cornet à la main], *tesseras agitans.*"[3] Looking at the world as it is, Diderot resigns himself to the fact that "the world belongs to the strongest." Rather, however, than submitting to that rule of force, he accepts life as an immense and protracted gamble undecided until the last roll of the dice. This disabused but hardly brooding statement clearly evokes his most famous literary creation of that same period: Jacques, the folk philosopher of fatalism. Without a dice cup waiting to be shaken one more time, Jacques' eight-day trip with his master is ruled by the similarly unknown yet irresistible dictates of a Great Scroll deciding whether he will ever finish the story of his life and his loves.

Fatalism and storytelling come together in *Jacques le fataliste* in a way that redefines both. Fatalism, *Le Robert* tells us, is "a doctrine acknowledging fate's complete control of events, of men, and of their actions."[4] It illustrates this definition with the Islamic concept *mektoub* ('it is written'), an example nicely appropriate to a novel where fatalism takes the form of Jacques' belief in the Great Scroll as a universal script containing every event of past, present, and future and whose dictates can neither be refused nor suspended. While everything may be predetermined at the objective level of events, there nonetheless remains for the individual fatalist the subjective uncertainty resulting from the fact that the scroll's dictates remain unknowable until they have taken place. Only after event A rather than B has taken place do we know that A was inscribed on the Great Scroll. Before the event, the individual concerned had no way of knowing which of the two alternatives was to take place. What is predetermined at the level of events is, for the individual fatalist experiencing those events, indistinguishable from a series of happenings ruled only by chance. From the viewpoint of the individual obliged to make decisions, fatalism finally offers no more consolation or instruction than a belief in pure chance.

Jacques le fataliste opens with an unidentified voice posing the question, "How had they met?"[5] The answer, offered by a second and equally unidentified voice, anticipates the conflict at work throughout the novel: "By chance, like everyone else [Par hasard, comme tout le monde]." Fatalism and chance, the one implying a strict determinism and the other an aleatory randomness, become indistinguishable at the level of the individual living life and obliged to make decisions in ignorance of the Great Scroll. For Jacques, reason and fantasy, the tactical corollaries of a belief in determinism on the one hand and a resignation to chance on the other, become one and the same: "It's that, not knowing what is written above, we know neither what we want nor what we do. So we follow our fantasy, which we call reason, or our reason, which is often only a dangerous fantasy that sometimes turns out well and sometimes, badly" (33). As would be the case for events explicitly recognized as chance, the unknowable script of the Great Scroll eliminates individual moral responsibility. When the girl accompanying the country surgeon is knocked off their horse during an argument over the gravity of knee wounds, Jacques suggests: "Don't be upset, my dear, it is neither your fault, nor the doctor's fault, nor mine, nor my master's. The fact is that it was written above that today, on this road, at this moment, the doctor would ramble on, my master and I would be surly, you would get a bruise on your head, and everyone would see your ass" (26). The principle governing Jacques' sense of responsibility for events as they happen is succinctly stated as he overcomes his frustration at being prevented from sleeping by the swarms of flies and gnats persistently circling around him: "Since something exists, it must necessarily be so" (251).

Jacques' situation is defined by the implicit dilemma of believing in an objective fatalism ruling the world and his subjective inability ever to be certain what will actually happen next. In so exuberantly portraying this impasse, Diderot expresses his own usually silenced doubts concerning those proud voices within the scientific communities of the eighteenth century that would dismiss chance as a ridiculous avatar of superstition. The adventures of Jacques and his master subvert any real distinction between chance and necessity. As Jacques Roger put it in his examination of Diderot's scientific thought: "For men caught up in the universal torrent, nothing more resembles the realm of

chance than a universe where everything is rigorously determined by everything. . . . Diderot's universe is a gigantic
dice game where everything is determined, where nothing
is known, and where the dice themselves change form in
the middle of the game."[6]

Jacques le fataliste's undoing of any strict boundary between chance and determinism takes place against a background of constant storytelling. Were the reader pressed
to describe the plot of this ultimately plotless novel, the
best summary would be that it is a story of stories: the story
of the master's attempts to extract from Jacques *l'histoire
de ses amours* and the parallel story of Jacques' sometimes
reluctant and sometimes impatient attempts to finish that
story in spite of its constant interruptions. All the secondary characters in this novel appear as pretexts for telling a
story and remain in it only so long as they have not arrived
at the end of their tale. Jacques telling the story of his
loves, the master telling the story of his manipulation by
Saint-Ouin, the hostess telling her story of Madame de
Pommeraye, and Des Arcis telling his story of the abbé
Hudson are only a few examples of the many characters
entering this work as sources of narratives whose delivery
and orchestration take place as a complex interplay of
sometimes oppositional, sometimes sequential, but always
interconnected storytelling voices. Like different constitu-
encies demanding to be heard, they clash, merge, separate,
swerve, and exit as a series of chaotic responses to the
listener's desire to hear a story, to escape what would otherwise be the boredom of life without story.

The act of storytelling is crucial to *Jacques le fataliste* at
another level. What distinguishes this work from the vast
majority of French novels of the eighteenth century is the
fact that Diderot situates the telling of these tales within an
explicit dialogue between an authorial voice and a second,
equally disruptive voice attributed to the hypothetical
reader. Just as the authorial voice will revel in its no longer

secret power over the potential infinity of chance events inflecting the stories we read—"You see, reader, that I am well on my way, and that it is completely up to me whether I make you wait one year, two years, or three years for the story of Jacques' loves" (24)—so also the voice of the hypothetical reader will freely interrupt, demand clarification of a detail, protest the use of a particular word, or ask that one story be abandoned in favor of another.

Including this meta-narrational discourse within the novel forces us, Diderot's actual readers, to assume a distanced, problematized relation to our own reading of the work. How, the question becomes, do we react when we find some version of ourselves as readers already included within the text? In an earlier study of *Jacques le fataliste*, I tried to analyze how Diderot's specific use of pronouns, verb tenses, performative discourse, and embedded narrations establishes this work as a sustained exercise of discursive irony redefining the mainstream tradition of realism, through which the eighteenth-century French novel most frequently defined itself.[7] Any attempt to understand this work's dialectic of chance and narration must include a careful attention to the paradoxes generated by the enclosure of all the various stories told within the ironizing parentheses of an explicit attention to the process of their telling.

The central paradox generated by this conflict between the stories told and the act of their telling is itself closely related to the work's key notion of fatalism. On the one hand, the novel's main character, Jacques, repeatedly insists that all the stories we hear—that of his loves as well as all the other tales—confirm his conviction that events are bound together by strict relations of cause and effect corresponding to the irresistible dictates of the Great Scroll. On the other, everything about the way we as readers actually come to hear these stories—our access to them through a second and always unpredictable level of authorial and lectorial interchange—consolidates an opposite impression of total indetermination, of a chaos alien to the operation of any real determinism.[8] To what extent, the question becomes, do these distinct and antagonistic levels of the work's signification redefine what this novel tells us about chance and storytelling?

Jacques' position—the fatalist's position—is easily described. For him, every event in his own as well as everyone else's story is one link in an unbroken chain. Understanding that chain, deciphering the inscriptions on the Great Scroll, consists in interpreting events according to a single ironclad rule. Given any event in a series, Jacques looks first to what immediately preceded it. Linking them he posits a 'since', the grammatical conjunction of causality. Returning to the original event, he then moves to the event immediately following it. Linking them he posits an 'in order that', the grammatical conjunction of purpose. The events remain as they were. What has changed is the space of interpretation between them. Once those interstices have been occupied by the projected functions of causality and purpose, the events' significance has been radically changed even though they themselves remain as they were. The fatalist, thanks to this grammatical alchemy, finds himself in a world majestically corresponding to everything he presumed it to be. What he leaves unsaid, of course, is the fact that this majesty is a construct grounded not in the events themselves but in the rule of *post hoc ergo propter hoc*, through which he has chosen to interpret their concatenation. Jacques and all the other storytellers in this novel are both within the stories they tell as their subjects and removed from them as their narrators. They are outside the events they relate because as they tell their stories, they view those past events from the promontory of a retrospectively secure belief in laws of causality and purpose linking each event in the narrative to its sequel.

But it is precisely that distance and control concomitant with the storytelling gesture that Diderot systematically subverts with his authorial incursions into the otherwise untroubled progression of the narrative sequences. For the fatalist, the fabric of life is a skein of intertwined but always separable threads spun out as linear concatenations of cause and effect. In order to tell a story, be it of his loves or of his captain's fate, Jacques need only isolate that strand from those around it and present it as a single, self-sustaining narrative sequence. Against that version of storytelling, in opposition to it, the repeated interruptions of the authorial and lectorial voices force the reader to an awareness of how artificial the linear sequence of narrative actually is.

An event is evoked. Rather, however, than allowing the readers to be carried along toward past and future on the fatalist's always secure bridges of cause and effect, Diderot mocks their desire for such clarity and insists instead that they sink into the indeterminate, chance-drive reality of the event as part of a flux teeming with relations to a multiplicity of contexts: the author's, the reader's, the other characters', as well as the associations any of them might make with what is being said. The traditional storyteller's version of events is a monolinear concatenation:

$$(1) \longrightarrow (2) \longrightarrow (3) \longrightarrow (4) \longrightarrow (5)$$

Diderot's version forces the reader to imagine instead a multidimensional entanglement of vectors and angles caught up within each other as a complex, irresolvable magma:

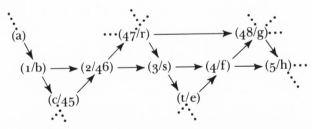

This second model, the one sustained by everything that is anomalous about *Jacques le fataliste*'s narrative diction, is in fact impossible to schematize. What this diagram tries to represent with its discontinuous imbrications of intermingled sequences is the fact that no event can occur with the kind of linear and univocal significance to which the traditional narrative model would reduce it. Compared, however, with the multiple registers of narration present in *Jacques le fataliste*, this diagram is inadequate not only because it limits the number of sequences represented but because it makes no attempt to reflect the two additional modes Diderot insistently points to as potentially pertinent to every event within the narrative: the conditional mode of what might have happened (e.g., the pseudo-episode of Jacques and his master's pursuit by the bandits Jacques has locked in their room) and the preterit mode of the multistoried past accompanying each element highlighted within the narrative sequence (e.g., the story of the friend of Jacques' captain and his many duels).

As conventional storyteller, the fatalist can narrate as he does only because he has reduced events to their role in one arbitrarily chosen sequence and excluded their references to all others outside it. Diderot, insisting on the disconcerting intrusions of the authorial and lectorial voices, underlines the fact that even the most apparently straightforward sequence—an eight-day trip by a man and his servant from no one knows quite where to Desglands's château—is at every moment subject to the chance interruptions of an infinity of other stories perfectly capable of becoming more important than the sequence they interrupt. As readers of this work, we are forced to realize that even the most innocent attempt to tell a story takes place against the background of a polylinear, multivocal, and aleatory reality upon which the traditional narrator carries out the most brutal surgery. The Great Scroll, the central symbol of the narrative gesture, may be, for Jacques, a readable and recitable text. For Diderot, on the contrary, any such script, its lines and letters everywhere twisted into and back upon each other, becomes a scenario of chaos, an exercise in pure chance, an unreadable text.

❦

Analyzing what he sees as the metaphysical illusion behind every attempt to approach the world as subject to
deterministic laws, the contemporary physicist Ilya Prigogine points out that such a position depends on assuming
the observer's ability to achieve a godlike independence of
the phenomena observed: "A description is objective to the
extent to which the observer is excluded and the description itself is made from a point lying *de jure* outside the
world, that is, from the divine viewpoint to which the human soul, created as it was in God's image, had access at
the beginning."[9] Jacques's perspective as fatalist, the storyteller's perspective, is that of someone who may seem to
be part of the events he narrates, but the very gesture of
narration establishes his point of view as separate from and
outside that onrushing stream of events. To tell a story, to
recite retrospectively what we now know was written on
the Great Scroll, is, no matter how humble a position the
fatalist's explicit philosophy might trace out for him, to
embark on an adventure of narrative representation. The
form of that representation, whatever the story's actual
content, sustains the illusion that the narrating voice can
somehow speak independently of the forces at work in the
tale it tells. Through its control over the narrated past, the
storytelling voice escapes the indeterminacy of the event
as a product of the lived moment. To tell a story is to
exercise a mastery over the listening audience through the
elaboration of a development and denouement that only
the narrator can provide. This sustained manipulation of
the listener's anticipation has the effect of consolidating,
in a way otherwise impossible, the storyteller's own sense
of identity as a unified instance of discourse able to retain the same—identity as *idem,* as a reiteration of same—
position of mastery over the entire course of the narration.
The storyteller preserves this identity, however, only so
long as the exercise of narrative mastery is authenticated
by the audience being addressed, by their docilely waiting
upon the storyteller's every word. To interrupt the storyteller or to anticipate the tale's ending—patterns repeat-

edly foregrounded in Diderot's text—is to subvert the narrator's mastery, to undermine the narrator's sense of identity as an instance of discourse held safe from the threat of chance.

Diderot's constantly interrupting authorial voice within *Jacques le fataliste* emphasizes everything the well-told tale would silence: the randomness of life as it is lived, as well as the narrator's status as a fragile and ever-changing perspective within the flux of an irresolvable whole refusing all pretense to separability and identity. Diderot's decision to enclose the already hopelessly intertwined tales told by Jacques and the other characters within a conflictual dialogue of authorial and lectorial voices eliminates the illusion on which the traditional storyteller's escape from chance is predicated. Forced down from the storyteller's promontory, the readers of *Jacques le fataliste* find themselves at one with a consciousness deprived of all access to the consoling vision of a Great Scroll to which they might relate as readers rather than letters.

In terms of its form as well as its content, *Jacques le fataliste* is a novel about storytelling. There is, however, an implicit contradiction between the dynamics of the successful story and Jacques' philosophy of fatalism. To enjoy a story is to be caught up in the suspense it generates, to be concerned with what will happen next to the character whose story is being told. The true fatalist, however, perfectly stoic as to whatever the next line of the Great Scroll may have to say, remains indifferent to the tugs of narrative suspense and identification. At one point in the novel Jacques openly mocks his master for how easily and absurdly he is overcome by the story's suspense. Jacques has arrived at the most poignant moment of his tale. Badly wounded at the battle of Fontenoy, he escaped from the cart of dead bodies in which he was being transported only thanks to the small sum of money he had received from his family before enlisting, which he was now using to pay

sovereign. It is, to the contrary, because the execution—an event for which the less sanguinary variant of *la fête* might well have been substituted—carries with it the precious premium of allowing its spectators, as they return to their private lives, to *faire un rôle*. That role will consist in their telling the story of what they have seen. They will do so, however, with the one all-important difference that it is now they who, as storytellers, will occupy the position of the monarch. It is they who will set the scene, assign roles, and control their audience's suspense. It is as storyteller that the spectator will go on to *rassembler ses voisins* and *se faire écouter*. Parallel to, yet vastly different, from the king's extraction of a bloodprice, storytelling provides a blissful reaffirmation of individual identity and importance. Even the most humble subjects will, for the time it takes to tell their tale, reign over and define themselves through an artful manipulation of their audience's fascination with what they have to say.

Jacques le fataliste speaks to its readers of a limit to our understanding of the world as a rationally ordered universe governed by laws of causality. As a meta-novel, it extends its subversion well beyond the "literary," as that category might arbitrarily be separated from larger concerns. Touching on those larger concerns, Michel Serres underlines what is at stake in this vision of the powers and limits of storytelling:

> Properly speaking, the rational is improbable. Law, rule, order, everything we mean by those terms, is only an improbability, as near as possible to what cannot happen [au plus près voisinage de ce qui ne peut pas avoir lieu]. The rational, miraculous, unbelievably rare and exceptional, borders on the nonexistent [adhère à l'inexistence], as close as possible to zero, to nothingness. What does exist is all the rest as a complement of increasing probability. What exists, and this is a tautology, is what is most probable. And

what is most probable is disorder. Disorder is almost always there.[11]

There is a parallel between everything Diderot forces his readers to remain so intensely aware of as they follow Jacques and his master during their eight-day trip and what Serres refers to as a fundamental conflict between the chaos of the real and the limiting power of the logos, the word, as the purveyor of a "story" attempting to dominate that chaos: "The core of the universe. Disorder as the great law beyond law. Stochastic myriads, the real. The real is not rational. It lacks both order and logos. It expires under the catastrophe of the rare logos [Il meurt par la catastrophe du logos rare]" (80).

Serres's statements are part of an analysis of the relation between literary and scientific discourse, between a discourse referring to other discourses and a discourse claiming to represent an independent reality. Juxtaposing Serres's view of scientific discourse with *Jacques le fataliste*'s meditation on narrative not only underlines their similarity but helps us to perceive an otherwise hidden dimension of Diderot's own work as the prime mover behind his century's most important contribution to the advance of science: the *Encyclopédie ou Dictionnaire raisonné des sciences, des arts, et des métiers*. As novel, meta-novel, or anti-novel, *Jacques le fataliste* offers its readers a vision of chance and indeterminacy, an understanding of the world's resistance to our attempts to impose upon it any system of reason, law, or determinism. Only a person as acutely aware of that resistance as Diderot, I would argue, could have committed himself to challenging it with so unparalleled a gesture of defiance and affirmation as his attempt to encircle and represent the whole of human knowledge. His initiation and overseeing of that labor of so many hands incarnated his hope of drawing together into a single text the whole of science, art, and technology in such a way that they might foster and fructify human endeavor for generations to come: "In effect, the goal of an encyclopedia is to bring together knowledge which is spread out over the surface of the earth, to reveal its overall organization to those with whom we live and to transmit it to those who will come after us."[12] From the time he wrote the initial prospectus to the *Encyclopédie,* Diderot made it clear that he intended to move beyond all existing systems, classifications, and hierarchies born of human error. The entire enterprise of the *Encyclopédie* was meant to initiate a series of innovative intersections and confluences within the turbulent flux of human knowledge. Far more an exhortation than a recapitulation, the *Encyclopédie* would be, not the fixed, predetermined *histoire de ce qu'on savait,* but, in a phrase borrowed from Francis Bacon, the future-oriented *histoire de ce qu'il fallait apprendre:*

> Nature offers us only specific things, infinite in number and without fixed and determined divisions. All things flow from each other through imperceptible nuances, and should there appear on the sea of objects surrounding us some few which, like the tips of rocks, seem to pierce the surface and tower over the others, they owe that advantage only to arbitrary systems, vague conventions, and exceptional events alien to their physical reality and the true foundations of philosophy.[13]

This distinction between a "history of what is known" and a "history of what must be learned" is essential to understanding not only Diderot's intentions as the editor of the *Encyclopédie* but also the profound coherence between that effort and the singularly anomalous redefinition of the novel represented by *Jacques le fataliste.* Diderot's novel demonstrates the inadequacy of any vision of human life as a predetermined, linear sequence of events unfolding according to some preordained purpose. Life, be it Jacques', the master's, or anyone else's, can never be lived as a "story," as the unproblematic enactment of some Great Scroll, some coherent narrative guided by a single, all-encompassing telos. In a similar fashion, Diderot's *Encyclo-*

pédie brings together an unintegrated multiplicity of elements whose value lies outside any overarching system imposed upon its parts. Refusing such integration, the whole retains its status as a purely alphabetical conglomerate whose constituent parts remain free to establish new and unsuspected relations each with the others. Only then is each free to combine and interact with all others according to an always potential and unlimited process of synergetic development and expansion.

Like *Jacques le fataliste,* the *Encyclopédie* represents an act of faith in a vital and generative disorder. Its promise of advances to come rests on its ability to operate beyond the constraints of any predetermined system. What distinguishes Diderot's *Encyclopédie* from that long tradition going from Vincent de Beauvais's *Speculum majus* to Furetière's *Dictionnaire universel* is its profound agnosticism, its refusal to subordinate its representation of human knowledge to the workings of any theological or teleological principle. As the reader of the *Encyclopédie* quickly discovers, the work's intricate system of cross references and referrals subverts any allegiance to a master meaning or integrating purpose assumed to be at work throughout human history. The paramount value guiding this work is an abiding faith in our potential to advance chaotically along the myriad, intertwining, and still untraced pathways of discovery. Diderot's commitment is to what he might initiate, never to what he might complete. The *Encyclopédie* is a call for discoveries to come. Arranged alphabetically, it only hints at the possible directions those advances might someday take. It leaves the way open to as yet unsuspected coincidences and confrontations among the investigations it would initiate. The power of Diderot's *Encyclopédie* lies in its refusal to subscribe to any predefined narrative of our developing knowledge, leaving it instead as an unfinished and unpredictable adventure of chance and serendipity in which each reader might become a participant.

There is a profound homology between the *Encyclopédie* as the untellable tale of scientific advances to come and

Jacques le fataliste as an encyclopedia of those forces inherent to the human condition that refuse the demands of the well-told story. *Jacques le fataliste*'s demolition of traditional narrative discourse parallels and confirms the *Encyclopédie*'s subversion of the teleological principles of order and purposefulness usually presiding over that genre's didacticism. More than anything else, it was this encyclopedic openness to the workings of chance and coincidence at every stage of the narrative sequence that led Diderot, as he wrote *Jacques le fataliste,* to so uncannily anticipate Paul Valéry's famous call for the ultimate novel, the novel that would free the genre from the illusory determinism apparently so inseparable from it: "It would perhaps be interesting to write for once a work that would reveal at each of its turning points all the imaginable alternatives, from which it would then choose the one option actually taken by the text. That would amount to substituting for the illusion of a single determination imitating reality that of the *possible-at-every-instant* [Ce serait là substituer à l'illusion d'une détermination unique et imitatrice du réel, celle du *possible-à-chaque-instant*]."[14]

Jacques le fataliste, by so insistently referring its reader back to the generative matrix of its form, accomplishes for the novel the same program of ironic subversion and synergizing coincidence that we find at the heart of Diderot's enterprise as the editor of the *Encyclopédie.* Both the traditional devices of storytelling and the conventional protocols of systematized knowledge reveal themselves as illusions refusing chance and opting instead for a congealed and ultimately mystifying exploitation of our need for narrative. While, Diderot tells us, that illusion may be consoling, the most exalting enterprise of human consciousness consists in its power to overflow and sweep aside the constraints of our always partial visions of causality, determinism, and order. Celebrating the fecundity of disorder, *Jacques le fataliste* becomes a veritable encyclopedia of the novel—a form risking itself within the praxis of an adventure governed only by chance.

Conclusion

As the eighteenth century's paramount literary genre, the novel played a central role in the Enlightenment's refusal of chance. The narrative portrayal of real life, what I have called the novel of experience, became the principal vehicle through which a growing reading public discovered a new model for understanding who they were and how they related to the world around them. As a narrative representation of interlocking causal sequences, the novel consolidated reason's claim that chance was an absurdity. The attentive reader was invited to learn from the adventures of the novelistic character that no matter what story was told, the individual consciousness remained incomplete and morally deficient so long as it refused to understand its specificity through the exemplary character as a legitimizing token of the aggregate. The experience offered and explicated by the novel was in this sense far more a creation than a representation, far more a product than a source. Evacuating the uncertainties of chance, the novel projected for its readers the illusion of a world beckoning them toward a socialized understanding of their individuality. The novel became for its Enlightenment audience the breviary of a new religion. It spoke to its readers of how they might find their place within the newly sacred order, not of any divinity beyond the human, but of the aggregate and the exemplary.

In reaction to this, some novelists, as we saw with Crébillon and Diderot, chose to speak differently of chance, acknowledging the singularity of the moment and the illusion of causality's integrating concatenations. These novelists did so, however, at the cost of finding themselves labeled as heretics, as grotesque deviants unworthy of descendance within the genre's legitimate filiation. Because they recognized chance as a force dissolving the syntheses of any enforced consensus, such novels could only be antinovels.

Mocking the certainties of all those Enlightenment communities born of the individual's effective annihilation within the exemplary, chance gave the lie to those reassuring algorithms of the aggregate presenting themselves to each as the necessary morality of all. To recognize the sway of chance was to recognize the individual as a consciousness inevitably outside any consensus all might be enjoined to obey and celebrate as the basis of their community. Chance spoke of the individual as a singularity and a solitude impervious to the counsels and imperatives of the average. For that, it had to be silenced.

I have argued in this study that our modernity, as fashioned by the Enlightenment, was constructed upon the systematic denial of chance. With the passing of the *ancien régime,* and in fact well before its actual disappearance in the fires of the Revolution, there expired a recognition and acceptance of chance that had cut across recognized class divisions. The traditional nobility, sustained by a sense of identity based on blood and birth, embraced the power of chance as it held sway over battlefield and gaming table. A predominantly rural third estate likewise accepted chance and fortune as uncontrollable and irresistible forces touching on and redefining all aspects of individual and communal life. The Enlightenment per se was the creation of another group which was neither of the traditional nobility nor of the countrymen. Whether philosophe, savant, or bourgeois—but most often some combination of the three—these new voices denounced and banished chance both as the moral degeneracy of the nobles' gambling and as the woeful ignorance of the peasants' superstition.

In place of chance, the ideology of the Enlightenment invited its anonymously egalitarian and soon-to-bestandardized audience to share in the proud adventure of life lived in a world fashioned by a panoply of sciences promising a previously unimaginable degree of control over the human as well as the material world. To an astonishing degree, the Enlightenment has delivered on that promise. The choice to which it stands as a monument is that of a world subject to rigorous, knowable, and manipulable laws of causality. Since the Enlightenment, the ambitious adventure of the physical and social sciences has redefined our most basic sense of what is real by surrounding us with an always more pervasive symbolic, artificial, and technologized world confirming within ever larger sectors of our daily lives the gospel of "scientific reason." In so doing, this brave new world has dismissed any attention to the force of chance as a perverse allegiance to the antiquated and the primitive. Only a fool or a madman, the spokesmen of our sciences tell us, would dare choose against the chance-excluding primacy of the rational and the determined.

Some voices have invited us to scrutinize more carefully the price we pay for this triumph of enlightened rationality. Pointing to the new dimensions of coercion accompanying the apparently beneficent triumph of science, Michel Serres has hypothesized that "all of our servitudes flow perhaps from there always having been someone to make us believe the real is rational. That is undoubtedly what power is."[1] Serres emphasizes the muted fact that behind the calmly universal rule of scientific law there is always an implicit *prise de pouvoir*, the empowering of a community of savants whose reign depends on their claim to represent and explicate what is really real.

The history of our civilization is in a very real sense the history of our claims to have understood the ultimate causalities at work in the world. Every such claim has been erected on a supposedly vanquished and no longer threatening cadaver of chance. A science is victorious only when, rather than to chance, it can point to its own hypotheses

as constituting an order of causality unlocking the secret
of how events have and will continue to occur. A science
assumes power only as its theorems, replacing chaos by
order, promise an escape from chance. In his introduction to a recent collection of essays continuing the debate
over scientific method that erupted among a number of
France's leading scientists and philosophers in the 1980
issue of *Le Débat,* Krzysztof Pomian suggests that we might
see the development of Western thought as having been
marked by the successive victories of four such models of
scientific thought.[2] Antiquity's belief in the movement of
the stars and planets as the basis of a universal determinism generated and empowered the science of astrology as a
first alternative to chance. The medieval and early modern
codifications of divine providence fashioned Christian theology as the dominant science of a determinism looking to
the dialectic of free will and predestination as the antithesis
of chance. The seventeenth through nineteenth centuries,
affirming an ever more complete allegiance to a view of
the world as an intricate interplay of material forces, saw
the consolidation of a Laplacian mechanical physics reducing chance to a delusion of the ignorant. Most recently, as
the emergence of quantum theory disqualified the Laplacian dream of absolute predictability at the level of the
individual, the locus of scientific truth has shifted to en-
sembles—of molecules, of persons, and of events—which,
once subjected to statistical analysis, can be expected to
reveal constants reducing chance to the docilely stochastic.

I have tried in this study to show how this imperialism
of the scientific was already at work in the paradigms of
the average and the normal shared by probability theory,
statistics, and the novel. Their insistence on understanding
the individual through the exemplary and the average testifies to the fact that our escape from chance came only
with an implicit but nonetheless real renunciation of our
individuality and our freedom. The Enlightenment has
made us heirs to a world everywhere arguing that there is

only danger, death, and insignificance in accepting our lives as a recalcitrance to the norm, as the exaltation of an idiosyncrasy embracing chance not as a humiliation but as our only escape from the tyrannies of reason, responsibility, and consensus.

Notes

1. My discussion of *le hasard* is indebted to Clément Rosset's analysis of that concept in his *Logique du pire* (Paris: Presses Universitaires de France, 1971); see esp. 71–122.

2. Jean Jacques, *L'Imprévu ou la science des objets trouvés* (Paris: Editions Odile Jacob, 1990), 11–12.

Chapter 1. THE TRIUMPH OF PROBABILITY THEORY

1. Georges Bataille, *Le Coupable,* in *Oeuvres complètes,* 12 vols. (Paris: Gallimard, 1970–88), 5:312.

2. Gerd Gigerenzer, Zeno Swijtink, Theodore Porter, Lorraine Daston, John Beatty, and Lorenz Krüger, *The Empire of Chance: How Probability Changed Science and Everyday Life* (Cambridge: Cambridge University Press, 1989), 292.

3. "Using geometry, we have so surely reduced it [the previously insoluble puzzle of chance] to an exact art that it shares its [geometry's] certainty and is ready to move boldly forward" (Blaise Pascal, *Oeuvres complètes de Pascal,* ed. Jacques Chevalier [Paris: Gallimard, 1957], 74). This claim is part of a two-page text usually entitled "Adresse à l'académie parisienne," in which Pascal briefly summarizes the various mathematical projects he was working on in 1654.

4. Ian Hacking, *The Emergence of Probability* (Cambridge: Cambridge University Press, 1975), 63–72.

5. Siméon-Denis Poisson, *Recherches sur la probabilité des jugements en matière criminelle et en matière civile* (Paris: Bachelier, 1837), 1.

6. René Descartes, *Oeuvres et lettres de René Descartes* (Paris: Gallimard, 1953), 142.

7. Renaissance skepticism is one of the key contexts for any study of the development of probability theory. On that subject see Richard H. Popkin, *The History of Scepticism from Erasmus to*

Spinoza (Berkeley and Los Angeles: University of California Press, 1979).

8. Christiaan Huygens, *Oeuvres complètes de Christiaan Huygens*, 22 vols. (The Hague: Martinus Nijhoff, 1888–1950), 14:56.

9. Pierre Rémond de Montmort, *Essai d'analyse sur les jeux de hasard* (Paris, 1713), vi–vii.

10. Abraham De Moivre, *The Doctrine of Chances* (London, 1718), cited in F. N. David, *Games, Gods, and Gambling* (New York: Hafner, 1962), 266.

11. For a broader investigation of how the Enlightenment tended to substitute a theoretical construct for the reality it claimed to explicate see Josué V. Harari, *Scenarios of the Imaginary* (Baltimore: Johns Hopkins University Press, 1987).

12. A. J. Ayer, "Chance," in *Scientific American* 213, no. 4 (October 1965): 46.

13. For a rapid summary of the implications of this law see the chapter "The Law of Great Numbers" in John Maynard Keynes, *A Treatise on Probability* (London: Macmillan, 1921), 332–36.

14. Emile Borel, *Le Hasard* (Paris: Presses Universitaires de France, 1947), 244–45.

15. On the development of statistics see Theodore M. Porter, *The Rise of Statistical Thinking* (Princeton, N.J.: Princeton University Press, 1986). For an analysis of the relation between the emergence of statistics as a science and the formation of the modern French state see Marie-Noëlle Bourguet, *Déchiffrer la France: la statistique départementale à l'époque napoléonienne* (Paris: Editions des archives contemporaines, 1988).

16. Pierre-Simon Laplace, *Essai philosophique sur les probabilités* (1814; reprint, Paris: Gauthier-Villars, 1921), 3.

17. Porter, *Rise of Statistical Thinking*, 5.

18. Georges Louis Leclerc Buffon, *Essai d'arithmétique morale*, in *Oeuvres philosophiques de Buffon*, ed. Jean Piveteau (Paris: Presses Universitaires de France, 1954), 456–88.

19. Lorraine Daston, *Classical Probability in the Enlightenment* (Princeton, N.J.: Princeton University Press, 1988), 126.

20. Denis Diderot and Jean d'Alembert, *Encyclopédie, ou Dictionnaire raisonné des sciences, des arts et des métiers* (1751–57; reprint [17 vols. plus plates and suppl. in 5 vols.], New York: Readex Microprint, 1969), 2:63.

Chapter 2. GAMBLING AS SOCIAL PRACTICE

1. The most popular of these were the famous Hôtel de Transylvanie, opened by prince François Rakoczi in 1714 (and immortalized in Prévost's *Manon Lescaut*); the Venetian embassy, which ran no less than four separate gaming rooms; and the basement room rented at the Luxembourg Palace by the entrepreneurial count de Modène, who equipped it to accommodate up to four hundred players at a time.

2. Quoted by the marquis d'Argenson in *Journal et mémoires*, 9 vols. (Paris: Renouard, 1859–67), 2:93. For a rich anecdotal study of who gambled where in France before the Revolution see Olivier Grussi, *La Vie quotidienne des joueurs sous l'ancien régime à Paris et à la Cour* (Paris: Hachette, 1985).

3. It should be remembered that the livre, in which most of the monetary sums referred to in this book are expressed, did not actually exist. As a money of account or *monnaie idéale*, it was a theoretical denomination whose value in relation to such coins as the écu, pistole, and louis varied during the *ancien régime*. For some sense of the value of the sums referred to, it can be noted that a professor earned 2,000 livres per year, and the average *rentier*, 3,000 to 4,000 livres.

4. Fougeret de Monbron, *La Capitale des Gaules ou la nouvelle Babylone* (Bordeaux: Ducros, 1970), 139–40.

5. Similar to contemporary roulette, these games involved the players' wagering on one or more numbers from a field of options, with the host-banker paying the winning bets and collecting the far more numerous losses. Biribi, for instance, was played on a cloth divided into seventy numbered squares. Each player would place his bets on a number and then draw a jetton from a deep velvet purse containing seventy numbered chips. If he drew his own number, the banker paid him sixty-four times the wager. Hoca was the same game with thirty numbers and a payoff of twenty-eight to one. The advantage to the amiable host serving as banker was, of course, enormous.

6. *Lettres de Madame, duchesse d'Orléans*, ed. P. Gascar and O. Amiel (Paris: Mercure de France, 1981), 118.

7. François Bluche, *La Vie quotidienne de la noblesse française au XVIIIe siècle* (Paris: Hachette, 1973), 87.

8. John Dunkley offers this as a possible explanation for the

popularity of gambling in the introduction to his critical edition of Regnard's *Le Joueur* (Geneva: Droz, 1986), 11.

9. Georges Mongrédien, *Louis XIV* (Paris: Albin Michel, 1963), 56.

10. D. M. Downes, *Gambling, Work, and Leisure* (London: Routledge and Kegan Paul, 1976), 14.

11. Guy Chaussinand-Nogaret, *La Noblesse au XVIIIe siècle* (Paris: Hachette, 1976), 119–59.

12. Robert Mauzi, "Ecrivains et moralistes du XVIIIe siècle devant les jeux de hasard," *Revue des sciences humaines* 90 (April–June 1958): 219–56; John Dunkley, *Gambling, a Social and Moral Problem in France, 1685–1792*, Studies on Voltaire and the Eighteenth Century, 235 (Oxford: Voltaire Foundation, 1985).

13. Frain du Tremblay, *Conversations morales sur les jeux et les divertissements* (Paris: A. Pralard, 1685); Louis Bourdaloue, *Sermon sur les divertissements du monde*, in *Oeuvres complètes*, vol. 2 (Tours: Cattier, 1865); Pierre de Joncourt, *Quatre lettres sur les jeux de hasard* (The Hague: T. Johnson, 1713).

14. Jean Barbeyrac, *Traité du jeu* (Amsterdam: Humbert, 1709); L.-A. Caraccioli, *Dictionnaire critique, pittoresque et sentencieux, propre à faire connaître les usages du siècle ainsi que ses bizarreries* (Lyon, 1768); Jean Dusaulx, *De la passion du jeu, depuis les temps anciens jusqu'à nos jours*, 2 vols. (Paris, 1779).

15. Dusaulx, *De la passion du jeu*, 1:133.

16. Edmund Bergler, *The Psychology of Gambling* (New York: Hill and Wang, 1957), 18.

17. Baldesar Castiglione, *The Book of the Courtier*, trans. Charles S. Singleton (New York: Doubleday, 1959), 127.

18. Oystein Ore, *Cardano: The Gambling Scholar* (New York: Dover, 1953), 194.

19. Roger Mettam, *Power and Faction in Louis XIV's France* (London: Blackwell, 1988), 45–81.

20. Diderot and d'Alembert, *L'Encyclopédie*, 2:502.

21. V. G. Kiernan, *The Duel In European History* (Oxford: Oxford University Press, 1988), 154.

22. Jean de La Bruyère, *Les Caractères de Théophraste traduits du grec avec les Caractères ou les Moeurs de ce siècle* (Paris: Garnier, 1962), 400.

23. Mauss's anthropological description of the gift and its role in larger structures of reciprocity has had a significant impact on historical studies during the last two decades. Examples of this

can be found in the group of articles entitled "Pour une histoire anthropologique: la notion de réciprocité," in *Annales* 6 (1974): 1309–80; in Natalie Zemon Davis, "Beyond the Market: Books as Gifts in Sixteenth-Century France," in *Transactions of the Royal Historical Society*, 5th ser., 33 (1983): 69–88; in Marvin Becker, *Civility and Society in Western Europe, 1300–1600* (Bloomington: University of Indiana Press, 1988); and in Jay M. Smith, *The Culture of Merit in Old Regime France* (Ann Arbor: University Microfilms, 1990).

24. Marcel Mauss, *The Gift: Forms and Functions of Exchange in Archaic Societies* (New York: Norton, 1967), 35.

25. Antoine Gombaud de Méré, *Oeuvres complètes*, ed. Charles Boudhors, 3 vols. (Paris: Editions Fernand Roches, 1930), 3:165.

26. Abbé Pluche, *Le Spectacle de la nature ou entretiens sur les particularités de l'histoire naturelle*, 8 vols. (Paris: Estienne, 1755–64), 6:118.

27. Marquis de Dangeau, *Journal*, 19 vols. (Paris, 1854–60), 7:309.

28. The French nobility's attitude toward participation in commerce and lucrative activity is a subject of great debate. Scholars such as Norbert Elias (*La Société de cour* [Paris: Calmann-Lévy, 1974]), François Bluche (*La Vie quotidienne*), and Roger Mettam (*Power and Faction in Louis XIV's France*) insist on the traditional view of the nobles' disdain for any involvement in commerce, while revisionist figures such as Guy Chaussinand-Nogaret (*La Noblesse au XVIIIe siècle*) and Simon Schama (*Citizens: A Chronicle of the French Revolution* [New York: Knopf, 1989]) see a nobility willingly and massively involved in financial endeavors. To a large extent these two schools are in fact talking about different and conflicting subsets within the nobility, subsets whose distinctness is nowhere more obvious than in their respective attitudes toward gambling.

29. For a modernized restatement of this argument see Jean-Marie Apostolidès, *Le Roi-machine: spectacle et politique au temps de Louis XIV* (Paris: Minuit, 1981).

30. Saint-Simon, *Mémoires de Saint-Simon*, 18 vols. (Paris: Editions Ramsay, 1977–79), 16:73–74.

31. Bernard de Fontenelle, *Eloge de Dangeau*, in *Oeuvres complètes de Fontenelle*, 5 vols. (Paris: Salmon, 1825), 2:54.

32. Michel Foucault, *Histoire de la folie* (Paris: Gallimard, 1972), 94.

33. For a general history of the lottery in France see Jean Leonnet, *Les Loteries d'état en France aux XVIIIe et XIXe siècles* (Paris: Imprimerie Nationale, 1963).

34. Daston, *Classical Probability in the Enlightenment*, 148–49.

35. Cited in *Dictionnaire des jeux*, ed. René Alleau (Paris: Tchou, 1964), 293 (s.v. "Loterie").

36. Barbeyrac, *Traité du jeu*, 286–87.

37. Hacking, *Emergence of Probability;* see esp. chap. 11.

38. Philip J. Davis and Reuben Hersh, *Descartes' Dream: The World According to Mathematics* (Boston: Houghton Mifflin, 1987), 19.

Chapter 3. LAW'S SYSTEM AND THE GAMBLE REFUSED

1. No convincing explanation of this pronunciation has yet been offered. The claim that the final *w* of Law's signature could easily be confused with a double *s* does not stand up to a scrutiny of actual documents. Alexandre Beljame's claim that the 'lass' pronunciation came as a popular French response to the Scottish custom of adding a final *s* to surnames as an abbreviation for 'son' ('Laws' for 'Lawson') is ingenious but unconvincing. See his "La Prononciation du nom de Jean Law, le financier," in *Etudes romanes dédiées à Gaston Paris* (Paris: Emile Bouillson, 1891).

2. There never was any Mississippi Company, as it has traditionally been designated. Law's colonial trading company was first known as la Compagnie d'Occident and later as la Compagnie des Indes.

3. J. G. A. Pocock, *The Machiavellian Moment: Florentine Political Thought and the Atlantic Republican Tradition* (Princeton, N.J.: Princeton University Press, 1975), 453–54.

4. These figures are taken from Herbert Lüthy, *La Banque protestante en France de la révocation de l'edit de Nantes à la Révolution* (Paris: SEVPEN, 1959), 276–82.

5. Edgar Faure, *La Banqueroute de Law* (Paris: Gallimard, 1977).

6. John Law, *Oeuvres complètes*, ed. Paul Harsin, 3 vols. (Paris: Librairie du Recueil Sirey, 1934): 2:166.

7. Lüthy, *La Banque protestante*, 27.

8. Adam Anderson, *An historical and chronological deduction on the origins of commerce* (1787; reprint, New York: Augustus M. Kelley, 1967), 123–24. Anderson is quoting here what he de-

scribes as the "sensible, familiar, and most plain simile" of one Archibald Hutcheson. This explanation was used by Peter M. Garber in his recent comparative study of Dutch tulipmania in 1637, the French Mississippi Bubble, and the English South Sea Bubble (see "Famous First Bubbles," *Journal of Economic Perspectives* 4 [1990]: 40).

9. In fact, the regent received 300 million immediately from this transaction, with the remainder scheduled to be paid out over a ten-year period.

10. Montesquieu, *Les Lettres persanes* (Paris: Garnier, 1960), 280. For translations from this text I have consulted J. Robert Loy's *The Persian Letters* (New York: World, 1961).

11. Emmanuel Le Roy Ladurie, *Les Paysans du Languedoc* (Paris: SEVPEN, 1966), 599–600.

12. Ange Goudar, *Histoire des Grecs ou de ceux qui corrigent la fortune au jeu* (London, 1758), vi–vii.

13. Montesquieu, *L'Esprit des lois*, 2 vols. (Paris: Garnier, 1961), 2:72. For translations from this text I have consulted Thomas Nugent's *The Spirit of the Laws* (New York: Hafner, 1966).

14. Saint-Simon, *Mémoires*, 16:98–99.

15. Paul-Emile Littré, *Dictionnaire de la langue française* (1877; reprint, Chicago: R. R. Donnelley, 1987).

16. Edmund Burke, *Reflections on the Revolution in France*, ed. J. G. A. Pocock (1790; reprint, Indianapolis: Hackett, 1987), 169.

Chapter 4. TOWARD A NOVEL OF EXPERIENCE

1. A. N. Kolmogorov, *Foundations of the Theory of Probability* (New York: Chelsea, 1950). The original German edition of *Grundbegriffe der Wahrscheinlichkeitrechnung* was published in 1933.

2. Ian Hacking, "Was There a Probabilistic Revolution?" in *The Probabilistic Revolution*, ed. L. Krüger et al., vol. 1, *Ideas and History* (Cambridge, Mass.: MIT Press, 1987), 45.

3. Pocock, *Machiavellian Moment*, 4.

4. For analyses of the roles of logic and rhetoric in the context of the probable as literary verisimilitude see Barbara J. Shapiro, *Probability and Certainty in Seventeenth-Century England* (Princeton, N.J.: Princeton University Press, 1983); and Douglas Patey, *Probability and Literary Form* (Cambridge: Cambridge University Press, 1984).

5. Buffon, *Essai d'arithmétique morale*, 461.

6. Ernest Coumet, "Le Problème des partis avant Pascal," in *Archives internationales d'histoire des sciences* 72–73 (1965): 245–72.

7. Davis and Hersh, *Descartes' Dream*, 24.

8. Daniel Defoe, *The Gamester* (London: J. Roberts, 1719), 12.

9. Diderot and d'Alembert, *Encyclopédie*, 3:105.

10. Cited in Georges May, *Le Dilemme du roman* (Paris: Presses Universitaires de France, 1963), 116–18.

11. Adolphe Quételet, *Sur l'homme et le développement de ses facultés*, 2 vols. (Paris, 1835), 1:21–22.

Chapter 5. JEAN DE PRÉCHAC AND THE NOBLE'S WAGER

1. Philippe Ariès, *L'Enfant et la vie familiale sous l'ancien régime* (Paris: Seuil, 1973); see esp. chap. 4 of part 1. Thierry Depaulis, "Le Jeu de cartes: quelques règles du passé," in *Playing Card* 13, no. 3 (February 1985): 74–80.

2. Diderot and d'Alembert, *Encyclopédie*, 1:289.

3. Jean de Préchac, *Les Désordres de la bassette*, ed. René Godenne (1682; reprint, Geneva: Slatkine, 1980), xii–xiii; translations are my own.

4. Very little was known of Préchac's life before the work of Robert Le Blant. See his somewhat exaggerated "Un Montesquieu Béarnais sous Louis XIV: Jean de Préchac," in *Revue Pyrénéenne*, 1928–32, 546–49, and especially his introduction to *Lettres de Jean de Préchac* (Pau: Lescher-Moutoué, 1940), 1–16.

5. Jean de Préchac, *L'Illustre Parisienne*, ed. René Godenne (1679; reprint, Geneva: Slatkine, 1979).

6. Henri Coulet, *Le Roman jusqu'à la Révolution* (Paris: Armand Colin, 1967), 273.

7. *Lettres de Jean de Préchac*, 40.

8. René de Ceriziers, *Le Héros Français, ou l'idée du grand capitaine* (Paris, 1645), 171; translations are my own.

9. Jean de Préchac, *La Noble Vénitienne ou la Bassette* (Paris: Claude Barbin, 1679), 44; translations are my own.

Chapter 6. CHANCE, READING, AND THE TRAGEDY OF EXPERIENCE: PRÉVOST'S *Manon Lescaut*

1. This definition is cited by Frédéric Deloffre and Raymond Picard in their edition of *Manon Lescaut* (Paris: Classiques Gar-

nier, 1965), 325; translations are my own. I have consulted D. C. Moylan's English translation in Richard Aldington's *Great French Romances* (New York: Duell, Sloan and Pearce, 1946).

2. The resistance by critics to an awareness of this appropriation of Manon by des Grieux is the subject of the feminist reading of Prévost's novel offered by Naomi Segal in *The Unintended Reader: Feminism and Manon Lescaut* (Cambridge: Cambridge University Press, 1986).

Chapter 7. THE IRONIES OF CHANCE: VOLTAIRE'S *Candide* AND *Zadig*

1. Diderot and d'Alembert, *Encyclopédie*, 2:1124.
2. Voltaire, *Candide*, in *Romans et contes de Voltaire*, ed. Henri Bénac (Paris: Garnier, 1960), 146; translations here of quotations from *Candide* and *Zadig* are my own. I have consulted Donald M. Frame's *Voltaire's Candide, Zadig, and Selected Stories* (Bloomington: Indiana University Press, 1961).
3. Jean Starobinski, *Le Remède dans le mal* (Paris: Gallimard, 1989), 123–43.
4. Ibid., 141.
5. Voltaire, *Dictionnaire philosophique*, ed. J. Benda and R. Naves (Paris: Garnier, 1961), 166; translations are my own.

Chapter 8. WRITING OF NO CONSEQUENCE: VIVANT DENON'S *Point de lendemain*

1. Vivant Denon, *Point de lendemain*, in *Romanciers du XVIIIe siècle*, ed. René Etiemble, 2 vols. (Paris: Gallimard, 1965), 2:385; translations are my own.

Chapter 9. THE MOMENT'S NOTICE: CRÉBILLON'S GAME OF LIBERTINAGE

1. Crébillon, *Le Hasard du coin du feu*, in *Oeuvres de Crébillon fils*, ed. Pierre Lièvre, 5 vols. (Paris: Le Divan, 1929–30), 1:250; translations are my own.
2. Diderot and d'Alembert, *Encyclopédie*, 1:361.
3. Crébillon, *Les Egarements du coeur et de l'esprit*, ed. René Etiemble (Paris: Gallimard, 1977), 73; translations are my own. I

have consulted Barbara Bray's translation in *The Wayward Head and Heart* (London: Oxford University Press, 1967).

4. Crébillon, *La Nuit et le moment*, in *Oeuvres de Crébillon fils*, 1:8; translations are my own.

5. Jean-Paul Sartre, *La Nausée* (1938; reprint, Paris: Gallimard, 1970), 61; translations are my own. I have consulted Lloyd Alexander's translation in *Nausea* (New York: New Directions, 1964).

6. See above, n. 3.

7. Jean Sgard, "La Notion d'égarement chez Crébillon," in *Dix-huitième siècle* 1 (1969): 241.

8. Paul Robert, *Dictionnaire alphabétique et analogique de la langue française*, 7 vols. (Paris: Le Robert, 1978), 2:403 and 3:228.

9. On this subject see Laurent Versini, *Laclos et la tradition* (Paris: Klincksieck, 1968), 461–63; and Philip Stewart, *Le Masque et la parole* (Paris: Corti, 1973), 157–60.

10. Crébillon, *L'Ecumoire ou Tanzaï et Néardarné*, ed. Ernest Sturm (Paris: Nizet, 1976), 208.

11. Fréron, in *L'Année littéraire* 3 (1754): 273, as cited by Clifton Cherpack in *An Essay on Crébillon fils* (Durham, N.C.: Duke University Press, 1962), viii.

12. The family histories written by or for the nobility in *ancien régime* France have received little scholarly attention. For a study of the genre in the context of seventeenth-century historical scholarship see Orest Ranum, *Artisans of Glory: Writers and Historical Thought in Seventeenth-Century France* (Chapel Hill: University of North Carolina Press, 1980). See also Jay M. Smith, "Birth, Merit, and the Uses of Family History," in Smith, *Culture of Merit in Old Regime France*, 46–86.

13. These figures are taken from Smith, "Birth, Merit, and the Uses of Family History," citing Gaston Saffroy, *Bibliographie généalogique, héraldique et nobiliaire de la France: des origines à nos jours* (Paris: G. Saffroy, 1974).

Chapter 10. CHANCE'S UNTELLABLE TALE:
DIDEROT'S *Jacques le fataliste*

1. For an attempt to interpret Diderot through Michel Serres's readings of Lucretius see Jeffrey Mehlman, *Cataract: A Study in Diderot* (Middletown, Conn.: Wesleyan University Press, 1979).

2. See Denis Diderot, "Projet de loterie," in *Oeuvres complètes*,

ed. H. Dieckmann, J. Proust, and J. Varloot, vol. 2 (Paris: Hermann, 1975), 440–54.

3. Diderot, *Eléments de physiologie,* in *Oeuvres complètes,* vol. 17 (1987), 516.

4. Robert, *Dictionnaire alphabétique et analogique,* 2:844.

5. Diderot, *Jacques le fataliste,* in *Oeuvres complètes,* vol. 23 (1987), 23; translations are my own. I have consulted J. Robert Loy's *Jacques the Fatalist and His Master* (New York: Collier Books, 1962).

6. Jacques Roger, *Les Sciences de la vie dans la pensée française du XVIIIe siècle* (Paris: Armand Colin, 1963), 633.

7. Thomas M. Kavanagh, *The Vacant Mirror: A Study of Mimesis through Diderot's "Jacques le fataliste,"* Studies on Voltaire and the Eighteenth Century, 104 (Oxford: Voltaire Foundation, 1973).

8. For an analysis of *Jacques le fataliste* in terms of this opposition see Aram Vartanian, *"Jacques le fataliste:* A Journey into the Ramifications of a Dilemma," in *Essays on Diderot and the Enlightenment in Honor of Otis Fellows,* ed. John Pappas (Geneva: Droz, 1974), 325–47.

9. Ilya Prigogine and Isabelle Stengers, *Order out of Chaos: Man's Dialogue with Nature* (New York: Bantam, 1984), 52.

10. Michel Foucault begins his *Surveiller et punir* (Paris: Gallimard, 1975) with a provocative analysis of the details of this execution and its implications for the practice of royal justice.

11. Michel Serres, *Hermès IV: La Distribution* (Paris: Editions de Minuit, 1977), 10.

12. Diderot and d'Alembert, *Encyclopédie,* 1:1156.

13. Denis Diderot, "Prospectus," in *Oeuvres complètes,* vol. 5 (1975), 91.

14. Paul Valéry, "Fragments des mémoires d'un poème," in *Oeuvres de Paul Valéry,* 2 vols. ed. Jean Hytier (Paris: Gallimard, 1957–60), 1:1467.

CONCLUSION

1. Serres, *Hermès IV,* 11.

2. Stefan Amsterdanski et al., *La Querelle du déterminisme* (Paris: Gallimard, 1990), 57–58.

Index

Designed by Jim Billingsley

Composed by Achorn Graphic Services, Inc.,
in Baskerville text and Bulmer display

Printed by The Maple Press Company
on 55-lb. Sebago Antique Cream
and bound in Holliston Roxite cloth

for his care by a dubious country surgeon. One evening, while taking a walk on his crutches, Jacques came upon a widow sitting next to a broken oil jar lamenting her and her children's ruin because the oil she has just spilled cost nine francs—more than she could hope to earn in an entire month. Taking pity, Jacques gave the woman twelve of his last eighteen francs. His reward for that act of charity came on his way back to the surgeon's when he was attacked by robbers who assumed that a man able to give away twelve francs must be carrying many times that sum. With Jacques now penniless, there is no doubt that the avaricious surgeon will throw him out. At this point in Jacques' story the master is overcome by the narrative suspense. Throwing his arms around Jacques' neck, he exclaims: "My poor Jacques, what will you do? What will become of you? Your predicament terrifies me" (100). Jacques' laconic reply to this outburst of emotion flowing from the master's identification with the story being told is a wry reminder that suspense grounded in the narrated past must always be qualified by the circumstances of the narration: "My master, don't worry. Here I am" (100).

The master may be comical in his fear for how things will turn out for someone in fact standing next to him, but his reaction is based on an identification with the story being told to which Jacques, as fatalistic as he may claim to be, is also eminently susceptible. Jacques can well proclaim that "when I cry, I often feel I am a fool" (100), but that does not stop him from breaking into tears as he tells the sad story of how his brother came to die in the Lisbon earthquake. If anything, Jacques' decision to give two-thirds of his money to the widow with the broken jar proves that he is particularly susceptible to an identification with her tale of woe. Even his still being alive to tell the master the story of his loves is the result of another character's decidedly antifatalistic identification with life's sad stories: it was because the wealthy Desglands identified with Jacques' generosity to the poor widow that he invited him to live at his château and saw to his care. In spite of his needling his master for identifying with the story being told, Jacques must finally recognize that same tendency as a real limit to his own fatalism: "I can't stop myself from crying or laughing. And that is what infuriates me. I have tried a hundred times" (100).

Just as there is a gap between the Great Scroll's determinism and the real world's chance, so also there is a gap between Jacques the devotee of fatalistic resignation and Jacques as he lives his life in the real world. Although these gaps may be denied at the level of proclaimed belief and philosophical statement, they become only more apparent at the level of feeling and action. Jacques' ultimate solution to this disparity between what he believes and what he does is a form of meta-fatalism, a second level of resignation accepting not only what is written on the Great Scroll but also the absurdity of his own reactions to that script: "I have decided to be just what I am. I realized, after thinking about it a bit, that it all comes down to almost the same thing if you add—what does it matter how one is? It is another kind of resignation, easier and more convenient" (101). Jacques admits to his master that in spite of his fatalism, he prays. His prayers are, however, of a particular sort: "Je prie à tout hasard" (178). This chance prayer, this prayer to chance, is the option of those who understand not only what they would wish themselves to be but what they in fact are: "It's that I am inconsequential and violent, that I forget my principles or my captain's lessons, and that I laugh and cry like a fool" (178).

It is, finally, only those able to laugh and cry like fools who can tell stories, listen to stories, and live within a reality redefined by the interplay of chance and story. Everything specific to this novel—the stories set at odds with one another, the arguments between author and reader—suggests that ours is a world of innumerable competing and interwoven stories soliciting our concern and offering in return some semblance of identity. To listen to any single story may be to enter a world of predetermined causalities following the script of their own Great Scroll; but, Did-

erot insists, to recognize the cacophony of the world as an
infinity of stories competing for our attention is to discover
the reality of chance as a force presiding over the narration
of those stories making us their own.

Jacques le fataliste's sustained meditation on fatalism, narration, and the reader/listener's identification with the
storytelling voice establishes this work as a reflection on
our paradoxical relation to the always storied yet always
aleatory world we share with our fellows. What is it, this
text asks, about telling and listening to stories, about the
isolation of order from chaos, of self from other, that
makes storytelling the most fundamental trope of human
communication? Why did Diderot compose this work in
such a way that our desire to hear a story is continually
frustrated and problematized rather than satisfied? Why
did he move outside the period's conventions of novelistic
representation to confront his readers with such baroque
permutations of the narrative gesture?

Addressing these questions extends *Jacques le fataliste*'s
significance beyond an experiment in narrative form to
the larger problem of understanding how our desire for
stories—those we tell as well as those we listen to—relates
to the social underpinnings of identity, order, and hierarchy. At one point in *Jacques le fataliste*, Diderot directly asks
what the social function of storytelling might be. Why, he
begins, do so many people delight in attending public executions—the gruesome rituals through which the *ancien
régime* reaffirmed its power to preserve order from chaos
and hierarchy from anarchy? The fact that people flock to
public executions, Diderot argues, must not be seen as
proof that they approve or ratify the political implications
of such violent spectacles. People attend them for the same
reason they are drawn to any event allowing them to tell a
story, to reassert their own identity within a generalized
economy of narrative exchange:

What in your opinion is the reason why people attend public executions? Inhumanity? You are wrong, the people are
not inhuman. That poor fellow whose gallows they gather
around, they would snatch him from the hands of justice
if they could. People go to executions looking for a scene
they can retell when they return to their neighborhoods.
That one or another, it doesn't matter, so long as they can
play a role, gather their neighbors around them, and make
themselves heard [pourvu qu'il fasse un rôle, qu'il rassem-
ble ses voisins et qu'il se fasse écouter]. Schedule an amus-
ing fair on the boulevards and you will see that the execution square will be empty. The people long for spectacles
and flock to them because they are amused while they take
place, and amused again by the stories they tell when they
get back home. (189)

This passage, for those who read *Jacques le fataliste* at the
time it first appeared in the *Correspondance littéraire*, evoked
that most notorious public execution of eighteenth-century
France, an event with which Diderot's career and the publication of his *Encyclopédie* were intimately connected: the
execution in 1757 of Damiens, the man who had raised
his knife against the person of the king as the ultimate
representative of the social order upon which the *ancien
régime* was founded.[10]

In analyzing the people's motives for being there, Diderot subtly calls attention to the fact that such public executions are the vehicle of a mystification, the pretext for a
tendentious misinterpretation of the people's presence
abusively justifying the actions of established authority. In
attracting a crowd whose presence apparently reaffirms
their allegiance to the outraged monarch, the public execution addresses itself to and exploits a desire whose real
object is in fact quite different from what this violent
spectacle of its satisfaction would seem to indicate. If
people flock to public executions, it is not, as royalist ideology would claim, because the people see themselves as
wronged by a crime perpetrated against the person of the